U.S. MARINES IN IRAQ, 2004–2005

INTO THE FRAY

U.S. Marines in the Global War on Terrorism

by
Lieutenant Colonel Kenneth W. Estes
U.S. Marine Corps (Retired)

History Division
United States Marine Corps
Washington, D.C.
2011

Other Publications in the Series
U.S. Marines in the Global War on Terrorism

U.S. Marines in Iraq, 2003: Anthology and Annotated Bibliography
U.S. Marines in Iraq, 2003: Basrah, Baghdad and Beyond
Det One: U.S. Marine Corps U.S. Special Operations Command
Detachment, 2003–2006
U.S. Marines in Iraq, 2004–2008: Anthology and Annotated Bibliography

PCN 106 0000 2300

Foreword

The following account represents one of the earliest efforts to chronicle Marine Corps operations in Iraq between 2004 and 2005. This was a significant period in the history of Operation Iraqi Freedom, seeing two battles fought over the city of Fallujah, the eruption of the Sadr revolt in an-Najaf, continuous counterinsurgency operations throughout Iraq, and initial efforts on the part of Marines to cultivate and forge alliances with the tribes of Iraq's al-Anbar Province.

Almost as soon as Saddam Hussein's regime collapsed in 2003, it became apparent to U.S. commanders that a second deployment of Marines to Iraq would be necessary to conduct security and stability operations. This monograph recounts the first two years of this second deployment during which Marines were responsible for Iraq's vast al-Anbar Province. This study focuses on I Marine Expeditionary Force's deployment in 2004 and II Marine Expeditionary Force's deployment of 2005, paying close attention to planning, counterinsurgency operations, and efforts to build civil-military relations with the Iraqi population. Particular attention is also paid to the first and second battles of Fallujah and the battle of an-Najaf.

This book was commissioned and written while U.S. forces were still engaged in combat operations in Iraq. Even now, just five years since the events recounted in this study, we already have a sense of the significance of these years and the Marine Corps' operations to the overall course of the war, and we can thank Dr. Estes for making this possible.

This History Division monograph is based on the occasional paper, "U.S. Marine Corps Operations in Iraq, 2003–2006" by the same author. This revision slightly differs from that original publication in a number of ways. First, it contains maps to help orientate and familiarize readers to Iraq, al-Anbar Province, and the two battles for Fallujah. Second, the new edition contains photographs depicting major commanders, combat operations, equipment, and civil-military operations. Third, several informative sidebars have been added to provide readers with detailed information on specific topics. And finally, references have been redacted into short bibliographical essays at the end of the book to give readers a concise overview of available documentary sources.

The author, Dr. Kenneth W. Estes, is a 1969 graduate of the United States Naval Academy who served in a variety of command and staff assignments in the U.S. Marine Corps before retiring as a lieutenant colonel in 1993. He earned his PhD from the University of Maryland in 1984 and has taught at Duke University and the U.S. Naval Academy. His publications include *The Marine Officer's Guide, Handbook for Marine NCOs, Marines Under Armor: The Marine Corps and the Armored Fighting Vehicle, 1916–2000,* and *A European Anabasis: Western European Volunteers in the German Army and Waffen-SS, 1940–1945.* He resides in Seattle, Washington.

Dr. Charles P. Neimeyer
Director of Marine Corps History

ISBN 978-1-78039-386-5

Preface

This is a story of Marines, missions, and machines. The deployment of the I and II Marine Expeditionary Forces in that sequence to Iraq during 2004–05 contains a surprising number of turns of events. These were largely successes, but the situations did not always appear so favorable at the time and often they required tenacious efforts, skills, courage, and stamina of Marines and their Navy and Army comrades to reach the desired outcome. The combat record of Marine Corps forces in Iraq brings great credit upon the Corps and the armed forces of the United States of America. But, as will be seen in the following pages, the combat record lies interspersed with a seemingly endless range of tasks undertaken by the battalions and the squadrons the Corps operated as it engaged in security and stabilization operations in al-Anbar and the surrounding provinces.

Nation-building has existed as a military mission for the U.S. Marine Corps at various junctures in its history. In contemporary usage, it has sent chills through the ranks of politicians, pundits, and observers and military leaders. Nevertheless, most of the activities of the Marine expeditionary forces in Iraq fell within the main lines of nation building in the classic sense. The restoration of order in the cities and towns, humanitarian assistance, training of security forces, and the facilitation of local government formed the bedrock of U.S. and Coalition actions in Iraq. In addition the concerted efforts by Multi National Forces–West to repair and reconstruct the urban infrastructure far exceeded the war damage Iraq sustained during the U.S. occupation in March–April 2003, and in reality began the long process of recovery from the extended period of deprivation suffered in the dictatorial regime that the U.S. actions had removed.

The emerging evidence of the 2004–05 campaign by Marine Corps forces and other elements of the U.S. Central Command will remain ripe for discussion and review by our institutions for decades to come. Few examples exist, however, of the extremes in operational employment experienced by the forces.

The military occupation of al-Anbar Province and its surroundings required the utmost of patience, perseverance, and fortitude, among many salient requirements. The cities and towns were damaged, inhabitants demoralized, and little vestige of civil authority remained. Hopes remained high, however, that the occupation would prove limited or even unnecessary and that the Iraqis would pick themselves up and begin a rebuilding process in the light of newly gained freedom. But as Marines took up new and unplanned responsibilities, various forms of insurgency began to build and present increasing security threats. For the Marines, nation building and combat operations would proceed in tandem, if not simultaneously for almost all of their service in Iraq.

The epic occupation of Iraq will long remain as one of the most novel military operations ever undertaken by a Marine Corps organization. It only capped, however, the extraordinary performances of I and II Marine Expeditionary Forces that remain as testimonials to the professionalism and preparedness of the U.S. Marine Corps in the beginning of the 21st Century.

A work of this kind necessarily depends on the help and advice of many people. The original concept of assigning this volume to an independent historian came from discussions in 2005 between then Lieutenant General James N. Mattis, commanding the Marine Corps Combat Development Center, and retired Major General Donald R. Gardner, president of the Marine Corps University. General Gardner launched the project and arranged for my appointment as a research fellow of his institution during 2006–08.

Officers and enlisted Marines of Inspector-Instructor, 4th Landing Support Battalion, Ft. Lewis, Washington, cheerfully provided office space and support for my research and writing. Their readiness to assist extended in many instances to their advice and valued explanations of current procedures and operational matters, including in several cases experiences in Iraq during the period treated by this work. In particular, I thank Lieutenant Colonel Richard C. Smith, Major Wesley E. Souza, Captain Gregory J. Chester, Captain Christopher J. Murphy, Sergeant Major Thomas Glembin, and Staff Sergeant M. E. Johnston.

At the Marine Corps History Division, I enjoyed the camaraderie and shared knowledge of Dr. Charles Neimeyer, director; Richard Camp, deputy director (2006-07); Colonel Patricia D. Saint, deputy director (2007-08); Dr. Fred Allison, oral historian; and Master Gunnery Sergeant Robert A. Yarnall, field historian. I received careful assistance from the Reference Section gang: Danny A. Crawford, Robert V. Aquilina, Lena M. Kaljot, Annette D. Amerman, Kara Newcomer, and Shelia Phillips. Julie H. Robert, a historical preservationist student at the University of Mary Washington, researched and edited the photographic collection printed with this work. The Marine Corps University Foundation and Marine Corps Heritage Foundation supported me with a combined fellowship in 2006-08, administered by retired Brigadier General Thomas V. Draude. The staff of the Archives Branch, Library of the Marine Corps, Gray Research Center at Quantico, principally Michael Miller, director, and Dr. Jim Ginther, manuscript curator, facilitated my use of their document collection. Scott A. Allen assisted me in understanding some of the contributions of the Marine Corps Systems Command to the campaign under study. I also received assistance from dozens of other Marines and civilians at Marine Corps Base Quantico. Approximately 20 officers undertook evaluation of this work in various draft stages.

Dr. Kenneth W. Estes
Marine Corps University
Research Fellow

Table of Contents

Chapter 1

The Return to Iraq

I Marine Expeditionary Force Prepares to Return to Iraq

The long, hot summer of 2003 drew to a close for the Marines in Iraq. Since the brief offensive of March and April had overthrown Saddam Hussein's regime, Marines had conducted an unplanned occupation and peacekeeping campaign. Lieutenant General James T. Conway's I Marine Expeditionary Force (I MEF) staff had announced the transition to "Post-hostility Operations" on 15 April, redeploying his forces to a new operating area south of Baghdad. Operation Iraqi Freedom shifted into security and stability operations aimed at facilitating humanitarian assistance and restoring civilian rule.

The summer had seen a dramatic reduction in Marine Corps forces in Iraq. 1st Marine Division commander Major General James N. Mattis had set the tone for the stability and security operations by drastically cutting his division troop list from some 23,000 to 8,000 Marines. He retained only seven battalions of infantry and two light armored reconnaissance battalions under a reduced division headquarters. These occupied seven key Iraqi "governorates" or provinces, working to reinstate local police and security functions and revive the municipal services and public utilities. The 3d Marine Aircraft Wing under Major General James F. Amos redeployed to the United States, leaving behind two detachments with 18 helicopters for support. The Marine Logistics Command under Brigadier General Richard S. Kramlich worked in Kuwait to reload materiel into ships and aircraft, supported the remaining units, and redeployed itself, leaving a special purpose Marine air-ground task force under Brigadier General Ronald S. Coleman to oversee the withdrawal of Marine forces in the theater.

On 3 September, General Conway held a transfer of authority ceremony with the Polish Army commander of the Multi National Division Center–South. The remaining Marines subsequently began their return to the United States. A 1st Marine Expeditionary Brigade command element briefly served as interim higher headquarters during this redeployment period. A further three weeks of patrolling and occasional fighting in an-Najaf fell to 1st Battalion, 7th Marines

before a turnover could be effected. The 1st Marine Division sustained no combat deaths during its stability and security operations campaign period. The last Marine Corps organization to reach home station, Company C, 4th Light Armored Reconnaissance Battalion, returned to Salt Lake City, Utah, on 9 December 2003, after three months in Iraq followed by a six-month Unit Deployment Program rotation in Japan.

Marines of the special purpose Marine air-ground task force (MAGTF) continued their mission into November along with a few other small elements, such as Detachment B of the 4th Air-Naval Gunfire Liaison Company, which supported the Multi National Division Center–South; 5th Platoon, Fleet Antiterrorist Security Team (FAST), providing security for the U.S. Embassy, Baghdad; and some 556 Marine Corps personnel remaining in Iraq and Kuwait. Before departing for the United States, General Mattis questioned Brigadier General Coleman about some of his equipment in the hands of the Marine air-ground task force. General Mattis thought he might need the equipment soon and set 10 November 2003 as the date when the entire division's personnel and equipment would be combat ready.

As the combat forces that conducted the original invasion and occupation phase left Iraq, the 13th Marine Expeditionary Unit (MEU) arrived in the Persian Gulf and reported to the Fifth Fleet on 29 September. These periodic and overlapping Marine Expeditionary Unit deployments operated as part of the theater reserve for the Combatant Commander, U.S. Central Command, Army General John P. Abizaid, during the remainder of Operation Iraqi Freedom. In this case, the 13th MEU operated with the British-led Multi National Division–Southeast. Landing elements included 1st Battalion, 1st Marines at Kuwait Naval Base and Umm Qasr. The Marine expeditionary unit then conducted anti-smuggling and security missions on the Faw Peninsula during 11–25 October.

Within a month of the change of command, Marine Corps Commandant General Michael W. Hagee asked General Conway to prepare his forces for another deployment to support Operation Iraqi Freedom II. Discussions in Washington D.C. had

1

At the relief in place ceremony at Camp Bablyon, Iraq, on 3 September 2003, Polish-led Coalition forces relieved the Marines of I Marine Expeditionary Force (I MEF).

advanced to the stage that a U.S. force rotation plan developed, and planners at Headquarters U.S. Marine Corps began to assess another deployment to Iraq. An initial request for three battalions quickly expanded, and within two months, 63 percent of I Marine Expeditionary Force (I MEF) was preparing to return.

Fielding I MEF for combat operations in Operation Iraqi Freedom caused considerable disruptions to the forces and supporting establishment of the Marine Corps during 2002–03. The staff of Headquarters U.S. Marine Corps estimated that providing such a force for another Iraq rotation would delay the normal unit deployment cycle another year, disrupt the maritime prepositioned shipping reconstitution by again drawing away essential equipment, and drastically impact the Marine Corps personnel policy governing deployment length, reserve mobilization, and the involuntary extension of tours of duty. All of these factors later affected retention in both active and reserve components.

Nevertheless, the Corps mobilized about 22,000 reservists by 1 May 2003 and retained over 10,500 on duty in mid-October. A planned maximum of 3,000 would remain on active duty after March 2004 by continued call-up and demobilization of reservists. Active duty end strength had also climbed because of "stop-loss" and "stop-move" manpower directives, reaching a peak of 179,630 Marines in July 2003. The number subsided to 177,756 at the end of September and presumably would return to the authorized 175,000 by March 2004.

Maintaining routine deployments to Okinawa had also required moving several battalions and aircraft squadrons from Iraq to the United States and then to Okinawa with 90 days or less at home station. Of equal concern to headquarters was the need to reconstitute the floating equipment pools carried in the three maritime prepositioned ship squadrons that had been used as part of the strategic deployment of I MEF to Kuwait at the end of 2002. The forecast estimated the basic reconstitution of the three squadrons by March 2004. The staff identified further challenges in replacing aviation ordnance, antitank missiles, and overcoming the depot overhaul backlog, but the larger question remained, that of supporting the next Marine Corps contingent in Iraq.

The shortfall in Coalition troops meant that the

United States would have to replace one or two Army divisions in March 2004. Although the final decision would not be made until the end of the year, the Joint Staff forecasted the need for three to six battalions each from the Army and Marine Corps. General Hagee decided to plan for the deployment of a Marine division built around six infantry battalions with commensurate aviation and logistics support.

The Commandant and his staff saw a key issue in the period of deployment and how it would affect the rest of the Corps. A seven-month deployment would permit much more flexibility in meeting global requirements while maintaining unit cohesion. He submitted the proposal to Secretary of Defense Donald H. Rumsfeld, who officially announced on 5 November 2003 that Marine Corps units would return to Iraq as part of the U.S. force rotations. Twenty-thousand Marines and sailors of I Marine Expeditionary Force would replace the Army's 82d Airborne Divi-

While Commandant of the Marine Corps from 2003 to 2006, Gen Michael W. Hagee provided leadership and guidance that laid the groundwork for the Marine Corps' return to Iraq in 2004.
Photo by Sgt Roman Yarek, Defense Imagery VIRIN: 050617-M-9114Y-037

sion by February 2004 as the primary force responsible for security operations in western Iraq. The deployment was expected to last seven months, with another 20,000-strong Marine force replacing them after that for another seven months.

On 27 November, General Hagee finalized the new deployment of Marines to Operation Iraqi Freedom. Marine Forces, Central Command, would be provided with a reduced Marine Expeditionary Force (Forward) for operations in Iraq. In addition to its command element, a reduced Marine division with nine infantry battalions would meet the requirements of the Joint Staff and of U.S. Central Command. The division would be accompanied by an aircraft wing and force service support group, both reduced and tailored for the smaller ground combat element.

The key components of General Hagee's guidance reflected the earlier concerns over the reconstitution of Marine Corps forces in the aftermath of the 2003 campaign. The seven-month unit rotation policy was the cornerstone of the 27 November 2003 planning guidance. Although the Army and other services worked their deployments to Iraq around a 13-month cycle, General Hagee wanted to maintain the by-now customary deployment of six to seven months to preserve the continuing operations of the Corps in its global commitments: the forward deployed III Marine Expeditionary Force (III MEF) in Japan and the smaller Marine expeditionary unit deployments from the east and west coast organizations to the Mediterranean and Pacific.

The Commandant authorized the Marine Forces Central Command planners to draw as required from the scheduled unit deployments to III MEF (except for the 31st Marine Expeditionary Unit [31st MEU]) for its force list. To meet material concerns, General Hagee requested the maximum use of in-theater equipment used by the 82d Airborne Division and 3d Armored Cavalry Regiment in their area of operations. Much of this was not common to Marine Corps unit tables of equipment, such as new counter-battery radars, uparmored wheeled vehicles, and various other items. Finally, with the exception of the first squadron that had been reconstituted—Maritime Prepositioned Squadron 3, based in the Marianas—General Hagee authorized the issue of equipment stored on Okinawa and with maritime prepositioned shipping squadrons.

The intended demobilization of the Marine Corps Reserve would prove temporary. Further deactivations continued past 17 December 2003, even as 3d Battalion, 24th Marines activated. But the activation of an infantry battalion as well as other units added

Photo by LCpl Andrew Williams, Defense Imagery VIRIN 030903-M-7837W-041

LtGen James T. Conway commanded I Marine Expeditionary Force through both the 2003 and 2004 campaigns in Iraq, and succeeded Gen Hagee as Commandant of the Marine Corps in 2006.

more than 3,000 reservists to the active force, not counting individual augmentations, by the time the 2002-03 activations had been demobilized by March 2004.

Problems in Iraq: The Emerging Insurgency: 2003–04

The fall of Saddam Hussein's Ba'ath regime in April 2003 marked the end of the first phase of the Iraq War. The next, signaled by a deadly insurgency against the Coalition occupation of Iraq, would begin almost immediately after. This phase of the war, characterized by irregular warfare and sectarian violence against Coalition forces and between Iraq's religious and ethnic groups, lasted considerably longer and presented many unanticipated challenges and obstacles to the U.S. military. Although the planning process by the United States for the invasion of Iraq

had exceeded a year, very little preparation for post-hostilities operations existed by the time major operations had ended in April. Most authorities assumed that the Iraqis would replace the Ba'ath regime with new leaders and that government bureaucracies would return to work and assist immediately in the recovery effort. With the end of the first phase of the war, however, the Coalition faced an Iraq whose political, civil, and economic institutions were in a state of disrepair and collapse.

At the same time as Coalition forces prepared for post-war reconstruction, United States Central Command initiated a rapid drawdown of forces stationed in the country. Most important, the Coalition Forces Land Component Command under Army Lieutenant General David D. McKiernan would transfer responsibility for stabilization to the Combined Joint Task Force 7. Converted from the headquarters staff of Lieutenant General Ricardo S. Sanchez's V Corps, the combined joint task force exercised command and control over a multinational force of more than 30 countries. Its responsibilities extended over all Iraq, and it reported directly to the new Coalition Provisional Authority under L. Paul Bremer III, the civilian governing agency established by the United States to oversee the establishment of a new Iraqi government. Coalition leaders hoped that both agencies would be able to create a new Iraq with reformed political institutions, a rebuilt infrastructure, and a reenergized society.

Hoping for a steady improvement in general conditions, Combined Joint Task Force 7's initial campaign plan of June 2003 anticipated decreasing opposition to the Coalition. According to this plan, the Coalition Provisional Authority would revive native institutions and governmental bodies at local and national levels. Meanwhile, ongoing U.S. military actions would decrease support for the old regime by destroying surviving paramilitary forces, and capturing, trying, and punishing former Ba'athists. The anticipated improvement of basic services and the transfer of Iraqi sovereignty to an interim government would further undercut the opposition of radical antiwestern religious groups and potential violence between different factions throughout the country. The end of combat would permit the repairing of damaged infrastructure and bring about economic recovery, thus promoting a newly emerging democratic government and discrediting antiwestern factions. Above all, both the Coalition Provisional Authority and Combined Joint Task Force 7 assumed that those Iraqi institutions, which had survived the combat phase as well as the final years of the Hussein regime, would continue to perform their usual security functions.

The overall goal for Iraq was to reduce the need for a long-term, large-scale U.S. military presence in the country. Creating a secure environment in which to hold local elections would encourage transition to local authority, allowing U.S. troops to withdraw from urban areas. American forces planned to move out of the cities into consolidated forward operating bases in late September 2003 and to be ready to conduct combat operations, assist or otherwise reinforce Iraqi security forces, and even expand the divisional zones of responsibilities as units such as the 101st Airborne Division, 82d Airborne Division, and the 3d Armored Cavalry Regiment began to redeploy to home stations. A single U.S. light infantry division would replace the multidivision occupation force that had been in place during the six months following the invasion. Thus, the new plan entailed the rapid training and development of robust Iraqi military forces, a capable police force, and an interim government. To help fulfill these goals, a program for training the new Iraqi Army would begin in August.

Nevertheless, these initial assumptions and plans proved too optimistic, forcing U.S. planners to devise a new campaign in August 2003 to confront the intensifying insurgency against the Coalition occupation. The insurgency had been growing at a rapid pace. Individual and organized criminal activities had appeared even before the occupation of Iraq began. In April 2003, soldiers of the 82d Airborne Division fired on a crowd of protesters in Fall, further inflaming hostility toward the U.S. presence in the country. The Coalition Provisional Authority's May 2003 decision to dissolve the Iraqi Army and dismiss all members of the Ba'ath Party from positions in the civil government removed thousands of Iraqis, most of them Sunnis, from positions of political power. Such measures created the impression that Sunnis would be a marginal group in the new Iraq and many former Ba'athists flocked to the ranks of the insurgency. Alongside former Ba'athists and regime supporters were more radical groups, such as fundamentalist paramilitary groups and international terrorist organizations.

In the new plan of Combined Joint Task Force (CJTF) 7, General Sanchez stated his mission was to conduct combat operations to destroy enemy forces and establish a secure environment while also engaging in stability operations to support the establishment of Iraqi sovereignty. The plan also entailed humanitarian assistance for the Iraqi population and restoring essential services to the communities. The protection of key sites and services, such as water, power, and sewage plants, would also contribute to general security and recovery. A large array of public works projects and conventional civil affairs programs would assist in restoring economic prosperity to Iraq and maintaining a sustainable quality of life, especially in the supply of power, fuel, water, and sanitation services. The reopening of Baghdad International Airport and introduction of a new currency were also major benchmarks. Finally, Combined Joint Task Force 7 planned to assist in the installation of viable and fair neighborhood, district, and city governing councils.

Due to the increasing intensity of the insurgency, continued combat operations would be significant features of the new plan. Under the concept of "an adapting enemy," the combined joint task force campaign plan anticipated an enemy capable of changing tactics and targets to avoid U.S. attacks and overcome improving security measures. The most likely enemy actions would come in the form of iso-

Army LtGen Ricardo S. Sanchez was commanding general of Combined Joint Task Force 7 and senior commander of coalition forces in Iraq from 2003 to 2004.
Photo by LCpl Andrew Williams, Defense Imagery VRIN 030903-M-7837W-040

Photo by SSgt Quinton Russ, USAF, Defense Imagery, VIRIN: 040324-F-9927R-001

Ambassador L. Paul Bremer III was head of the Coalition Provisional Authority and the chief civilian official in Iraq from May 2003 until the transfer of sovereignty in June 2004.

lated and random attacks. Less likely, but much more dangerous, would be the enemy mounting an organized, well-targeted, and highly lethal attack. In addition, planners recognized the potential for the enemy to disrupt reconstruction of the country with political assassinations.

Realizing the Coalition would be unable to rapidly eradicate resistance to the U.S. presence in Iraq, Sanchez and his staff proposed long-range plans to defeat the former regime forces, to neutralize extremist groups, and to reduce crime by 50 percent. To accomplish these goals, Combined Joint Task Force 7 would establish, equip, and train a large Iraqi security force; municipal police; battalions of the Iraqi Civil Defense Corps; and thousands of Facilities Protection Service guards. Planners assumed that only extremist groups, the most unpredictable enemy, would remain likely opponents by the time of the turnover to relief forces in 2004.

The end result, proposed in the August campaign plan, was a safe and secure environment created by a much more vigorous level of U.S. activities. Combined Joint Task Force 7 concluded that the initial deployments for combat under Operation Iraqi Freedom would need to be extended by a full year with

a relief anticipated sometime in the spring of 2004.

The Force Takes Shape

The I MEF and 1st Marine Division operational planning teams worked on the force structure, framed the mission, and formulated tasks and organizations from late September through 19 October 2003. They then identified units to be provided for operations in Iraq by mid-December. The I MEF command element would require its usual detachments of civil affairs, intelligence, force reconnaissance, communications, radio, air-naval gunfire liaison, and Army psychological operations units, all gathered under the administration of the I MEF Headquarters Group. The 1st Marine Division, under the command of Major General James N. Mattis, organized its combat power around two reinforced infantry regiments (regimental combat teams), each with three infantry battalions (with a light armored reconnaissance battalion standing as the third battalion in one regiment), a combat engineer company, and a combat service support detachment. The division also had an artillery battalion transformed into a provisional military police unit, a tank company, and an assault amphibian company.

The 3d Marine Aircraft Wing (Forward), commanded by Major General James F. Amos, planned to employ a single aircraft group. With the exception of tanker and liaison aircraft detachments, it would include no manned fixed-winged aircraft, entailing three medium-lift helicopter squadrons, one heavy-lift helicopter squadron, and two light-attack helicopter squadrons. An unmanned aerial vehicle squadron and an air defense battalion also accompanied the group for air control and ground support. Brigadier General Richard S. Kramlich's 1st Force Service Support Group (Forward) organized separate groups for the eastern and western sectors of I MEF's planned area of operations, the vast al-Anbar Province. Each was to support one regiment, with the remaining assests allocated to a brigade service support group for the rest of the force. An engineer contingent included a naval mobile construction battalion (the "Seabees"), three engineer and engineer support companies, and several companies of military police.

Between 26 August and 9 September 2003, the Army's Task Force Baghdad conducted Operation Longstreet in al-Anbar and northern Babil Provinces, revealing key insurgent sanctuaries and infiltration routes. Consequently, U.S. Central Command commander, Army General John P. Abizaid, planned to augment the Marine Corps deployment with an Army brigade combat team, additional infantry battalions, a small boat detachment, and a requirement for counter-battery radars.

While the members of the I MEF, who returned to

their home stations in 2003, were all veterans of combat, stability, and security operations, many units had to be disbanded because of transfers and expired terms of service. Replacements had to be obtained and trained. Training schedules, family support, and maintenance programs were designed to maximize leave, to retain cohesion, and to preserve combat readiness. The 1st Marine Division recuperated at its California home bases but toiled anew to refurbish its materiel and to prepare personnel for future operations. On 5 January 2004, the 1st Marine Division was rated fully mission capable. At a cost of $79.9 million, extensive planning and much effort, the division was prepared for immediate deployment.

The 1st Force Service Support Group, reformed in November 2003 into the "expeditionary template" organization, was long under study in the Marine Corps. This measure sought to change the combat service support echelon of Marine Corps forces from ad hoc units that had to be reorganized for each deployment, defined by existing conditions, into permanent organizations with designated commanders and staffs, exercising command and control both in garrison and when deployed. Intended for a nine-month "proof of concept" period, 1st Force Service Support Group commander, Brigadier General Kramlich, ordered the creation of Combat Service Support Group 11, led by the commander of the transportation support battalion, and Combat Service Support Group 15 as a general support group, led by the commander of the supply battalion. This program would ultimately lead to the redesignation of the Marine expeditionary force's combat support element as a Marine logistics group in November 2005.

Although the rotation units for the second six-month deployment had yet to be identified, General Conway sent his final force list for Operation Iraqi Freedom II to General Abizaid on 12 December 2003. This organization initially contained no artillery, except for that organic to the U.S. Army 1st Brigade, 1st Infantry Division. Marine Corps and Army infantry were cross-attached, with the 2d Battalion, 4th Marines, joining the brigade and the Army's 1st Battalion, 32d Infantry, attached to Regimental Combat Team 1. The Marine Corps infantry contingent had grown in barely a month to a total of eight infantry battalions, one reconnaissance battalion, and one light armored reconnaissance battalion. The Army brigade contributed three more

MajGen James N. Mattis, commander of 1st Marine Division 2003–04, was already a veteran of Marine Corps operations in Afghanistan and Iraq when I MEF returned to Iraq in the spring of 2004.

Photo by LCpl Christopher R. Rye, Defense Imagery VIRIN: 031007-M-6237R-024

Photo by LCpl Jonathon T. Spencer, Defense Imagery: 040422-M-2900S-023

MajGen James F. Amos (right), commander of 3d Marine Air Wing from 2003 to 2004, speaks with Capt Shawn Miller of Marine Wing Support Squadron 273 while deployed to al-Anbar province in April 2004.

battalions, including an armor battalion that was partly reformed as vehicle-mounted infantry. This task organization was augmented, near the time of embarkation, with artillery batteries A and E, 11th Marines. These two batteries arrived on 28 February 2004 and drew 18 howitzers from the prepositioning ships supporting the deployment. Counter-battery fires against indirect fire attacks from the insurgents became the initial mission for these two batteries. Later, when needs became more urgent, the equipment aboard the maritime prepositioned shipping would permit very rapid reinforcement of the Marine division. In addition to the forces under I MEF control were two bridge companies drawn from II Marine Expeditionary Force (II MEF) and Marine Reserve Forces, a detachment of light attack helicopters to operate out of Balad Air Base, and two Navy surgical companies.

Al-Anbar Province and the Insurgency

In October 2003, the Joint Staff decided that the Marine Corps would relieve the Army's 82d Airborne Division. The area of operations included the large al-Anbar Province and the northern Babil Province, which was the heart of the Sunni Triangle and the anti-Coalition insurgency west of Baghdad. The region posed challenges unlike those I MEF faced during the stability and security operations campaign it conducted in the summer of 2003. While the northern Babil area was familiar to Marine veterans of 2003, al-Anbar Province was not. I MEF and division operations planning team studied the province intensely, paying particular attention to terrorist infiltration routes, termed "rat lines," extending from Syria to the major cities of Fallujah and Ramadi.

Al-Anbar Province was an active center for the insurgency where its vast expanses served as an infiltration route, training ground, and sanctuary. It was also a latent flash point with cities such as Fallujah known throughout Iraq as a center of religious fundamentalism and general hostility to the central government, whether it was the Ba'ath Party, Coalition Provisional Authority, or the Iraqi Interim Government. The original 2003 U.S. offensive through this area had focused on enveloping Baghdad, thus bypassing most of the major population centers of the province. As a result, those elements that would constitute the bulk of the anti-Coalition insurgency, such as veterans of the Republican Guard, Iraqi Intelligence Service, and the Ba'ath Party, remained relatively cohesive and unscathed by the initial invasion. After initial combat operations ended, a single armored cavalry regiment was assigned to patrol a vast area the size of North Carolina. Such a weak presence squandered the war's gains and allowed an enemy sanctuary to flourish. The region was also a stronghold of Iraq's Sunnis, and many of its population feared loss of status and marginalization as a result of Hussein's fall, de-Ba'athification, and the Coalition Provisional Authority's plan to empower Iraq's Shi'a majority. Although most of the population did not actively work against the Coalition forces, many did render support to the former regime loyalist movements.

Al-Anbar Province's geography helped make it a safe haven for insurgents. Both its natural river and man-made highways transformed it into a transit hub for insurgent groups. Since the province shares

Photo by LCpl Samantha L. Jones, Defense Imagery VIRIN: 041115-M-3658J-011

BGen Richard Kramlich, commanding general of 1st Force Service Support Group, talks with Marines at Camp Fallujah in November, 2004.

lengthy frontiers with Saudi Arabia, Jordan, and Syria, insurgents could easily find cross-border sanctuaries outside of Iraq. Age-old smuggling routes, tribal associations reaching across the political borders, and

Marines from the 24th Marine Expeditionary Unit establish a perimeter in Qalat Sukkar, Iraq in 2003 as civilians gather to welcome them as they secured the town. As they returned to Iraq, the Marines of I MEF could draw on almost a century's worth of experience conducting counterinsurgency operations.

Photo by SSgt Bryan Reed, Defense Imagery, VIRIN: 030413-M-0175R-089

History Division Map

In 2003, Marines had been primarily responsible for operations south of Baghdad; however, beginning in 2004, Marine Corps deployments were based in the vast al-Anbar Province in Iraq's west.

active support from Ba'athist Syria provided the insurgents a steady supply of money and sanctuaries. Radical elements could infiltrate the country, relying on counterfeit documents, safe houses, and training areas.

The insurgents also had a ready source of munitions and arms. U.S. Army sources identified 96 known munitions sites and indicated innumerable uncharted ones in the province. A large portion of Iraq's arms industry was centered in the area—particularly in al-Ameriyah, Al Mahmudiyah, and Iskandariyah. Although some localities faced arms shortages and the price of weapons increased as a result of Coalition actions, the enemy had few supply problems for its commonplace weapons: AK-47 rifles, explosives, ammunition, mortars, and rocket-propelled grenades (RPGs).

Building on Experience and Corporate Memory: the Marine Corps and Counterinsurgency

As challenging as the new operations in al-Anbar Province would be, the stability and security operations conducted during the summer of 2003 had demonstrated that the Marine Corps' approach to counterinsurgency, based on nearly a century's worth of experience, remained relevant. These experiences would continue to influence Marine Corps plans for their return to Iraq in 2004. On 18 January 2004, General Conway delivered a presentation to the Marine Corps Association Ground Dinner in which he outlined the new challenges that the Marines would face in their second deployment. He asserted that the leadership had to remember several factors. For example, whereas the Marines had been responsible for an area comprised mostly of Shi'a in 2003, the population in the new area of operations would largely be Sunni. Therefore, an important part of the expeditionary force's approach would involve finding a way to mitigate the perceived political losses suffered by the Sunnis as a result of the fall of the Ba'ath regime. In keeping with I MEF's successful experience in 2003, the Marines would focus on the Iraqi people—providing security and a better quality of life for the population and preparing the Iraqi people to govern themselves.

General Conway noted that I MEF's approach would be based on three major lines of operation: security and stability operations, information operations, and civil affairs. The goals of these operations were far reaching and wide ranging, and included eliminating destabilizing elements, establishing training programs for Iraqi security forces, developing an aggressive information campaign that promoted local confidence and established effective means of disseminating information, identifying and securing funding and resources for civil affairs initiatives, establishing local government, reducing unemployment, and ultimately preparing for the transition to Iraqi

sovereignty. Success would be measured by the extent to which the Iraqi people could assume responsibility for their own security. The failure of any of these elements would pose increasing difficulties and dangers for the Coalition forces and the Iraqi population.

While the situation in al-Anbar Province in 2004 would be markedly different from the one Marines confronted in southern Iraq in 2003, General Conway nevertheless noted that those earlier experiences would play an important role in the coming mission. He highlighted the successful accomplishments of 2003, noting that Marines demonstrated the mental and physical ability to shift rapidly from combat to stability operations and were able to conduct both simultaneously. General Conway pointed out that the culture of the Marine Corps as an infantry force with strong, small unit leadership enhanced the Marines' ability to effectively perform stability operations in southern Iraq. Battalion commanders exercised total authority in their areas of responsibility. Frequently, no one doctrine governed particular problems, and commanders adapted to their unique situation. The expeditionary force deployed a significant infantry capability, and Marines made sure to patrol the streets so that they could be seen by the locals and reassure Iraqis looking for a safe and secure environment.

The need to build good relations with the local population had been critical, and General Conway reminded his audience of the several accomplishments Marines had achieved in 2003. Operating from the belief that the quickest way to win the support of adults was to improve the quality of life of their children, Marines tried to move quickly to accomplish any project that benefited Iraqi children. These included making children aware of unexploded mines and constructing and repairing playgrounds and schools. Related to this, the Marines of I MEF had focused on consulting Iraqis and included them in the decision-making process as they set priorities for reconstruction projects. The Marines' philosophy of inclusion gave the Iraqis a sense of having a stake in their own future and confidence in American concern for their welfare.

A "trust relationship" thus formed between Marines and Iraqis. The fact that the Shi'a formed the majority of the population in much of the I MEF area of operations in 2003 proved significant. Harshly oppressed by the former regime, they demonstrated more sympathy for the Coalition than their Sunni neighbors to the north, and Marines conducted themselves in a manner to preserve good will with the Shi'as.

To build good relations with the local population,

Marines worked to manage the levels of violence. If fired upon, Marines achieved immediate fire superiority. The I MEF human exploitation teams constantly worked to collect information, which was then combined with other data to form a useful intelligence picture. When sufficient intelligence allowed targeting, Marines quickly killed or captured those who resisted.

One result of their efforts to build strong relations with the local population was that Marines were able to work with the local police forces, thus allowing I MEF to leave the built-up areas and towns. The Marine quick reaction forces always stood ready to provide "on call" support, but this was seldom necessary. The Iraqis in the Marines' area of operations soon began to police themselves. They prevented looting, destroyed improvised explosive devices, and in some cases conducted raids on criminals and former regime loyalists in their areas.

Chapter 2

The Deployment

The planners of I Marine Expeditionary Force (I MEF) and its subordinate units worked on the force deployment in November 2003 and in December began to develop the details of the strategic movement of all units identified for deployment. In addition to the forces under I MEF control, several additional units deployed for duty with Combined Joint Task Force 7. These included two bridge companies drawn from II Marine Expeditionary Force (II MEF) and Marine Reserve Forces, and a detachment of light-attack helicopters to operate out of Balad Air Base. Two Navy surgical companies also deployed to Kuwait, operating under control of Commander, Marine Forces Central Command.

As in previous campaigns in the Persian Gulf, the Marine Corps forces, deploying for the 2004 campaign in Iraq, shipped their equipment and a relatively small number of personnel by way of Navy and military sealift shipping while the bulk of personnel and some cargo traveled via strategic airlift. Only two Navy ships took part in this phase, each a highly capable amphibious assault ship: the USS *Bataan* (LHD 5) from the Atlantic Fleet and the Pacific Fleet's USS *Boxer* (LHD 4). Fifty-five helicopters deemed immediately necessary for the relief of the aviation component of the Army's 3d Armored Cavalry Regiment were loaded onto these ships. The remaining 59 helicopters, in various states of disassembly, were shipped in the military sealift ships (24 helicopters) and strategic airlift (35 helicopters). The *Boxer* and *Bataan* sailed on 14 and 23 January 2004 from their ports of embarkation. Between 18 January and 28 February, ten Military Sealift Command ships sailed from their ports, all taking approximately a month for the transit. Additional equipment for I MEF, principally vehicles drawn from maritime prepositioned ships—USNS *1stLt Baldomero Lopez* (T-AK 3010), MV *Pvt Franklin J. Phillips* (T-AK 3004),and MV *PFC William B. Baugh* (T-AK 3001)—awaited the arrival of the troops in Kuwait. These ships arrived 10 February–5 March and comprised the lead elements and main body of the I MEF forces. Though small numbers of personnel continued to arrive in Kuwait through 13 March, the main effort was preparing the relief in place of 3d Armored Cavalry Regiment, planned for 20 March,

and the 82d Airborne Division, planned for 4 April.

Assembling the force in bases and camps in Kuwait proved as complex as the deployment of I MEF to the theater the previous year. The early 2004 relief in place for U.S. forces saw 12 Army brigades and two Marine Corps regiments replacing 17 Army brigades, most of which used the Kuwait expeditionary camps and training locales for three months as the sites for the relief in place. An early problem was the minimum requirement for 7,500 bed spaces at Camp Udari to support the 1st Marine Division through the standard joint processing known as Reception, Staging, Onward movement and Integration of forces (RSOI). Reduced to 3,500 beds at Camp Udari, I MEF staff found 1,000 additional beds each at Camps Victory and New York. The remaining shortfall could only be filled by moving two regiments into camps, training areas, and on to the border assembly areas. In all, I MEF used six camps, three ports, and two air facilities during its RSOI phase.

After all Marines assembled in their assigned units and were issued equipment, they went to the range area to test fire crew-served weapons and systems unloaded from shipping and storage, and conducted final battle training. The convoys were dispatched in sequence by the 1st Marine Division, which also performed security functions for most convoys of the I MEF headquarters group and the 3d Marine Aircraft Wing. A three-day training period provided detailed preparation for safe and secure convoys. The convoy commanders formed, loaded, armed, and rehearsed their convoys for the first day and a half under the coordination of the division's operations staff. On the afternoon of the second day, each commander received the latest route and intelligence briefings, conducted a certification briefing for the division's chief of logistics, and got the assigned departure and convoy clearance information. For the final 24 hours, the convoy remained under a safety stand-down calculated to ensure rested personnel and well-prepared equipment for the single-day movement into the area of operations destinations.

In addition to the convoys, intratheater air transportation lifted selected units and equipment from Ali al-Salem Air Base to several air facilities in the

Marine F/A-18 Hornet fighter-bombers from Marine All-Weather Fighter Attack Squadron 224 sit on the flight line of al-Asad Air Base, Iraq.

new area of operations. The six newly arrived Lockheed KC-130F Hercules refueler-transport aircraft of 3d Marine Aircraft Wing supported this lift as well as the wing's internal missions.

I MEF headquarters established a garrison at Camp Fallujah, outside the city of the same name. The 1st Marine Division set up headquarters in the al-Anbar capital ar-Ramadi, at Forward Operating Base Champion, which would soon be renamed Camp Blue Diamond. The aviation combat element was based at al-Asad Air Base, and the 1st Force Service Support Group was housed south of Fallujah at Camp Taqaddum airfield.

The initial ground deployment into Iraq saw Regimental Combat Team 7 occupy al-Asad Air Base and deploy its units in the western half of the I MEF area of operations, while Regimental Combat Team 1 occupied Camp Fallujah, taking responsibility for the easternmost section of the area. The Army's 1st Brigade, 1st Infantry Division, remained at Ramadi with additional responsibilities for the vast and less populated area stretching south to the Saudi Arabia frontier, later called Area of Operation Manassas.

The planning by I MEF before returning to Iraq essentially sought to build on what had been widely assumed was a successful period of stability and security operations by the 82d Airborne and 3d Armored Cavalry Regiment. In particular, the Marine plan hinged on a strong "first 60 days" as the best method to maintain and continue progress toward a secure and independent Iraq.

To maintain continuity in security and stability operations between the 82d Airborne and I MEF, the relief in place outlined in I MEF orders sought to replace Army units sequentially, from the smaller up to larger units. This process also took place geographically from west to east, as Regimental Combat Team 1 and 3d Marine Aircraft Wing first relieved the Army's 3d Armored Cavalry Regiment of the huge western section of al-Anbar Province as well as airspace management responsibilities handled by the regiment's air cavalry squadron. Then 2d Battalion, 4th Marines, reported to the Army's 1st Brigade of the 1st Infantry Division followed by the relief of 3d Brigade, 82d Airborne, by Regimental Combat Team 1.

The Marines of I MEF at all levels carried out essential operations with their counterparts in the 82d Airborne. These operations consisted of the so-called "right seat, left seat" rides in which incoming I MEF leaders and Marines patrolled with the soldiers of the 82d Airborne, then exchanged roles and took over the operations with 82d Airborne personnel still in place to provide assistance and advice. Each unit then transferred the responsibility and authority for the district or sector. Before such transfer of authority occurred, the incoming Marine Corps units assumed security of all vital infrastructure and institutions in their assigned sectors. They introduced themselves to local, Coalition, and non-governmental organization leaders, supervised local infrastructure projects, assumed responsibilities for equipment, and continued the ongoing process of collecting and disposing of weapons and unexploded ordnance.

In each case, the transfers of authority occurred well before the deadlines. General Conway recognized the need for an accelerated relief of Army units deployed in Iraq and promised all due speed. The early dispatch of Regimental Combat Team 7 from Camp Udari paid off, as it completed its relief of 3d Armored Cavalry Regiment on 15 March, five days ahead of schedule. As part of the transfer, 3d Marine Aircraft Wing assumed responsibility for airspace management and aviation support for the area of operations. On 21 March, General Mattis relieved the commander of the 82d Airborne Division, Major General Charles H. Swannack Jr., and assumed responsibility for ground operations in the Marines' area of operations, named Atlanta in Marine Corps orders and plans. The 1st Force Service Support Group relieved the 82d Airborne Division Support Command on 22 March. The 3d Brigade, 82d Airborne Division, was relieved on 28 March, seven days ahead of schedule.

Though the Marines of I MEF met General Conway's expectations, al-Anbar Province also lived up to its reputation as a tough area of operations, and as such, Marines conducted combat operations for several days before the transfers of authority took place. By 14 March, insurgents inflicted 11 casualties upon the 1st Marine Division. On 18 March, insurgents fired rockets at 3d Marine Aircraft Wing's al-Asad Air Base killing one Marine and wounding three. A bombing killed a second Marine on 25 March 2004.

Equipping I Marine Expeditionary Force

Although the Marines newly arrived in al-Anbar considered themselves better prepared and organized

The 3d Marine Aircraft Wing used Boeing-Vertol CH-46 Sea Knight (pictured below) and Sikorsky CH-53 Super Stallion helicopters in Iraq. Both types received new armor and other upgrades upon returning there in 2004.

Photo by LCpl William L. Dubose III, Defense Imagery, VIRIN: 060530-M-9529D-001

Photo by LCpl Kevin C. Quihuis Jr., Defense Imagery VIRIN: 030410-M-5753Q-094

Capt Tom Lacroix, commanding officer, Company C, 1st Battalion, 7th Marines, speaks on the radio while accompanied by radio operators Cpl Kenny Bergain (left) and LCpl Travis Ball during the clearing of Qadawi Baghdad in 2003. All are wearing the Interceptor Multi-Threat Body Armor System Outer Tactical Vests.

for the stability and security operations missions than in the 2003 campaign, the Marine Corps equipment needs had increased. The brief period of occupation duty in mid-2003 allowed no time for incorporating new technologies and engineering into the force. By 2004, however, the experiences of U.S. and Coalition forces had generated a comprehensive set of new equipment requirements. Thus, the second deployment presented a range of new equipment requirements. Stability and security operations demanded increased numbers of vehicles of all types, yet the force lacked funding for maintenance and facilities that more equipment would require.

Aircraft survivability problems dated from the initial combat phase of the 2003 campaign, necessitating the installation of modernization systems. The completion schedule anticipated for installing most of these systems did not cover the initial part of the 2004 deployment of aircraft from 3d Marine Aircraft Wing. The special schedule developed for the Aircraft Survivability Upgrade resulted in the installation of lightweight armor kits and a ramp-mounted machine gun into the Sikorsky CH-53E Super Stallion heavy-lift helicopters by mid-April. The 36 Boeing-Vertol CH-46 Sea Knight medium-lift helicopters received infrared jammer upgrades and lightweight

armor kits beginning in April and July, respectively. The six KC-130Fs also received infrared jammer upgrades in April. Much more time would be required, however, to deploy the highly desired AN/AAR-47(2) missile warning set and AN/ALE-47 countermeasures dispenser into the light-attack squadrons. Only the larger aircraft had these capabilities.

The hope that I MEF could obtain special equipment needed for the 2004 deployment from units departing Iraq would fall far short of expectations despite a U.S. Central Command directive to leave all "uparmored" High Mobility Multipurpose Wheeled Vehicles (HMMWV)—"Humvee" models M1114, M1116, and M1109—and all tactical vehicles fitted with bolt-on armor or ballistic doors. The 82d Airborne Division turned over 83 uparmored Humvees, but the Marine expeditionary force required 250. Of the highly desired Warlock radio frequency jammers used to counter improvised explosive devices, only 25 could be gained from Combined Joint Task Force 7 sources; the Marine Corps required 61.

As in the case of the 2003 campaign, the supporting establishment of the Marine Corps, chiefly Marine Corps Systems Command, employed rapid acquisition under the Urgent Universal Need Statement (UUNS) process. Commanders of forces assigned for the 2004 campaign received instructions in November 2003 to request material required under UUNS to General Conway for consolidation and forwarding. Ultimately, the Marine Requirements Oversight Council reviewed the requests and recommended actions to the Commandant. The initial requests before the 2004 deployment totaled approximately $170 million, in comparison to approximately $100 million provided for the entire 2003 campaign.

The requirement for uparmored Humvees took immediate priority. The Marine Corps Logistics Command produced steel doors for delivery to the deploying units until more permanent solutions could be approved and acquired through joint service and Marine Corps specific programs to produce armor kits and new production vehicles. As I MEF returned to Iraq, the 2004 Urgent Universal Needs Statement items already included the following (See Table 2-1):

In addition to compiling the initial requirements, Systems Command deployed liaison teams to the I MEF staff to assess new requirements and accelerate the UUNS process.

The tandem requirements of human body armor and armor kits for utility vehicles became more pressing in both military and political arenas after combat continued in 2003 as the Iraqi insurgency gained mo-

Table 2-1: Urgent Universal Needs Statement Items

Item	Number
Marine Expeditionary Force Combat Operations Center	1
Medium-level vehicle hardening:	
Door protection	3,049
Underbody protection	3,638
Ballistic glass	2,704
Temporary steel plating	2,144
Position locating systems:	
Blue force tracker	100
EPLRS with M-DACT	50
Combat identification devices:	
Glo tapes	40,000
Phoenix Jr. strobe lights	5,000
Thermal combat imaging panels	2,163
Dust abatement systems	6
Night vision devices	882
PRC-148 radios	1,294
Advanced combat optic gun sights	3,724
M240G/TOW dual mount	97
Tropospheric satellite support radios	22
Medium tactical vehicle replacement-MTVR center seats	325
Checkpoint force protection kits	50
PRC-150	34
Personal role radios	1,487
"Dragon Eye" unmanned aerial vehicle	35
Handheld translation devices	300
Satellite-on-the-move capability	110
Mobile generator for forward resuscitative surgery system	4
PRC-150 remotes	48
PAS-13 thermal sights	855
Vehicle barrier nets	50
Lightweight body armor	1,080
"Sophie" thermal binoculars	20
22 Kw generators	17
Vehicular mounts for PRC-150	36
Explosive ordnance disposal capabilities:	
Protective suits	60
PSS-14 detectors	74
Percussion actuated nonelectric disruptors	15
Large package X-ray apparatus	7
Blast tents	15
Blast rings	15
Marking foam	500
Robot capability	15
AN/PAQ-4C infrared night sights	182
Data distribution system upgrade	20
Large LVS trailer capability	20
Ditching machine	4
Air-Naval Gunfire Liaison Company communications suites	4
Battlefield tire changing systems	2
Technical control facility	2
Automated Deep Operation Coordination System servers and laptops	
2d MAW group-level Combat Operations Center	5
KIV-7 encryption devices	7
PRC-117F radios	22
Deployable rapid assembly shelters for satellite terminal	10
MTVR trailers	20
Semiautomatic sniper rifle	18
Tactical photo reproduction capability	4
Bed netting	25,000
Data distribution system servers	16
Test stand	1
Bridge erection boat trailer	17
Lightweight all-terrain vehicles	53

mentum after the declared "end of major combat operations." Armoring a fleet of utility vehicles never intended for use in close combat was a requirement new to the logistics system, and the system's response proved predictably slow as casualties increased. Likewise, distribution of the new Interceptor body armor system to the troops was only partially complete at the time of the 2003 invasion, and priorities of issue left large numbers of combat units with older design armor vests. Moreover, defective quality control and the delays in providing upgrades to Interceptor components (heavier insert plates and additional side and shoulder protection) exacerbated the political uproar. The American government and military underestimated the scope and ferocity of the insurgency and the personal protection that fighting insurgents would require. The military laboratories and systems commands responded with designs encompassing almost total protection for vehicles and persons alike.

The "hardness" or armor of Humvees remained a critical problem for all U.S. troops, including Marines as three different levels of protection appeared in the uparmored Humvees, but only one of which offered

Photo by Sgt. Jeremy M. Giacomino, Defense Imagery VIRIN: 080709-M-6668G-021

Fighting the insurgency requried upgrades to the armor on High-Mobility Multipurpose Wheeled Vehicles (HMMWVs or Humvees). These adapted vehicles, such as this M1114, were known as "up-armored" Humvees.

adequate protection against the improvised explosive devices employed by the enemy. As a result, some units procured locally fabricated steel plates to augment the minimal protection offered by the unarmored Humvee. So scarce were the uparmored Humvees that Marines began to improvise simple, additional protection, such as hanging bags containing Kevlar plates salvaged from vests and vehicles on the exterior of the otherwise thinly constructed doors of their Humvees, thus making their vehicles into "Hillbilly Hummers."

Personal body armor consisted of two types during the initial stages of the 2003-04 campaign. The superior Interceptor System, used by front-line troops, gradually replaced the older vests worn by Marines during 1st MEF's 2004 deployment. The older design was the Personnel Armor System Ground Troops (PASGT) vest that had replaced the obsolete vinyl and ballistic plate combination of the older M-1969 Fragmentation Protective Body Armor. The PASGT ballistic filler consists of 13 plies of treated (water repellent) aramid Kevlar 29 fabric and improved the M-1969's protection against fragments.

The more effective Interceptor Multi-Threat Body Armor System consistes of two components:a Kevlar-weave outer tactical vest, which can stop a 9mm bullet, and ceramic small arms protective inserts (SAPI) or plates. The 16.4-pound system of vest with removable throat and groin protectors (8.4 pounds) and insertable front and rear plates (4 pounds each), can defeat the 7.62mm round common to the insurgents' primary AK weapon types. Straps and Velcro fasteners allow attachment of personal equipment. The 2003 Armor Protection Enhancement System added sections to protect the neck, arms, and groin. The later Deltoid Extension protected the sides of the rib cage and shoulders but added pounds, provided less ventilation, and limited body movement.

As the more than 20,000 Marines and sailors of I MEF filled their new positions for the 2004 campaign, equipped as well as the hurried measures and changing military environment permitted, the age-old problem remained: Who was the enemy; where was he; and what were his intentions?

Chapter 3

Early Operations in Al-Anbar Province

Al-Anbar Province

At 53,208 square miles, Iraq's al-Anbar Province occupies 32 percent of the nation's total area, and is the country's largest province. Nevertheless, the province is largely an unpopulated desert with most of its 1.3 million inhabitants densely packed along the Euphrates River, which cuts through the northern part of the province. Most of the inhabitants, who account for 4.9 percent of Iraq's total population, are Arab Sunnis of the large Dulaym tribal confederation. The province's capital is ar-Ramadi.

The river brings life to one of the harshest environments in the world. The region's subtropical temperatures range, on average, from 90 to 115 degrees Fahrenheit in summer to less than 50 degrees Fahrenheit in the winter. All of the province's major cities sit along or near the Euphrates' banks: Husaybah, al-Qaim, Haditha, Hit, Ramadi, and al-Fallujah. From Husaybah, where the river enters Iraq from Syria, it progresses in a fairly eastwardly direction for a little more than 50 miles before taking a sharp turn south at the city of Rawah. Between there and Haditha is Lake Qadisiyah, an artificial creation of the Haditha Dam. From Haditha, the Euphrates snakes southeasterly through the eastern part of the province before exiting east of Fallujah. Just south of Ramadi lie the lakes al-Habbaniyah and al-Milh, filled with Euphrates water by canal. Lake Tharthar, supplied with Tigris River water by canal, lies between the rivers. Down river from Ramadi are irrigation canals and most of the pumping stations. About 140 miles from Ramadi the Euphrates splits into two branches, al-Hillah and al-Hindiyyah. The latter forms the main channel and provides irrigation for rice crops, while al-Hillah, separated among numerous canals, provides irrigation to the east and south.

The western desert, an extension of the Syrian Desert, rises to elevations above 1,600 feet. Further south, the Southwestern Desert (al-Hajarah) contains a complex array of rock, wadis, ridges, and depressions. Through this region, running in a fairly direct east-west direction from Syria and Jordon is a highway and rail network that transforms the province into a bridge connecting Iraq's most populated regions and capital to Saudia Arabia, Jordan, and Syria.

Al-Anbar Province, especially Ramadi and Fallujah, reflects the strong tribal and religious traditions of its inhabitants. Saddam Hussein was constantly wary of the volatile nature of the area. Depending on which approach was most expedient, the Ba'ath regime would alternate between openly supporting the tribal groups through patronage and using the tools of governance to isolate them. If it meant being able to exert greater control over the region, the regime was happy to curtail provincial authority to better patronize the al-Anbari tribes. Iraq's oil wealth enhanced the ability of the ruling clique to bypass government institutions. The revenue generated by oil deepened the system of patronage, as funds were controlled by the central figures of the regime who funneled money and public works to loyalists. Tax revenue, already tainted by corruption, became secondary to oil wealth. Sunnis benefited the most from this system. In any case, the regime took more interest in population centers closer to Baghdad, leaving most of the province untouched. Such conditions and policies weakened governmental power in the province. Crippled by persistent corruption, undercut by deal-making between the ruling regime and tribal sheikhs, and monitored by an ever present, heavy-handed security apparatus, the civic institutions of al-Anbar Province fell into disrepair until the collapse of Saddam Hussein's regime in April 2003.

The province stood rife with insurgent and criminal activity at the time I MEF took up its security and stabilization task, and its major cities of Ramadi and Fallujah were centers of anti-Coalition resistance. Amid this hostile environment, the Coalition had labored to deliver on its promises to restore security, essential services, government, and a viable economy to the people of al-Anbar Province. However, it only had limited resources to apply to its appalling situation.

Initial Deployment

The I Marine Expeditionary Force's area of operations in al-Anbar Province—code named Atlanta—was further divided. During the first two weeks of March 2004, Colonel Craig A. Tucker, commanding Regimental Combat Team 7, deployed his maneuver

An AH-1W Super Cobra and UH-1N Huey from Marine Light Attack Helicopter Squadron 167 fly near the Euphrates River at al-Taqaddum during April 2009.

battalions throughout the newly designated Area of Operations Denver to cover several population centers as well as known infiltration routes used by enemy forces to cross the Syrian frontier into Iraq. The area covered most of the province's western region. The line companies went to Camp Hit, near the Euphrates city of Hit. One line company then deployed to the more distant Camp Korean Village, at ar-Rutbah, from which the borders with Jordan and Syria could be observed. The 3d Battalion, 7th Marines, as well as elements of the 1st Light Armored Reconnaissance Battalion and 1st Force Reconnaissance Company made Camp al-Qaim their base. A small detachment of the 1st Force Reconnaissance Company remained at al-Asad Air Base. After a brief stay at the air base, the 3d Battalion, 4th Marines, moved to Camp Haditha and Patrol Base Rawah, northwest of the Haditha Dam.

Major General James F. Amos deployed his 3d Marine Aircraft Wing (Forward) to five facilities to provide four aviation functions—aerial reconnaissance, assault support, command and control of aircraft and missiles, and offensive air support—throughout Area of Operations Atlanta. Elements of Marine Wing Headquarters Squadron 3, Marine Aircraft Group 16, Marine Wing Support Group 37, and Marine Air Control Group 38 were based at al-Asad Air Base with forward air support elements at al-Taqaddum Air Base, al-Qaim, Mudaysis, and Camp Korean Village. Al-Asad Air Base had two medium-lift helicopter squadrons; one and one-half heavy-lift helicopter squadrons, a light-attack helicopter squadron, a tanker-transport detachment, and a tactical air con-

trol center. Al-Taqaddum hosted the other medium-lift helicopter squadron and part of the light-attack squadron. The three other sites hosted a medevac helicopter detachment, and assault support and attack helicopter detachments were placed there to meet tactical needs.

Support for the aviation element built up rapidly. Air Force C-130s and 3d Marine Aircraft Wing KC-130s moved over 462 tons of aviation ordnance for operations. One hundred tons of aviation equipment was dispersed to the al-Taqaddum Air Base, al-Qaim, and Korean Village sites to support forward arming and refueling activities. Maintenance and spare part logistics began immediately, and an aircraft engine pool was established with the assistance of depot support from Naval Air Facility, Sigonella, Italy. Upon taking responsibility for the expeditionary force's area of operations, the 3d Marine Aircraft Wing acted as the responsible agency for air command and control from ground level to 11,500 feet above it.

The 1st Force Service Support Group provided Combat Service Support Battalions 1 and 7 from Combat Service Support Group 11 for the direct support of the two regiments of the 1st Marine Division and based the bulk of its units and resources at Camp al-Taqaddum. Combat Service Support Group 11 also provided direct support as required to the Army's 1st Brigade, 1st Infantry Division. Under the operational control of the 1st Brigade at Ramadi was the 2d Battalion, 4th Marines. Brigadier General Kramlich employed Combat Service Support Group 15 as the general support provider at Camp al-Taqaddum and Brigade Service Support Group 1 functioned as his

Most of al-Anbar Province is uninhabited desert, and the magnitude of this 2005 sandstorm striking al-Asad Air Base attests to its harsh environment. The storm originated far to the west at the Syrian-Jordanian border.

landing force support party in Kuwait. Upon arrival at Camp al-Taqaddum, the group received vital reinforcements from 3d Battalion, 24th Marines, for local security, and on March 20 the Army's 120th Engineer Battalion (Heavy) reported for operations, providing myriad support ranging from fortifying the camp to disposing of enemy ordnance.

At the same time, the 1st Marine Division completed its movement from Kuwait using the command post established in Ramadi as noted above, where the Army's 1st Brigade, 1st Infantry Division, patrolled the Area of Operations Topeka. The 1st Brigade, 1st Infantry Division, under the command of Colonel Arthur W. Conner Jr., deployed its 1st Battalion, 16th Infantry, and 2d Battalion, 4th Marines, at Ramadi, where the 1st Battalion, 5th Field Artillery, equipped with M109A6 Paladin self-propelled howitzers, was also stationed. Conner operated 1st Battalion, 34th Armor, out of Hibbinaya, halfway between Ramadi and Fallujah. Battery I of 3d Battalion, 11th Marines, converted to military police duty, operated from a camp at Madaysis from where it could monitor the Saudi Arabia border crossing at Ar'ar Wadi. A Marine expeditionary force order designated this zone Area of Operations Manassas. Last to move into its base in Iraq, Regimental Combat Team 1 occupied Camp Fallujah, sending battalions to cover its Area of Operations Raleigh.

Regimental Combat Team 1 commander Colonel John A. Toolan detailed 2d Battalion, 1st Marines, to Camp Baharia, just east of Fallujah, and 1st Battalion, 5th Marines, to Camp Abu Ghraib, west of the town, Abu Ghraib. He also covered the sector in north Babil Province with 2d Battalion, 2d Marines at Al Mahmudiyah and with the Army's 1st Battalion, 32d Infantry, 10th Mountain Division, at Camp Iskandariya. The 1st Reconnaissance Battalion, less one company assigned to Regimental Combat Team 7, was also based at Fallujah but oriented its actions throughout the area of operations. The units in Area of Operations Raleigh were also responsible for conducting operations in the suburbs of Baghdad. These included stopping insurgents from attacking Baghdad airport, Abu Ghraib Prison, north Babil, and Iraqi national highways 8 and 9. The Camp Dogwood logistics support area of the Army, located 40 kilometers southwest of Baghdad, also required local security support for its garrison.

1st Marine Division commander Major General James N. Mattis set the tone for the new campaign with a forthright message to his command (see sidebar). In it, he drew from the Marine Corps' legacy of fighting small wars, illustrating continuity between the Marine's current mission in Iraq and to the Central American interventions of the 1920s and 1930s. He warned the Marines to overcome the insurgents' attempts to drive a wedge between the Americans and Iraqis, and ordered his forces to "First, do no harm," when it came to the Iraqi civilian population. General Mattis did not evade or soften the difficul-

Letter to All Hands

We are going back into the brawl. We will be relieving the magnificent soldiers fighting under the 82d Airborne Division, whose hard won successes in the Sunni Triangle have opened opportunities for us to exploit. For the last year, the 82d Airborne has been operating against the heart of the enemy's resistance. It's appropriate that we relieve them: When it's time to move a piano, Marines don't pick up the piano bench—we move the piano. So this is the right place for Marines in this fight, where we can carry on the legacy of Chesty Puller in the Banana Wars in the same sort of complex environment that he knew in his early years. Shoulder to shoulder with our comrades in the Army, Coalition Forces and maturing Iraqi Security Forces, we are going to destroy the enemy with precise firepower while diminishing the conditions that create adversarial relationships between us and the Iraqi people.

This is going to be hard, dangerous work. It is going to require patient, persistent presence. Using our individual initiative, courage, moral judgment, and battle skills, we will build on the 82d Airborne victories. Our country is counting on us even as our enemies watch and calculate, hoping that America does not have warriors strong enough to withstand discomfort and danger. You, my fine young men, are going to prove the enemy wrong—dead wrong. You will demonstrate the same uncompromising spirit that has always caused the enemy to fear America's Marines.

The enemy will try to manipulate you into hating all Iraqis. Do not allow the enemy that victory. With strong discipline, solid faith, unwavering alertness, and undiminished chivalry to the innocent, we will carry out this mission. Remember, I have added, "First, do no harm" to our passwords of "No Better Friend, No Worse Enemy." Keep your honor clean as we gain information about the enemy from the Iraqi people. Then, armed with that information and working in conjunction with fledgling Iraqi Security Forces, we will move precisely against the enemy elements and crush them without harming the innocent.

This is our test—our Guadalcanal, our Chosin Reservoir, our Hue City. Fight with a happy heart and keep faith in your comrades and your unit. We must be under no illusions about the nature of the enemy and the dangers that lie ahead. Stay alert, take it all in stride, remain sturdy, and share your courage with each other and the world. You are going to write history, my fine young sailors and Marines so write it well.

Semper Fidelis,
J. N. Mattis,
Major General, U.S. Marines

---

ties of the Marines' task, declaring that the mission would be "hard, dangerous work." The current mission would be their Guadalcanal and Hue City, and would define the Marines' legacy in the early 21st Century.

At this point, the Marine Corps had deployed some 24,500 men and women to Iraq, approximately 24,300 under I MEF, drawn from Atlantic and Pacific bases, augmented by 5,500 Navy construction and Army troops. Some 3,900 Marines and sailors of Marine Corps Reserve organizations were serving on active duty with about 80 percent deployed to Iraq. Another 1,900 individual augmentees from the Reserves served throughout the Marine Corps.

The Iraq Insurgency

The earliest classification of a post-hostilities threat group was that of "former regime loyalists." These included Ba'ath Party members, former Iraqi soldiers, and remnants of the Fedayeen Saddam, a radical paramilitary group loosely recruited into the Iraqi defense establishment. The insurgency also included extremist groups, such as the Wahhabi movement, the Iraqi Islamic Party, and pro-regime tribes. These could be augmented by outside actors, including international terrorists interested in exploiting the unrest and U.S. vulnerabilities.

The insurgency continued efforts to reorganize under various groupings to force the withdrawal of Coalition forces and to regain power within Iraq. It operated throughout several cities within the Sunni Triangle from Ramadi in the west to Baghdad in the east and Mosul in the north. The U.S. and Coalition bureaucracy later coined successive terms according to the political climate—"Anti-Coalition Forces" and "Anti-Iraqi Forces" were favorites of political figures loath to acknowledge the existence of a genuine Iraqi insurgency against U.S. and allied forces.

The insurgents proved well armed. Although initially poorly trained, they were soon able to execute lethal attacks against the Coalition forces and Iraqis who sided with them. The intelligence services considered the former regime forces as compatible with other groups, such as foreign fighters, transnational terrorists, pro-Saddam tribes, radical Kurdish factions, and Islamic extremists throughout Iraq. Former regime loyalist elements continuously attempted to gain favor in militant Sunni neighborhoods throughout Iraq. They used private homes to conduct meetings and cache their weapons. During the initial period of its occupation of Iraq, the Combined Joint Task Force 7 staff considered Ba'athist leadership cadres and old regime forces as the primary threat to Coalition operations. They probably were responsible for the majority of ambushes against "soft" targets, such as convoys, and symbolic centers of the interim government, such as police stations and council meeting locations.

While many of the anti-Coalition organizations drew their ranks from secular nationalists and former supporters of the regime, other groups were organized along religious lines. Wahhabist influences remained strong with the Sunni tribes in the vicinity of Fallujah with some support among their co-religionists within Baghdad. A radical religious organization with origins in Saudi Arabia, Wahhabists preach non-tolerance of infidels, jihad against Coalition forces, and martyrdom in the name of their goals. Baghdad

In his Commander's Intent, 1st Marine Division commander MajGen James N. Mattis characterized the new mission in Iraq as a moment that would define the Marine Corps, akin to the battles of Iwo Jima and Hue City.

Photo by LCpl Henry S. Lopez, Defense Imagery VIRIN: 030312-M-0523L-003

Table 3-1: Marine Corps Forces In Support of Operations Iraqi Freedom II–April 2004

I MEF (Fwd), Kuwait	116
I MEF (Fwd), Iraq	29,579
I MEF (Fwd), Qatar	13
2d Medical Battalion, Kuwait	161
Fox Vehicle Detachment, Kuwait	12
Total I MEF (Fwd) assigned forces	29,881
U.S. Navy (22d NCR) and Army (1st Brigade)	(5,565)
Total I MEF (Fwd) Marine Corps forces	24,316
1st FAST Company (-), Baghdad	116
Detachment B, 4th Air-Naval Gunfire Liaison Company	33
Element, MarForCent, Bahrain	6
Marine Corps Element, Land Component Command, Arifjan, Kuwait	3
National Intelligence Support	15
Other	14
Total U.S. Marine Corps	24,508

Sunni and Ba'ath party members typically remained more secular in thought than Wahhabists but they would occasionally cooperate as a matter of convenience. U.S. and Coalition forces identified elements of several recognized terrorist organizations in Iraq, and these groups may have received support from the former regime. Some of the Islamic extremist organizations suspected in the enemy ranks included al-Qaeda, Ansar al-Islam, Hezbollah, and Wahhabis.

The insurgency was not only confined to militant Sunni groups, however. Shortly after the fall of the Ba'ath regime, radical Shi'a militias began to gain momentum and popularity. For example, the Supreme Council for the Islamic Revolution in Iraq (a Shi'ite political party and armed militia) took advantage of the security vacuum to increase influence throughout Iraq. In addition, the collapse of the Ba'athist regime helped increase the relative influence of Ayatollah Sistani and other important clerics of the key Shi'ite holy cities of an-Najaf and Karbala. The renewed emphasis on an-Najaf as a center of the Shi'a religion— the largest in Iraq—countered the former influence of Iranian clerics seeking to fill the void, thus causing undoubted friction between Shi'ite elements.

While Iran traditionally supported all Shi'a organizations, the Supreme Council's goal of creating an Iraq independent of Tehran left it somewhat at odds with the Islamic Fundamentalist Republic. The Badr Corps, the military arm of the Supreme Council, re-

Militant Sunnis and Shi'a, secular Ba'athists, and foreign fighters all took part in terrorist attacks against Coalition forces. Roadside bombs, such as the one whose aftereffects are depicted here, were a common weapon deployed by insurgent groups.

tained much stronger ties to Tehran, however, and it continued to stage demonstrations openly hostile to the Coalition. The Badr Corps' followers in Iran reportedly crossed into Iraq with Iranian intelligence agents within their organization. Many observers believed that the corps placed arms stockpiles in the Shi'a sections of Baghdad and other cities to the south. The Supreme Council later changed the name of its militia to the Badr Organization, connoting a more peaceful and political emphasis, but it remained a significant military presence in Iraqi public life.

Other religious organizations, while not directly rising against U.S. and Coalition forces, remained vital sources of support for the insurrection and other forms of opposition to them. The Howza (religious seminaries teaching Islamic theory and law once banned under Saddam Hussein) had three key elements for the Shi'a: the premier religious school in the Shi'a religion located in an-Najaf, a body of leaders that guided the direction and conduct of the Shi'a religion, and the mutually shared goals of all Shi'as. All Shi'a-based organizations opposing the Coalition forces had some affiliation with the Howza, including

Table 3-2: I Marine Expeditionary Force Combat Power (On Hand/Ready)–April 2004

Aviation					
AH-1W	UH-1N	CH-46E	CH-53E	KC-130F	RQ-2B Pioneer
34/25	18/13	34/27	24/19	6/5	8/7
74%	72%	79%	79%	83%	88%
Ground (USMC)					
HMMWV (Antitank)	HMMWV Hardback	Amphibious Assault Vehicle	Light Armored Vehicle	Tank M1A1	Howitzer M198
103/94	403/365	39/37	118/89	16/16	18/18
91%	90%	95%	75%	100%	100%
Ground (Army)					
Tank M1/A1/A2	Bradley Fighting Vehicle M2/A1/A2	HMMWV M1064	Howitzer, M109A6	Scout HMMWV	
14/13	30/28	8/7	6/6	128/124	
93%	93%	88%	100%	97%	

the SCIRI, Badr Corps, and the Iranian Dawa Party. Several persons claimed to speak on behalf of the Howza, such as the influential religious leader Muqtada al Sadr, son of a murdered Shi'ite cleric, and Ayatollah Sistani.

Marines Establish Their Presence

By 20 March 2004, the 1st Marine Division had completed its relief of the 82d Airborne Division in al-Anbar and northern Babil Provinces. Regimental Combat Team 7 went into action first. Its patrols and limited offensive actions ranged far, and the 1st Light Armored Reconnaissance Battalion reportedly put the equivalent of 2.5 years worth of peacetime mileage on its General Motors-Canada light-armored vehicles during its first month of operations. Security was scarce, and resistance against U.S. and Coalition forces in the region was persistent. The first casualties in the division came from an improvised explosive device deto-

nated on 6 March against a vehicle in the 3d Battalion, 7th Marines, sector, injuring two Marines.

Two days later, Marines launched their first offensive action of the year when 3d Battalion, 7th Marines, and the 1st Squadron, 3d Armored Cavalry Regiment, conducted a cordon and search of a house in Husaybah. Regimental Combat Team 7's discovery of 10 improvised launchers and 60 57mm aerial rockets arrayed around Camp Korean Village was sobering. On 15 March, Syrian border guards fired with small arms on Marines of Company L, 3d Battalion, 7th Marines, near the Husaybah border crossing point. The Marines responded with rifles, heavy and light machine guns, and a tube launched, optically tracked (TOW) antitank missile shot. One Marine was wounded while three Syrian border posts were damaged or destroyed. Investigations by local Iraqi guards proved that the Syrians had opened fire first and that neither side had crossed the frontier at any point.

Iraq's al-Anbar Province was divided into Areas of Operation. I MEF's (code named Atlanta) included Area of Operations Denver (western region), Area of Operations Topeka (Ramadi and its surrounding area), Area of Operations Raleigh (Fallujah and surrounding areas), and Area of Operations Oshkosh (al-Taqaddum).

I MEF Briefing Map, Adapted by History Division

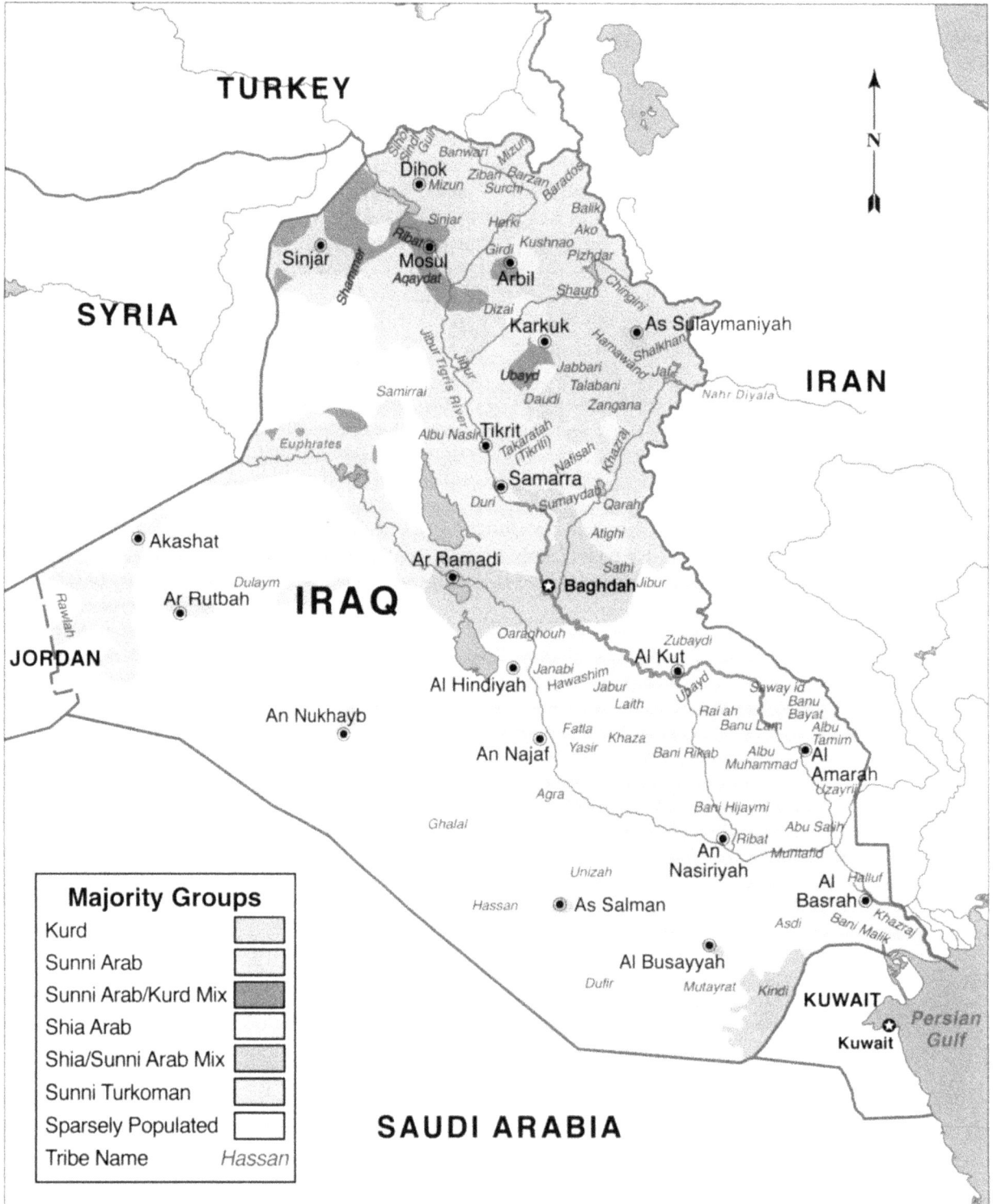

Majority Groups

Kurd
Sunni Arab
Sunni Arab/Kurd Mix
Shia Arab
Shia/Sunni Arab Mix
Sunni Turkoman
Sparsely Populated
Tribe Name   *Hassan*

History Division Map

Although al-Anbar is geographically the largest of Iraq's provinces, it is the least populated, with most of its inhabitants living along the Euphrates River. The majority of its inhabitants are Sunni Arabs of the Dulaym tribe.

The regiment executed operations across Area of Operations Denver that focused on identifying and capturing enemy mortar men, explosive device planters, and foreign fighters. Colonel Tucker's primary task remained to interdict the infiltration of foreign fighters joining the Iraqi insurgent effort by using the so-called "rat lines" from the porous Syrian border and the "white wadi" emerging from the border with Saudi Arabia. In the vital security area around al-Asad Air Base, Regimental Combat Team 7 executed a coordinated raid using special operations personnel with Marines of the al-Asad garrison to capture suspected insurgents conducting rocket attacks on the base.

To establish a presence north of the Euphrates and destroy key insurgency command and control areas, the 3d Battalion, 4th Marines, moved into Rawah on 21 March. Both mounted and dismounted patrols by joint U.S.-Iraqi teams reinforced border security and sought to deny emplacement and detonation of explosive devices along various routes. On 19 March, the regiment reported that a patrol from 3d Battalion, 7th Marines, stopped and seized a vehicle containing several grenades, RPG-type rockets, launchers, and machine gun ammunition. Three of the six suspects fled the vehicle, and three were detained. On 22 March, Marines from the same battalion again stopped a sin-

gle vehicle for violating curfew, and the search of the vehicle uncovered one U.S. identification card, a cellular phone, two handheld global positioning devices, and a mortar firing table printed in Arabic. Two individuals were arrested and brought to Camp al-Qaim for further questioning where they provided intelligence for a follow-on cordon-and-knock mission that brought no further discoveries.

In Rawah, the 3d Battalion, 4th Marines, conducted patrols with local police and began its campaign to secure the town. Far to the southwest in Area of Operations Denver, Marines of 2d Battalion, 7th Marines, conducted joint dismounted security patrols with the Rutbah Iraqi Civil Defense Corps Company. The 1st Force Reconnaissance Company tracked high-value insurgents and planned raids, maintained border observation, and deployed snipers as required. All units produced information operations aimed at calming and reassuring the local populace, while spreading the fruits of civil affairs projects and other assistance pro-

The disposition of U.S. and allied forces in Iraq is shown as reported in a Pentagon press briefing on 30 April 2004.

Pentagon Press Briefing, April 30, 2004, http://www.defenselink.mil/DODCMSShare/briefingslide/52/040430-D-6570C-006.jpg

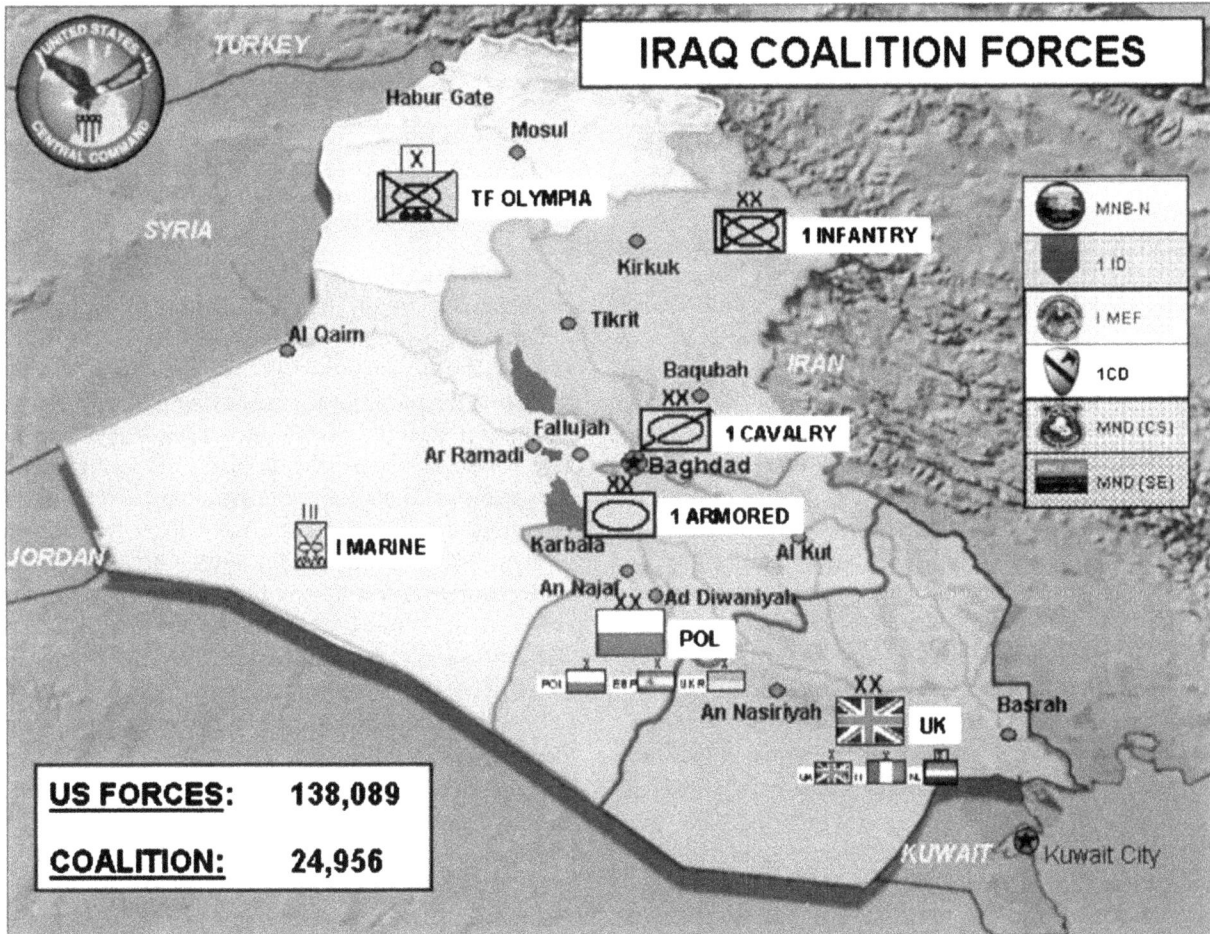

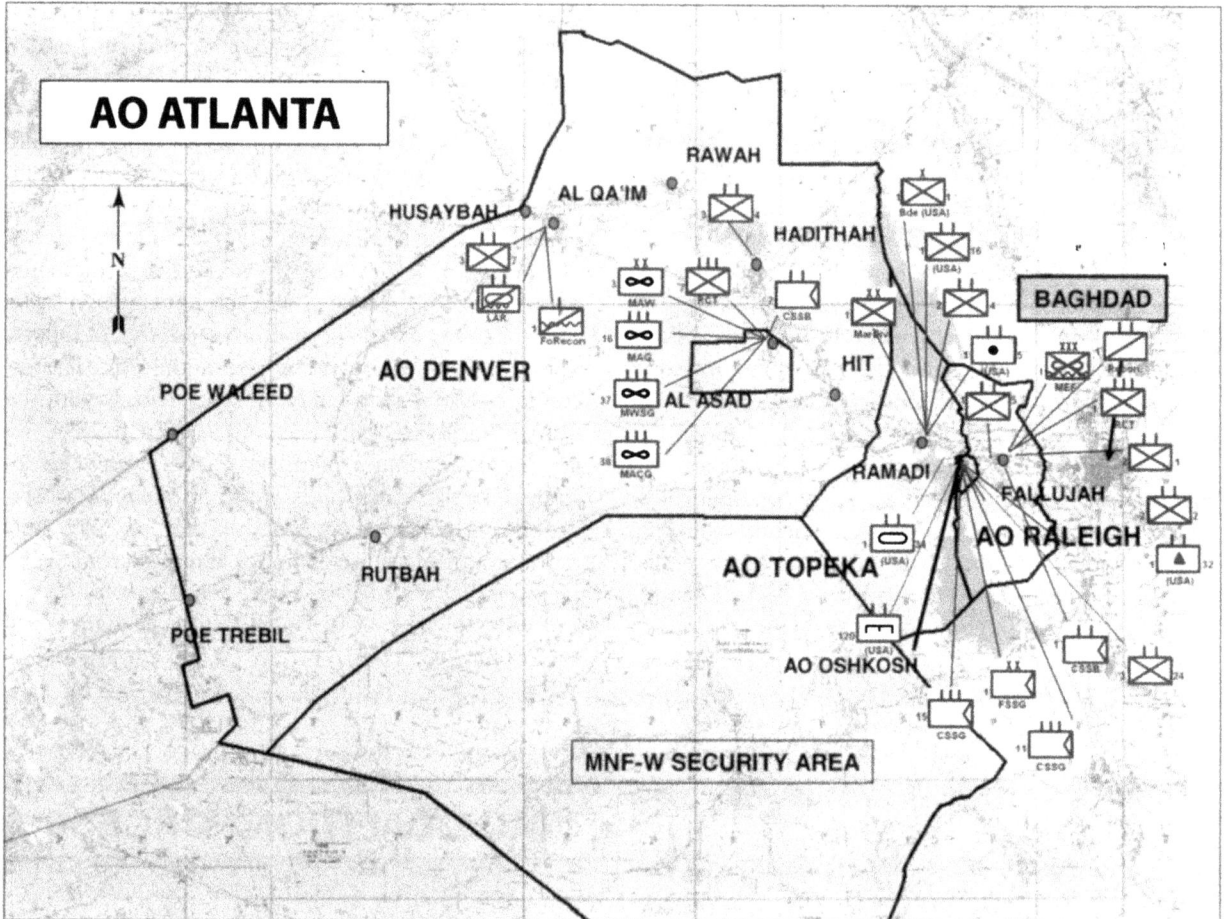

AO ATLANTA

AO DENVER

AO TOPEKA

AO RALEIGH

AO OSHKOSH

MNF-W SECURITY AREA

BAGHDAD

RAWAH

AL QA'IM

HUSAYBAH

HADITHAH

HIT

RAMADI

FALLUJAH

POE WALEED

RUTBAH

POE TREBIL

AL ASAD

I MEF Briefing Map, Adapted by History Division

Initial Deployment of I Marine Expeditionary Force (Forward) Units, March 2004.

grams. In this manner, the regiment executed General Mattis' intention of dual-track operations to kill insurgents and to help support the Iraqi people.

During this first partial month of operations (5–31 March) in Area of Operations Denver, Regimental Combat Team 7 experienced 24 mine or improvised explosive device attacks, found 73 other devices before they could be detonated, and received 27 indirect- and 26 direct-fire attacks. Four Marines died in action and 51 were wounded in this introduction to the new area.

The 1st Brigade, 1st Infantry Division, continued to center its main effort on Ramadi, bolstered considerably by the attachments of 2d Battalion, 4th Marines, and the provisional military police battalion formed by 3d Battalion, 11th Marines. The brigade's eastern boundary with Regimental Combat Team 1 moved to the western bank of the Tharthar Canal with Regimental Combat Team 1 assuming responsibility for the battlespace north of the Euphrates near Saqlawiyah. The military police company, transferred from the 4th Marine Division to 3d Battalion, 11th Marines, operated

the detention facility in Ramadi and made its first detainee transfer on 24 March, transporting 15 captives to Camp Fallujah. As the unit moved, a bomb exploded. The detonation produced no casualties, and the subsequent search of a house in the vicinity led to the capture of four rifles, electrical switches, and a large pile of wire. The brigade had two other such devices explode in its sector the same day. One of these explosions injured two Marines, and the other targeted an Army M1A1 Abrams main battle tank. The search of the area by the Army's 1st Battalion, 34th Armor, led to the killing of two insurgents, one of whom had an AK-47 rifle and a detonating device. Such events continued across the operating areas, taxing the men and women of each regiment or brigade to remain vigilant and ready for action.

Other 1st Brigade operations included security sweeps against surface-to-air missile teams operating around al-Taqaddum, convoy escort for units passing between the two Marine regiment sectors, and covering the withdrawal of the last elements of 82d Airborne

Division to Balad Air Base, north of Baghdad. Continuing operations in Ramadi included sweeps, check points, raids, and watching for highly-placed insurgent leaders.

The movement of Regimental Combat Team 1 from Kuwait took place during 14–21 March, and the regimental commanders and staff began work with the 3d Brigade, 82d Airborne Division, at Camp Fallujah to effect the "right seat, left seat" turnovers at all levels. During this process, Colonel Toolan received operational control of the 1st Battalion, 32d Infantry, from the 1st Brigade, 1st Infantry Division's Colonel Arthur W. Connor. Along with 2d Battalion, 2d Marines, the soldiers would cover north Babil province. The external security responsibility for the Abu Ghraib Prison fell to 1st Battalion, 5th Marines, and Colonel Toolan's other two battalions operated outside of Fallujah to isolate it from infiltration. 2d Battalion, 1st Marines, covered the north

and east, while 1st Reconnaissance Battalion was responsible for the southern sectors. The unenviable mission for the Marines and soldiers of Regimental Combat Team 1 consisted of stabilizing a large area that included the most volatile town in the notorious Sunni Triangle, Fallujah.

Roughly nine square miles in size, the city sits like a trapezoid along the Euphrates' eastern bank with parallel northern and southern boundaries. As the Euphrates approaches the city, the river takes a sudden turn in a northeasterly direction. Almost immediately, however, the river returns to its southeasterly course. The peninsula formed by this course change forms an arrow-like formation aimed at the city's northwestern district, the Jolan Quarter. On the peninsula's eastern side are two parallel bridges that run into the city. The southern bridge carries Highway 10 over the Euphrates. The road runs through the city center and bisects High-

Fallujah is bounded on the west by the Euphrates River, a rail line on the north, and Highway E1 on the east. Highway 10 bisects the city, running east and west.

2d Topographic Platoon Map, Adapted by History Division

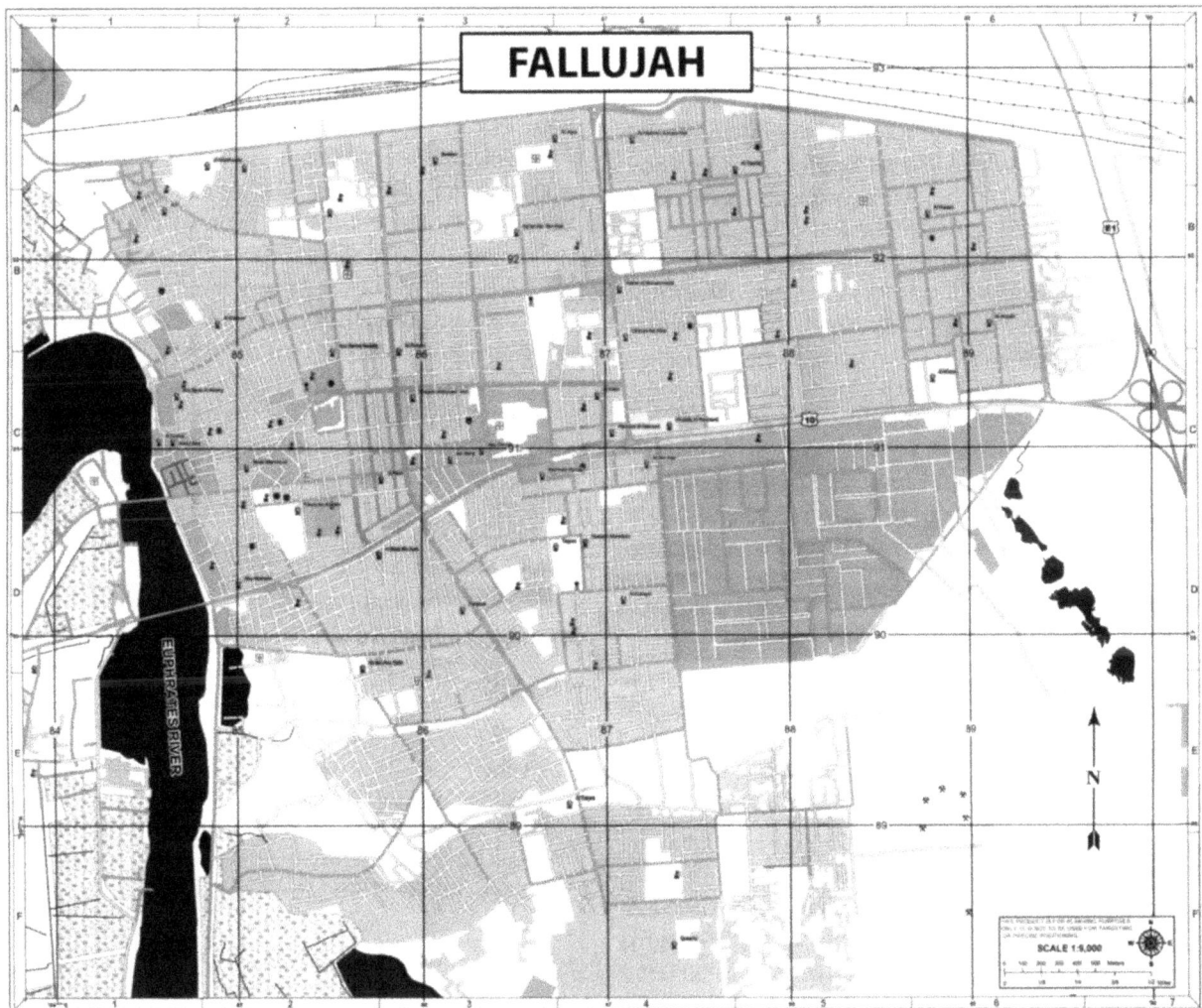

way E1 just outside the eastern city limits.

On 18 March, insurgents attacked the Regimental Combat Team 1 and 3d Brigade, 82d Airborne Division command groups in Fallujah along Highway 10. A week later, two more attacks on the highway within 15 hours of each other hit a special operations unit and a Marine Wing Support Squadron 374 convoy. Colonel Toolan ordered 2d Battalion, 1st Marines, to secure the cloverleaf intersection with Highway 1, which runs north-south on the eastern side of the city, and the northeast portion of the city adjacent to Highway E1. At dawn on 26 March, one rifle company of 2d Battalion, 1st Marines, seized control of the cloverleaf. Traffic was stopped and diverted around Fallujah, and E and F Companies entered the northeast portion of the city. The insurgents responded to their approach by launching coordinated mortar and small arms ambushes throughout the day against the Marines who engaged the insurgents in numerous firefights. On 27 March, at the request of the city council, 2d Battalion, 1st Marines, pulled its forces from that portion of the city but retained surveillance over the cloverleaf. The next day, the battalion reoccupied the intersection, remaining in place through the end of the month to prevent further attacks on convoys.

Under these less than auspicious circumstances, the transfer of authority with the 3d Brigade, 82d Airborne Division, and that of the two divisions as well, took place on 28 March at Camp Fallujah. Throughout the week, 23–31 March, insurgents struck the camp with indirect fire, and Abu Ghraib Prison received the same treatment for three days. On 30 March, insurgents ambushed a convoy from the 1st Force Service Support Group near Fallujah. The next day, a patrol from 1st Reconnaissance Battalion discovered a cache of 300 mortar rounds southwest of Fallujah. As difficult as these early experiences in al-Anbar Province had been for the 1st Marine Division and its supporting aviation and service contingents, hopes remained high that a sustained and determined Marine Corps presence could bring improved conditions to the chaotic province.

Among the many technological advantages Marines exploited in this campaign was the much improved intelligence capability that had been developed over two decades. The 2003 campaign in Iraq had seen the baptism of fire for the Marine Corps intelligence battalion formed in the MEF headquarters group under normal organization. Accordingly, the 2d Intelligence Battalion established its Tactical Fusion Center with the division command post at Camp Blue Diamond and proceeded to operate information cells as low as the company level in the ensuing campaign. The Tactical Fusion Center combined in a single place the intelligence from

higher echelons of national and military intelligence services with the data from the many sources of local Marine Corps and Army units. Overall, the positioning of the Tactical Fusion Center adjacent to the divisional operations center provided situational awareness unprecedented even by standards of the 2003 accomplishments.

General Mattis signaled his appreciation of the situation near the end of March. Colonel Tucker's Regimental Combat Team 7 had successfully positioned units to interdict the primary rat line. Concurrently, Colonel Toolan's Regimental Combat Team 1 had moved aggressively against the enemy center of gravity in Fallujah, while Colonel Conner's 1st Brigade preempted insurgent force efforts to disrupt the authorities of al-Anbar Province. The Marines wanted to increase human intelligence, fused with all sources, to create opportunities for strikes against the insurgent networks.

General Mattis saw in the opposition a combination of classic insurgent tactics and terrorist activities, and these had increased during the turnover. Not only were the more plentiful road convoys attacked, but also violence in urban and rural areas across the province heightened. Increased patrol activity into areas not normally covered had produced attacks by both improvised explosive devices and direct fire. In no case, however, did the insurgents demonstrate any interest in assaulting the new arrivals. Instead, they had fallen before steady Marine infantry pressure and return fire.

The opening of the I MEF stability and security operations campaign in March ended with an insurgent ambush that left four U.S. security contractors killed and mutilated on the Highway 10 bridge in west-central Fallujah, prompting U.S. offensive actions in reprisal. The initial campaign plan for stability and security operations would give way to full-spectrum combat operations for Marines and soldiers in Iraq and not exclusively in the I MEF zone.

General Mattis Urged His Division Onward

Demonstrate respect to the Iraqi people, especially when you don't feel like it. As the mission continues, we will experience setbacks and frustrations. In many cases our efforts will seem unappreciated by those we are trying the hardest to help. It is then that small unit leaders step up and are counted. Keep your soldiers, sailors and Marines focused on the mission and resistant to adversarial relationships with the Iraqi people . . . We obey the Geneva Convention even while the enemy does not. We will destroy the enemy without losing our humanity.

Chapter 4

The First Al-Fallujah Battle and Its Aftermath

The offensive actions carried out by Regimental Combat Team 1 on 25–27 March succeeded in sending a message to the people of al-Fallujah that the Marines were there to stay. While setting back the civil affairs process in the city, Marines felt they were effectively dealing with the situation.

As noted, the 1st Marine Division had developed a measured, phased approach to stabilizing the al-Anbar region that combined kinetic operations, information operations, and civil affairs actions to show the residents of Fallujah both the carrot and the stick. This planning was described in a division order prepared for the regimental combat team called Fallujah Opening Gambit. Despite these and other measures, however, events in the city forced the division to confront a range of new circumstances and unanticipated challenges.

Operation Vigilant Resolve (3–30 April 2004)

On 31 March 2004 insurgents ambushed four armed security contractors from the firm Blackwater USA. The Americans died amid a volley of hand grenades. A mob gathered, desecrated the bodies, set them afire, and hung two of them from the nearby Old Bridge spanning the Euphrates River. World media broadcast the hanging bodies, and the American and western public saw shocking footage of charred and almost unrecognizable bodies as residents of the city cheered and danced. Less known was the cooperation of local Iraqis who helped the Marines of 2d Battalion, 1st Marines, recover the remains of three victims that night and the fourth the following day.

After a series of conferences with the White House and the Secretary of Defense, Lieutenant General Ricardo S. Sanchez, commander of Combined Joint Task Force 7, directed the Marines to undertake immediate military action. On 1 April 2004, Sanchez's deputy director of operations, Army Brigadier General Mark Kimmitt, promised an "overwhelming" response to the Blackwater deaths, stating that "we will pacify that city." In the midst of calls for vengeance including options of destroying what little critical infrastructure remained in the city, both I Marine Expeditionary Force commander, Lieutenant General

James T. Conway, and 1st Marine Division commander, Major General James N. Mattis, cautioned against rash action. In the division's daily report, General Mattis' assistant division commander, Brigadier General John F. Kelly, strove to temper the call for immediate offensive action:

As we review the actions in Fallujah yesterday, the murder of four private security personnel in the most brutal way, we are convinced that this act was spontaneous mob action. Under the wrong circumstances this could have taken place in any city in Iraq. We must avoid the temptation to strike out in retribution. In the only 10 days we have been here we have engaged the "good" and the bad in Fallujah everyday, and have casualties to show for our efforts. We must remember that the citizens and officials of Fallujah were already gathering up and delivering what was left of three victims before asked to do so, and continue in their efforts to collect up what they can of the dismembered remnants of the fourth. We have a well thought out campaign plan that considers the Fallujah problem across its very complicated spectrum. This plan most certainly includes kinetic action, but going overly kinetic at this juncture plays into the hands of the opposition in exactly the way they assume we will. This is why they shoot and throw hand grenades out of crowds, to bait us into overreaction. The insurgents did not plan this crime, it dropped into their lap. We should not fall victim to their hopes for a vengeful response. To react to this provocation, as heinous as it is, will likely negate the efforts the 82d ABD paid for in blood, and complicate our campaign plan which we have not yet been given the opportunity to implement. Counterinsurgency forces have learned many times in the past that the desire to demonstrate force and resolve has long term and generally negative implications, and destabilize rather than stabilize the environment.

Sanchez' headquarters ordered immediate offensive action to re-establish freedom of maneuver in

Photo by 1st Lt Esteban Vickers, DVIDS, VIRIN 080410-M-2385J-003

On 31 March 2004, four Blackwater USA civilian contractors were ambushed and killed by insurgent forces in Fallujah. Their bodies were burned and mutilated and two were hung from this bridge (pictured here in 2008).

Fallujah on 1 April. At I MEF headquarters, General Conway directed General Mattis to establish 12 checkpoints around the city using local Iraqi Civil Defense Corps and police personnel to prevent any movement into or out of the city by younger males. Iraqi paramilitary personnel, at this time still considered to be reliable, manned seven of the checkpoints positioned as inner cordons, and Marines of Lieutenant Colonel Gregg P. Olson's 2d Battalion, 1st Marines, and Lieutenant Colonel Brennan T. Byrne's 1st Battalion, 5th Marines, set up five outer checkpoints to complete the ring around the city. As this was occurring, the two Marine battalions began moving significant combat power to the northeast corner of the city, near the Jolan District.

On 3 April, General Sanchez issued his order for Operation Vigilant Resolve. The mission aimed to deny insurgents sanctuary in Fallujah and to arrest those responsible for the Blackwater killings. The two Marine battalions moved into positions around the eastern and northern portion of Fallujah to seal the outer cordon of the city. The Marine and Iraqi positions continued to be fired upon and the friendly Iraqis soon fled. The Iraqi 36th Commando Battalion was subsequently dispatched to replace the fleeing Iraqi forces. A specially trained unit augmented and mentored by the U.S. Army's Special Forces to fight alongside American troops, the commandos would acquit themselves well in combat during the weeks ahead.

In his commander's comments of 3 April, General Mattis raised the difficulties of conducting offensive operations in Fallujah:

My intent is to then enter the city from two directions, which will draw fire from guerillas and put us in a position to exploit our own well considered and conditions-based operation. There are over 250,000 inhabitants in the city, the vast majority of whom have no particular love for the Coalition, but are also not insurgents. From a moral, ethical, legal, and military perspective, we will fight smart: We do not have to be loved at the end of the day, this is a goal that is no longer achievable in Fallujah, but we must avoid turning more young men into terrorists. We will also avoid doing what the insurgents, terrorists, and foreign fighters, and "Arab Street" all expect, and that is the thoughtless application of excessive force as if to strike out in retribution for the murders.

General Mattis and his division staff planned decisive operations to bring Fallujah under control while simultaneously maintaining the counterinsurgency operations in nearby Ramadi and the rest of al-Anbar and north Babil Provinces to prevent conceding any advantage to the insurgents.

His orders called for a four-phase operation to be implemented by Colonel John A. Toolan's Regimental Combat Team 1. In Phase I, the regiment would begin sustained operations in Fallujah beginning 0100 on 5 April with a tight cordon of the city using two battalion-sized task forces in blocking positions and traffic control points on all motorized avenues

of approach. This stage included raids against high value targets and the photography shop that printed the murder photos. Phase II entailed continuous raids against targets inside the city from firm bases established within northern and southern Fallujah. Messages concerning the operation would be broadcast informing citizens of measures necessary to protect themselves and families from harm and thanking the local population for their cooperation and for information leading to the death or capture of insurgent forces. In Phases III and IV, Regimental Combat Team 1 would, at the moment of the commander's choosing, attack and seize various hostile sectors in the city, integrating and eventually turning operations over to Iraqi security forces.

Colonel Toolan ordered his two battalions, the regiment's supporting tank company, assault amphibian company, and its artillery battery into their battle positions in the early morning hours of 5 April. The 1st Reconnaissance Battalion swept to the north and east of the city to target insurgents seeking to fire mortar rounds and rockets into Marine positions. Company D, 1st Light Armored Reconnaissance Bat-

Col John A. Toolan (left), commander of Regimental Combat Team 1, and 3d Battalion, 1st Marines, commander LtCol Willard Buhl, discuss progress made by their forces during Operation Vigilant Resolve.

Photo by LCpl Jordan F. Sherwood, Defense Imagery, VIRIN 040813-M-0706S-030

A Marine M1A1 Abrams main battle tank blocks access into Fallujah to isolate insurgent forces operating inside the city during Operation Vigilant Resolve.

talion, moved north to cover Highway E1. Marines of Company B, 1st Combat Engineer Battalion, and Navy Mobile Construction Battalion 74 constructed a berm around southern Fallujah, further isolating the battle area.

As Captain Kyle Stoddard's Company F, 2d Battalion, 1st Marines, occupied its position, insurgents engaged his 2d Platoon and combat engineer detachment with RPG-type rocket launchers and small-arms fire. An Air Force AC-130 gunship arrived on station and coordinated with the battalion for fire support. When the AC-130 had stopped firing, the Jolan District lay ablaze, and the enemy threat had disappeared.

With 2d Battalion, 2d Marines, blocking any escape to the south of Fallujah, the assault of the city commenced on 6 April with 2d Battalion, 1st Marines, attacking the Jolan District in the city's northwest corner while 1st Battalion, 5th Marines, attacked west from its positions south of the cloverleaf connecting

Marines from 2d Battalion, 1st Marines, set up a perimeter in the streets of Fallujah during Operation Vigilant Resolve.

Photo by GSgt Chago Zapata, Defense Imagery, VIRIN: 040812-M-0095Z-074

An Iraqi soldier of the 36th Commando Battalion, Iraqi Special Operations Forces Brigade, waits to participate in a joint operation in Najaf Province in August 2004. The battalion was one of the few Iraqi units to not desert during Operation Vigilant Resolve, and elements of the force fought alongside 2d Battalion, 1st Marines, in Fallujah's Jolan District.

Highways E1 to 10 into the industrial Sin'a District. General Mattis planned to pinch the insurgents from two directions, adding a steadily increasing pressure. The fighting in late March had determined that the enemy lacked the resolve and the fighting skill to stop advancing Marine rifle units. A progressive advance into the city would exploit insurgent weaknesses and lead to their wholesale collapse.

As Marines entered the city, Colonel Toolan's estimation of the enemy's posture proved consistent with his expectations. The moves from north and southeast into the city each night drew immediate fire from insurgents, revealing their locations, and thus allowing the Marines to destroy them. The Marine battalions attempted to integrate Iraqi Civil Defense Corps troops into the blocking positions and new Iraqi Army units into Marine battalions as rapidly

as possible. Marine commanders, Coalition authority representatives, and civil affairs officers advised the civil, tribal, and religious leaders about the situation. These locals predicted dire consequences if the Coalition continued to move into the city. But the Coalition's response to the city's leaders was that their predictions lacked credibility and that they bore major responsibility for the present conditions in Fallujah. The information operation campaign used public service announcements, handbills, and notifications to the mayor, city council, sheiks, and police. These announcements stated that a curfew would be imposed and enforced between 1900–0600.

As operations proceeded, General Mattis signaled his concern about I MEF's southern boundary because a revolt in Baghdad led by Shi'a cleric Moqtadre al-Sadr threatened I MEF's communications to the south and east. Elements of al-Sadr's militia (also termed the Mahdi Army) moved astride the Euphrates near al-Musayyib on the Karbala-Baghdad highway. Iraqi police managed to restore order, but the uprising remained a serious portent of the future.

By 6 April, the inadequacy of Iraqi paramilitary forces could no longer be denied. Most of the 2,000 Iraqi soldiers and police theoretically deployed to support the 1st Marine Division had deserted as soon as, or even before, the fighting began. The 2d Battalion, New Iraqi Army, for instance, took fire while convoying from Baghdad on 5 April and refused to go into action with some 38 percent of its forces disappearing at once. Many of these Iraqi soldiers reportedly entered insurgent ranks. Only the 36th Iraqi Commando Battalion/Iraqi National Guard Battalion (400 troops with 17 U.S. Special Forces advisors) stayed the course, working alongside 2d Battalion, 1st Marines, in Jolan. The 506th Battalion of the Civil Defense Corps proved unsteady but useful at manning exterior checkpoints, but no other Iraqi soldiers served in this action. The Civil Defense Corps' 505th Battalion, for instance, never reported for operations.

On 6 April, General Mattis decided to order in an infantry battalion from Regimental Combat Team 7. At the same time, he expressed frustration with the Iraqi security force program:

> A primary goal of our planning to date has been to "put an Iraqi face" on security functions as quickly as possible. With three weeks on the ground, reporting and experience has indicated that all Iraqi civil security organizations—police, Iraqi Civil Defense Corps and border force—are generally riddled with corruption, a lack of will, and are widely infiltrated by anti-

Coalition agents. In one case we have reporting that an entire unit located in Fallujah has deserted and gone over to the insurgent side. Their treachery has certainly cost us killed and wounded.

There are a number of explanations for this turn of events, not the least of which is that until now the forces have been little more than a jobs program. We are only now asking them to man their posts, to step up and be counted, and it would seem many are either voting with their feet—or their allegiance.

Starting on 7 April, Regimental Combat Team 1 attacked continuously for 48 hours, killing and routing those insurgents who had stayed to fight. Fighting at times was at close range, no more than 25 meters at best. The Marines continued to push. The 1st Battalion, 5th Marines, moved through the southeastern district sectors of the city proper and controlled 1,500 meters of Highway 10 west of the cloverleaf. The 2d Battalion, 1st Marines, continued attacking in its corner of the city, expanding to the south and west. A mosque gave special resistance to 1st Battalion, 5th Marines, with small arms and rocket-launcher (RPG) fire, leading to a coordinated assault to seize it, killing one insurgent and taking three prisoner. Route E1 remained open for Coalition traffic to the north of the city. Late on 7 April, the reinforcing battalion from Regimental Combat Team 7, the 3d Battalion, 4th Marines, began to move from al-Asad Air Base to Fallujah, where it would join Regimental Combat Team 1 for the fight by the following afternoon.

Marines fought in full-scale urban combat for almost six days for the first time since 2003. The insurgents proved to be an adaptive force, using small three- to five-man teams, shoot-and-run tactics, and sniper fire revealing some skill. They also used indiscriminate mortar, artillery rocket, and handheld rocket-launcher fire at a safe distance from Marine positions. They displayed organized battle order and command and control using cellular phones, pigeons, and visual signals. Cached weapons and equipment in numerous locations throughout the city allowed them freedom of maneuver.

Marines saw numerous cases of civilian observers cueing insurgents to their movements, thus exploiting the rules of engagement under which Coalition troops fought. In any case, after Marines achieved superior firepower, insurgents retreated and attempted to blend with the civilian populace, allowing them to fight another day.

Supporting arms proved essential even when Marines engaged in close quarters combat. Lieutenant Colonel Olson characterized it by stating that "wave after wave of close air support aircraft: Air Force F-16C, and AC-130, Marine AH-1W Cobras and UH-1N handled the mission load." Throughout the entire month of April, Captain Brad S. Pennella's Battery A, 1st Battalion, 11th Marines, shot 30 counter-fire missions against insurgent mortar and artillery rocket positions, and fired 14 missions to support the infantry.

Marines of 2d Battalion, 1st Marines, patrol the streets of Fallujah during Operation Vigilant Resolve in April 2004.

Photo by LCpl Kenneth E. Madden III, Defense Imagery, VIRIN: 040405-M-5505M-041

Photo by A1C Alicia M. Sarkkinen, USAF, Defense Imagery VIRIN 031125-F-7392S-030

Under pressure from the Iraqi Governing Council and the Coalition Provisional Authority, the head of U.S. Forces Central Command, Army General John P. Abizaid, (center), ordered a suspension of offensive operations in Fallujah on 9 April 2004.

In addition, Company C, 1st Tank Battalion (Captain Michael D. Skaggs), attached a platoon to each infantry battalion in direct support. Repeatedly, under steady RPG and small arms fire, the M1A1 tanks rolled into enemy territory and demolished enemy personnel and equipment.

Combat in Fallujah demonstrated many unusual characteristics. Outside of the city's industrial Sina'a District, residential buildings make up most of its more than 50,000 buildings. The brick or concrete homes typically are one or two stories high with flat roofs, enclosed courtyards, and perimeter walls. While some neighborhoods have a normal grid pattern, the Jolan District revealed twisted alleyways and jumbled streets, repeated to an extent in the industrial southeast.

The narrow streets and walled enclosures channeled attacking Marine rifle squads, but the enemy engaged in little street fighting, preferring to hole up and fight from ambush inside the houses themselves. By doing so, they avoided exposure to Marines placed in overwatch, observation, and sniper positions. The walls of the typical house resisted grenade fragments, requiring each room to be cleared individually.

The windows typically were barred; doors, gates, and even internal barricades were reinforced, making some houses miniature forts, requiring multiple shots of multipurpose assault weapons, rockets, and tank guns to breach or reduce.

The houses offered multiple entry and exit points at the front, kitchen, side, or rear, enabling insurgents to move easily through the residential areas. Their tactics frequently relied upon arms caches in many houses, enabling them to move unarmed between them in the guise of innocent civilians and then set up ambushes. After they were inside, Marines usually found the same layout: the front door opened to a small entryway with twin doors leading into two sitting rooms. Beyond these one encountered interior doors opening to the central hallway, where all first floor rooms led. In that hallway stood the typical stairwell to the second floor, containing more rooms and an exterior stairwell to the rooftop.

The increased security focus and operational tempo in the division's zone fostered an additional operational planning effort to develop preliminary operations in and around Fallujah to support the main effort. The intelligence analysis identified three key cities harboring and supporting enemy activities: Saqlawiyah, Karmah, and Jurf as-Sakhr. The staff made plans for combined operations in these cities. With Colonel Toolan and his staff focused on Fallujah, General Mattis activated the division's alternate command group "Bravo." Led by 1st Marine Division assistant commander, General Kelly, "Division Bravo" moved to north Babil Province and assumed command of the two infantry battalions there. These would play a key role in establishing a secure environment for the ongoing Arba'een pilgrimage, which brought hundreds of thousands of Shi'a faithful into Karbala. Some operational planning teamwork later occurred to conduct a relief in place by the Army's 1st Armored Division, which was by then beginning to engage in operations to the south of Baghdad.

As Marines poised and repositioned for further operations on 9 April, orders arrived from General Sanchez to cease all offensive operations in Fallujah. L. Paul Bremer III and the Coalition Provisional Authority had prevailed upon General Abizaid, head of Central Command, to order a cease-fire at the behest of the Iraqi Governing Council (IGC) in Baghdad. The halt was to allow IGC council representatives the opportunity to negotiate the enemy's surrender. Politics brought Regimental Combat Team 1's momentum to a stop. Marines received the order to cease offensive operations with some disbelief.

The insurgents' use of information warfare played a role in the cessation of operations. Although the Marines of Regimental Combat Team 1 were achieving considerable gains, the insurgency was able to effectively employ the media to stir up opposition to the Coalition campaign. In addition to the insurgents' surprising mobility and strength, the insurgents displayed an excellent grasp of information operations. Their propaganda reached television and radio stations, appeared on the Internet, and spread through the streets by word of mouth. Some groups distributed fliers and videos alleging Coalition atrocities and insurgent successes. Arab satellite news programming, especially the ubiquitous Al Jazeera, highlighted the "excessive force" of the Marines and soldiers of 1st Marine Division, making allusions to the Israeli actions in Palestine as further denunciation. With no western press embedded with I MEF forces and the streets too dangerous for independ-

Although the combat operations in Fallujah garnered the most attention in April 2004, intense fighting also took place in al-Anbar's capital, Ramadi (pictured here in 2008), during the same month.

Photo by Cpl Jeremy M. Giacominol, Defense Imagery VIRIN: 080423-M-6668G-022

Photo by SSgt D. Myles Cullen, USAF, Defense Imagery, VIRIN: 040628-F-0193C-009

While the transfer of sovereignty from the Coalition Provisional Authority to the Iraqi Interim Government on 28 June 2004 occurred ahead of schedule, the country was far from stable or secure. U.S. Ambassador to Iraq, L. Paul Bremer III, was photographed shortly before departing Iraq after the transfer.

ent reporting, the media battlefield fell to the insurgents.

The Iraqi Governing Council caved in to pressures within and without its chambers. Three of its members resigned in protest, and five others threatened the same. Bremer met with the Council on 8 April and received the opinions of the Sunni members that Operation Vigilant Resolve amounted to "collective punishment" and that even more massive demonstrations of resistance and opposition were in the offing.

Bremer was already under pressure to deal with the al-Sadr revolt, and the British had criticized him for his heavy-handed approach in Fallujah. He also knew that the Abu Ghraib Prison scandals were about to become public knowledge. Thus, he probably decided to cut his losses. For him, the larger objective of returning sovereignty to the Iraqis by 30 June likely took precedence.

An uncertain siege continued for three weeks. On 8 April 2004 the newly arrived 3d Battalion, 4th Marines, launched an attack from Fallujah's northeast, oriented southwest. As it took up the main effort, the other two battalions continued to reduce insurgent pockets of resistance. The enemy fired rockets and mortars from the city center but had by then lost all of its initial defensive positions. Not surprising to the Marine Corps battalions, the insurgents remaining within the city limits tried to use the cease-fire to their advantage. Colonel Toolan tightened the cordon on the city to prevent the insurgents from withdrawing from the city and to block reinforcements. The 36th Iraqi Commando Battalion continued to fight alongside the Marines, distinguishing itself as the sole Iraqi unit to prove itself in combat. Meanwhile, the Iraqi 505th Battalion manned checkpoints under supervision on the outskirts of the city.

Captain Jason E. Smith led his Company B, 1st Battalion, 5th Marines, through some of the heaviest fighting in the industrial area during the formal offensive operation. He returned to the offensive again on 13 April. The insurgents surrounded the attached 3d Platoon, Company A, which lost an assault amphibious vehicle and took several casualties. Leading the rescue effort, Smith guided his convoy toward the smoke of the burning vehicle and then dismounted, racing to the first vehicles to lead his Marines to the trapped platoon. With total disregard for enemy fire, he coordinated attacks on the insurgents. Organizing a defensive perimeter and evacuating casualties, he supervised the recovery of the disabled tracked vehicle and coordinated the withdrawal as part of the rear guard.

Following the cease-fire, representatives from I MEF, the Coalition authority, and Iraqi organizations began to negotiate with the insurgents, but little

Photo by Sgt Paul L. Anstine II, Defense Imagery VIRIN 040314-M-5150A-024

In April 2004, units from Colonel Craig A. Tucker's Regimental Combat Team 7 were sent to Area of Operations Raleigh to relieve Regimental Combat Team 1 at Fallujah.

progress was made. Marines had to defend themselves from repeated insurgent cease-fire violations. On 25 April, both General Conway and General Mattis met with former Iraqi Army generals to discuss the possible formation of a military unit in Fallujah. The negotiations produced the Fallujah Brigade, which gained the quick approval of the military chain of command. By 28 April the Fallujah Brigade had begun assembling and on the 30th, a turnover led to the phased withdrawal of the 1st Marine Division from Fallujah. While Bremer protested the creation of the brigade, even more serious problems emerged by the end of April that overshadowed his misgivings. For General Conway, the unusual negotiating opportunity allowed at least a bad solution to an insoluble dilemma because the 1st Marine Division no longer had authority to continue the assault and to clear the city, and it lacked the manpower and other resources to manage a prolonged siege.

Insurgency in Al-Anbar Province
April 2004

The 1st Marine Division fought its first battle for Fallujah well but with considerable political interference. The ensuing days saw a widespread rise in violence and opposition to occupying forces, in some instances reflecting the rising temperatures and the public's frustration with the squalid conditions in the city. In other cases, violence was planned by anti-Coalition factions and insurgents. In al-Anbar Province, insurgent groups rallied to support their brethren remaining behind in the city, spurred by the Fallujah insurgent and foreign fighter leaders who escaped in the first days of April. But another crisis overshadowed the difficulties of soldiers and Marines in that province, one with considerable political impact.

The relatively young but influential Moqtadre al-Sadr, scion of a Shi'a clerical dynasty, enjoyed increasing power and popularity after the overthrow of Saddam Hussein's regime. Having served as a symbol of Shi'a resistance to the former regime, he continued as a resistance leader by opposing the U.S. and Coalition occupation of Iraq. In 2003 he formed a militia, which became known variously as the Sadr Militia or the Mahdi Army, and announced a shadow Shi'a government in al-Kufah, where he intended to establish government ministries. Al-Sadr continued to pose obstacles to the Coalition Provisional Authority's plans for a transition to Iraqi self-rule via the Governing Council, and on 5 April 2004, Coalition authorities closed his newspaper and called for the leader's ar-

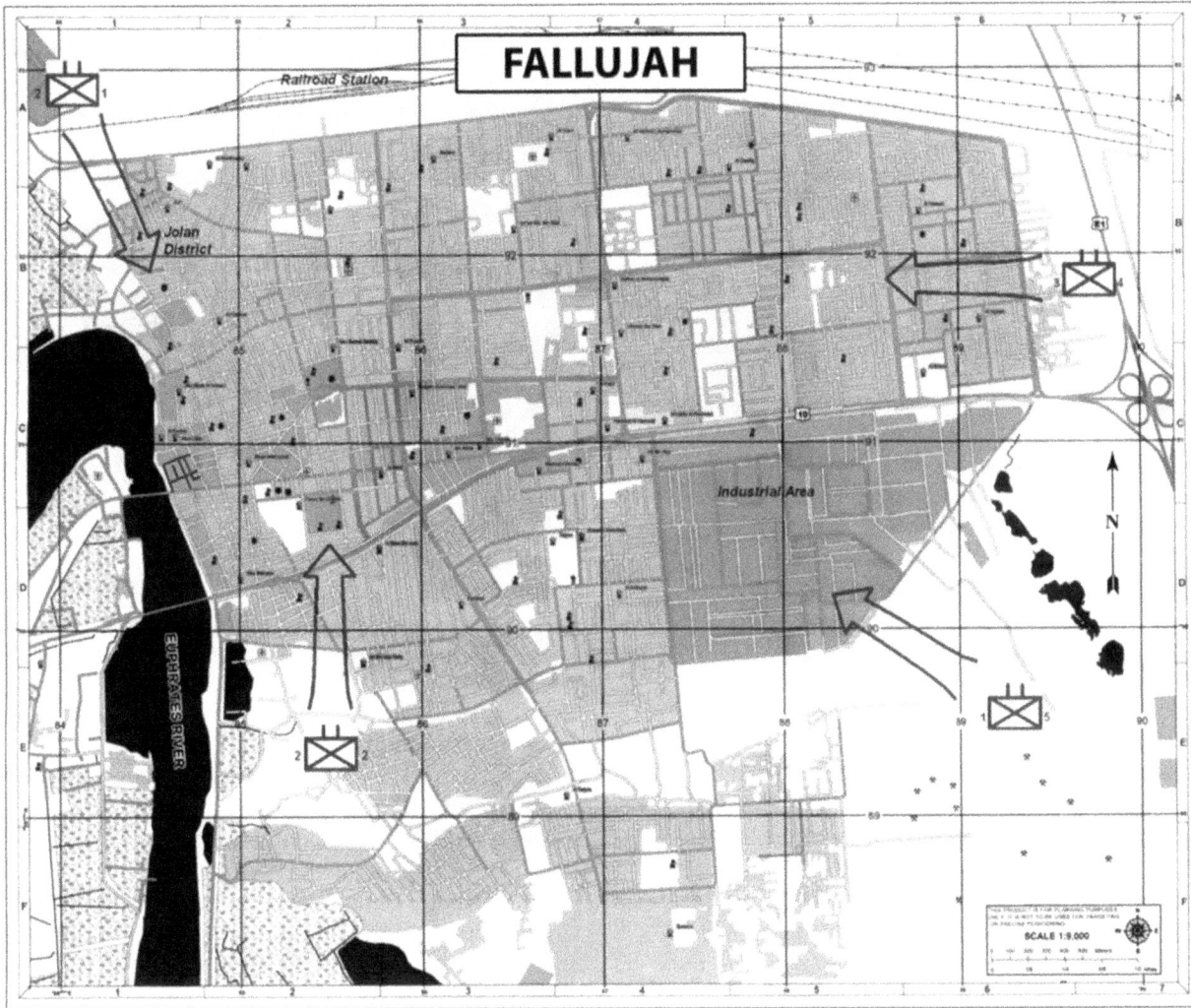

FALLUJAH

2d Topographic Platoon Map, Adapted by History Division

Operation Vigilant Resolve, April 2004.

rest on various charges. At the same time, thousands of Iraqis in Baghdad (he was the de facto ruler of the Sadr City section of Baghdad) and the Shi'a cities of al-Kut, Karbala, ad-Diwaniyah and an-Najaf took to the streets to support al-Sadr, while his militia seized government buildings and police stations in a major uprising and challenge to the Coalition Provisional Authority.

For the first time in a year, cannon and gun fire resounded through the streets of the city. The 1st Armored Division halted its redeployment movements on 6 April, having turned over the garrison mission to the 1st Cavalry Division. General Sanchez issued orders to the 1st Armored Division to deploy combat units south of Baghdad with warnings of further actions to come. He ordered Operation Resolute Sword on 7 April against the Mahdi Army:

The Mahdi Army is declared to be a hostile

To provide better leadership over the Iraq War, the Combined Joint Task Force 7 was replaced by the Multi National Force–Iraq and the Multi National Corps–Iraq in the summer of 2004. In July 2004, Army LtGen Ricardo S. Sanchez was relieved as senior commander in Iraq by Army Gen George W. Casey Jr. (shown below testifying before Congress in 2005).

Photo by TSgt Myles D. Cullen, USAF, Defense Imagery VIRIN: 050623-F-0193C-022

Photo by Cpl Matthew S. Richards, Defense Imagery, VIRIN: 040812-M-4358R-052

Marines from the 11th Marine Expeditionary Unit participate in a joint raid with Iraqi Security Forces against the forces of Moqtada al-Sadr in an-Najaf, August 2004.

force; Coalition forces are authorized to engage and destroy the Mahdi Army based solely upon their status as members of the Mahdi Army. There is no requirement for members of Mahdi Army to commit a hostile act or demonstrate hostile intent before they can be engaged. Muqtada al-Sadr is the leader of Mahdi Army. Positive identification of Mahdi Army targets must be acquired prior to engagement.

With the dispatch of 3d Battalion, 4th Marines, to Regimental Combat Team 1 in support of Operation Vigilant Resolve, General Mattis sensed that the division had reached the end of its resources. Yet he suspected that an emerging danger to the east and south remained with the al Sadr revolt; he wrote on 8 April:

> The current tempo and widespread enemy surge across our operations area has this division stretched. We are moving aggressively against the enemy across our zone but there are enemy forces operating in areas where we have no forces and the Iraqi security forces are impotent. We lack sufficient forces to fully address the enemy in the area north of Camp Fallujah (vicinity of al Karma), Jurf al Sukr, Northern Babil and the rocket belt south of Fallujah and Abu Ghraib prison. We will address those enemies once we free up forces so we can destroy their sanctuaries. Additional forces to command

and control the Northern Babil fight, a regiment headquarters, a tank company (personnel only), and one USMC infantry battalion have been requested by separate correspondence.

In northern Babil Province, two U.S. battalions under the 1st Marine Division sought to maintain the flux of events between the Fallujah and al-Sadr uprisings. The U.S. Army's 1st Battalion, 32d Infantry, focused on securing routes for the Arba'een pilgrimage of the Shi'a. This required ambushing insurgents setting explosive devices, mounting patrols along routes in the zone, and supporting the traffic control points manned by the Iraqi Civil Defense Corps. When feasible, patrols of 1st Reconnaissance Battalion moved in from its usual areas south of Fallujah to counter insurgent indirect fire and booby trap teams.

While escorting a convoy into al-Anbar Province, the reconnaissance battalion's 2d Platoon, Company B, ran into a well-concealed and fortified position southwest of Fallujah. When Captain Brent L. Morel, the platoon commander, saw his lead vehicle smashed by a rocket, he ordered his other two vehicles to flank the insurgent position. As insurgent mortar and machine gun fire increased, Captain Morel led an assault across an open field and up a ten-foot berm into firing positions from which the reconnaissance Marines eliminated 10 insurgents at close range and forced the others to flee. Continuing the assault against the other insurgents who continued to pin down the convoy, Captain Morel received a fatal burst of automatic weapons fire. Leadership fell to team leader Sergeant Willie L. Copeland III, who continued the assault by fire with his five Marines while shielding and attempting to save the life of his captain. Under the cover of hand grenades, they withdrew to safety with Morel's body. In the same action, Sergeant Lendro F. Baptista led his three-man team against more insurgent positions, single-handedly killing four of them at close range while directing fire against several others. He then personally covered the withdrawal of the team to safety with his own firing.

In Area of Operations Topeka, the soldiers and Marines with the Army's 1st Brigade, 1st Infantry Division, fought feverishly against insurgents rallying to support the fighting in Fallujah. Fighting in Ramadi reached a new level of intensity, with 6 April being the worst day, when 12 Marines of 2d Battalion, 4th Marines, died in an urban firefight against insurgents operating in small groups that initially attacked the government center. The battalion succeeded in defending the government buildings, assisting in extracting Coalition authority officials, and pushing the attackers into the eastern side of the city.

At 1048 on 6 April, Company G received small arms and RPG fire in the al-Malaab District. The patrol, pursuing the attackers, cordoned off the buildings in the area, when small arms fire erupted. Two squads engaged the enemy, and the battalion sent its quick reaction force. At approximately 1145, Company G received more fire and at 1205 was pinned down in a house. The quick reaction force moved to the area in support but was engaged by insurgent forces as well, one block east of Company G. Captain Christopher J. Bronzi, the company commander, led his Marines in the ensuing 24 hours of action, personally destroying several enemy fighting positions and repeatedly exposing himself to small arms and grenades. At one point on the sixth, he led a fire team into a fire-swept street to recover the body of a fallen Marine.

At this time the battalion received notice from 1st Marine Division that three mosques in the area had called for "jihad." At approximately 1330 an explosive device was reported in Company E's sector, on the eastern outskirts of the city, and while cordoning off the area the company received small arms fire. At approximately the same time just to the east, one of the battalion's sniper teams set up near the Euphrates River was attacked by 12 to 15 men. At approximately 1400, a Company E patrol was ambushed. A quick reaction force was dispatched to reinforce the patrol when it engaged with the enemy still further to the east of the city. Two Humvees were hit, and its platoon commander was critically wounded. Under heavy machine gun and rocket fire, squad leader Corporal Eric M. Smith assumed command of the pla-

A number of captured weapons and munitions found and seized by Marines during vehicle inspections conducted throughout an-Najaf Province were displayed before being destroyed in August 2004.

Defense Imagery, VIRIN: 040821-M-555Z-001

toon and led the Marines 50 meters across open ground, where they set up in a few fighting holes placed along Route 10. Smith then ran back across the field to evacuate his platoon commander and the platoon's weapons. Employing machine guns from the platoon's seven-ton truck, Smith led a counterattack against the insurgent force and relieved another squad that had been pinned down. When an Army mechanized infantry platoon arrived, Corporal Smith coordinated the evacuation of casualties and withdrew the platoon to the company command post.

The battalion determined that fighters came into Ramadi on motorcycles and in pickup trucks, met at a central location (likely the soccer field), and informed the town's people that they were going to attack U.S. forces that day. On the spot interrogation revealed that the insurgents forced residents out of their homes as the fighters prepared to engage the Americans. When the fighting subsided, the insurgents made a planned withdrawal on motorcycles and possibly in boats on the Euphrates back to their base camps.

The launching of Operation Vigilant Resolve ignited festering insurgent cells that had planned incursions of these types. Having stirred up a hornet's nest across al-Anbar Province, the Coalition forces found themselves extended beyond tolerable limits. The insurgents established ambushes, roadblocks, emplaced explosive devices, and fired all kinds of weapons indirectly at Coalition forces. As part of their efforts to cut lines of communications, they moved against key bridges, including the Tharthar Bridge over the canal of the same name.

These were dark hours for the U.S. and Coalition position in Iraq, and the political-military direction of the campaign to clear Fallujah of insurgents demonstrated considerable weakness and discord. As planned, the "transfer of sovereignty" between the Coalition Provincial Authority and Iraq did occur on 28 June 2004. Bremer had advanced it two days ahead of schedule to forestall further difficulties, and he departed Iraq minutes after the ceremony. With the establishment of Iraqi sovereignty, the U.S. led Coalition Provisional Authority dissolved itself and legal authority devolved upon the appointed Iraqi Interim Government. The United States and Coalition forces continued to operate under the "all necessary measures" language of the U.N. Security Council resolutions that identified the state of conflict existing in Iraq and the need for the multinational force to conduct operations and to detain individuals to help establish a secure environment.

In wake of the First Battle of Fallujah and the par-

allel al-Sadr rising in April, the transition to Iraqi sovereignty on 28 June 2004 took on a rather hollow ceremonial character. The equally symbolic raising of the American flag over the new U.S. Embassy in Baghdad by Marines, marking the first time the American flag had flown there in 13 years, did herald some significant changes in U.S. policies and plans for the future. But the idea of sovereignty had little meaning in Iraqi streets. Still ahead lay several months of fighting and many casualties to restore a semblance of order in Iraq. The lessons were hard, but Marines knew from the moment the battle was terminated on 30 April that they would need to return to Fallujah. Nominally, I MEF reported 27 U.S. killed in action and more than 90 wounded in the first Battle of Fallujah, but Army and Marine Corps casualties, in related incidents in Ramadi and the area surrounding Fallujah, were just beginning to show the extent of their losses. In April, the 1st Marine Division alone suffered 48 Marines, two soldiers, and one Navy corpsman killed in action, and the wounded in action totaled 412 Marines, 43 soldiers, and 21 sailors. Little information exists on casualties for the few Iraqi forces fighting with the Coalition. Enemy losses can never be known, but are estimated by some intelligence sources as 800 Iraqis killed, which undoubtedly included noncombatants.

Regimental Combat Team 7's Counterstrike in Operation Ripper Sweep (14 April–1 May 2004)

Thwarted in their efforts to eradicate the insurgents from Fallujah, General Conway and General Mattis turned to the many instances of insurgency in the surrounding areas of the province. The Army's 1st Brigade, 1st Infantry Division, worked unceasingly to maintain a semblance of order in Ramadi, using the full panoply of raids, cordons, and various types of patrolling and ambush actions. In the western areas of the province, Regimental Combat Team 7 continued to interdict insurgent transportation routes while also raiding suspected insurgent cells across the Euphrates valley between al-Qaim and Rawah.

Beginning on 10 April, General Mattis' staff began to work with Colonel Craig A. Tucker's Regimental Combat Team 7 to develop a plan to move a key part of the regiment into Area of Operations Raleigh. It would relieve Regimental Combat Team 1 of its responsibilities outside Fallujah and deal with the incipient insurgent activity in the towns and countryside surrounding that city. Tucker had his staff devise a plan to free sufficient combat power from the camps and duties in western al-Anbar Province and to move it with the regimental tactical command post to positions in its eastern areas.

The resulting plan juggled the missions of I MEF's many units. The 3d Marine Aircraft Wing would have to assume responsibility for security of Camp Korean Village to free the 1st Light Armored Reconnaissance Battalion, which was leaving the border crossings Trebil and Wallid uncovered (the crossings remained closed for most of the month during the Fallujah crisis). The Azerbaijani company stationed at Camp Haditha Dam would be reinforced with only a detachment from 3d Battalion, 4th Marines, and a small craft company. The Taqaddum security battalion, 3d Battalion, 24th Marines, replaced 2d Battalion, 7th Marines, at Camp Hit. At Camp al-Qaim, only 3d Battalion, 7th Marines, remained to counter insurgents at the Syrian border zone. The Haditha Dam and Hit zone formerly occupied by 2d Battalion, 7th Marines, was covered by Task Force Walsh (Major Bennett W. Walsh—who commanded the 1st Small Craft Company) consisting of L Company, 3d Battalion, 24th Marines; Company C, 1st Combat Engineer Battalion; the 1st Small Craft Company; a platoon left by 1st Light Armored Reconnaissance Battalion; a platoon of military police; detachments of volunteers; and the Azerbaijani company. The regiment's executive officer, Lieutenant Colonel John D. Gamboa, took command of what became known as Regimental Combat Team 7 West at the main command post during the regiment's offensive foray around Fallujah. As part of this offensive, General Mattis assigned Tucker an additional mission of clearing the right bank of the Euphrates along Route 10 as far as the peninsula west of Fallujah, closed for several days because of explosive devices and ambushes.

The force taken by Colonel Tucker on this operation consisted of his tactical command group, the 2d Battalion, 7th Marines; 1st Light Armored Reconnaissance Battalion; 3d Platoon, Company C, 1st Tank Battalion (attached at the time the Fallujah battle began); Battery E, 2d Battalion, 11th Marines; and a platoon from the 1st Force Reconnaissance Company. General Mattis clarified his plan on 13 April:

> The division is stretched thin with the route security mission coupled with the Fallujah cordon. These missions tie down a significant portion of our maneuver assets and the sooner we receive direction about the anticipated resolution of Fallujah negotiations, the better. While accepting a short term risk in the west permits us to move against several enemy sanc-

tuaries and dominated areas in area Raleigh, Regimental Combat Team 7 must return to the western operating area in approximately seven to ten days or we will face setbacks along the rat lines that may negate our successes further east. Limiting defensive route security missions and maintaining the cordon around Fallujah for as short a period as possible are tactical imperatives; we need to return to the offensive as rapidly as possible.

As the task force organized by Colonel Tucker began to assemble at al-Asad Air Base, the situation continued to deteriorate as the division reported on the 13th: "the two companies of effective Iraqi Civil Defense Corps from the 507th Battalion have essentially quit."

The division's order of the day for 14 April set out the mission for Regimental Combat Team 7. Colonel Tucker issued his orders for Operation Ripper Sweep which would be conducted in three initial phases:

> At al-Asad: rearm, refit, refuel and rehearse in preparation for upcoming operation in support of the division's efforts at Fallujah. Depart al-Asad at 1400 on 15 April for area Raleigh. At 0600, 16 April, commence the attack astride the main routes from Taqaddum, clearing the insurgents from the southwest of Fallujah through al-Amirah. Continuing on order to clear Jurf as Sakhr, preparing for further operations in the security zone of Regimental Combat Team 1.

At 0600 on 16 April, the Ripper Sweep forces began the offensive with 1st Light Armored Reconnaissance Battalion attacking southeast where a blocking position was established to support the follow-on clearance by 2d Battalion, 7th Marines, between al-Taqaddum and Fallujah. Insurgent resistance remained minimal. The only notable contact during the clearance occurred when 1st Light Armored Reconnaissance units were engaged by small arms from a fuel truck while south of Fallujah. The Marines suspected a vehicular bomb and destroyed the truck with 25mm cannon fire, wounding both occupants, who received immediate medical evacuation. At 1300 on 18 April, 2d Battalion, 7th Marines, and 1st Light Armored Reconnaissance Battalion continued the attack into the center of al-Amiriyah town, covered overhead by Air Force F-16 Fighting Falcon fighter-bombers and Marine Corps AH-1W Cobra attack helicopters. The reaction to the Marines who entered al-Amiriyah in their armored vehicles was warm, despite the fact that intelligence had reported the town was a sanctuary for insurgents. Colonel Tucker said of the locals' reaction to the Marines, "it was like liberating France." The picture began to develop that the "bow-wave" caused by the overwhelming offensive capability of the task force had driven insurgent elements out of the entire zone well before the Marines arrived. Among several detainees the task force captured the eighth ranking person on Regimental Combat Team 1's high value target list.

General Mattis reacted positively to the restoration of free movement from al-Taqaddum into and south of Fallujah, linking with the main surface communications to Kuwait. He ordered Regimental Combat Team 7 to continue movement as far as Jurf as Sak, linking with 2d Battalion, 2d Marines. General Kelly's Division Bravo group had extended that battalion to cover any move by al-Sadr militiamen toward the division's flank. General Mattis communicated the following:

> Following Regimental Combat Team 7's actions this week, we will be driving the tempo throughout most of area Atlanta. Regimental Combat Team 7 will then return to the west and reestablish its dominance. The relief in place with 1st Armored Division in North Babil, freeing up two battalions, and the arrival of additional tank and assault amphibious vehicle companies will enable us to maintain the momentum we are now developing in the east. More importantly, we will have the forces necessary to exploit our success with persistent presence in key areas. It will soon be clear that Blue Diamond is the dominant tribe in the al-Anbar Province.

Tucker's task force spent a day at Camp al-Taqaddum and Camp Fallujah conducting maintenance and preparing to continue with Operation Ripper Sweep. At 0400 on 22 April the force took its offensive to the left bank of the Euphrates against al-Karmah, which the 3d Battalion, 4th Marines, had discovered was an insurgent base after the initial Fallujah cease-fire. Once again, 1st Light Armored Reconnaissance Battalion led the offensive, followed by 2d Battalion, 7th Marines. In a street-by-street search-and-clear operation, the two battalions again encountered no insurgents but found numerous weapons caches and 57 explosive devices. On 24 April the force moved to Camp Fallujah, while some rifle companies remained in al-Karmah and continued operations until the end of the month.

Because of actions taken by both Regimental Combat Team 1 and the Army's 1st Brigade, 1st Infantry Division, to support the Regimental Combat Team 7 task force in its attack, the al-Karmah action amounted to a division-level fight. With the exception of the two battles for Fallujah, large-scale operations of this kind were uncommon On the 20th, the division transferred responsibility for northern Babil Province to the 1st Armored Division, which was then in the middle of its campaign against the al-Sadr uprising in the Karbala-Najaf-Kut region. The Division Bravo command group returned to the division, and the two battalions—2d Battalion, 2d Marines, and 1st Battalion, 32d Infantry—reverted to Regimental Combat Team 1 and 1st Brigade, 1st Infantry Division, respectively. The battalions were welcome reinforcements for their actions around Fallujah and Ramadi. The 2d Battalion, 2d Marines, formally relieved Tucker's Regimental Combat Team 7 of its mission at al-Karmah on 25 April. The next day, 2d Battalion, 7th Marines, moved back to Area of Operations Denver to reestablish its presence in Hit and Haditha.

Although Operation Ripper Sweep officially terminated at this point, the task force remained at Camp Fallujah until 1 May, while Colonel Tucker and his staff planned a cordon of Fallujah in anticipation of a renewed attack by Regimental Combat Team 1 to destroy remaining insurgent forces in the city. With the creation of the Fallujah Brigade, however, General Mattis put these operations on hold. On 1 May, the remaining Regimental Combat Team 7 forces departed Camp Fallujah and returned to al-Asad Air Base and Camps al-Qaim and Korean Village to resume stability and security operations there. Western al-Anbar Province had not remained quiet during the regiment's foray around Fallujah. Task Force Walsh worked hard in its economy of force mission in the Hit-Haditha zone, and the 3d Battalion, 7th Marines (the sole infantry battalion remaining in Area of Operations Denver), encountered considerable action in Husaybah and al-Qaim throughout the month.

The ambitious sweep by Regimental Combat Team 7 around Fallujah found few insurgents, but succeeded in restoring the tactical initiative to the 1st Marine Division, opening land communications routes, and scattering any insurgents who either planned ambushes or hoped to join the insurgents in Fallujah.

Restoring Balance in Al-Anbar Province

The festering problem of Fallujah would not see resolution until after the U.S. forces had accom-

Marines from Company C, Battalion Landing Team, 1st Battalion, 2d Marines, 24th Marine Expeditionary Unit, conduct a cordon-and-search operation in North Babil Province in September 2004.

plished their unit rotations in mid-2004. In April and May, reinforcements requested by General Mattis began to arrive, with Company B, 1st Tank Battalion, joining the Fallujah cordon on 25 April, and Company B, 3d Assault Amphibian Battalion, joining Regimental Combat Team 7 at al-Asad Air Base on 13 May.

At the same time the first Marine reinforcements began to arrive, a major shift occurred in the overall command of the Coalition effort in Iraq. Since the creation of the Combined Joint Task Force 7, it had become clear that the full reconstruction effort in Iraq was too large a project for what was initially a corps-sized staff. General Abizaid responded to this by placing Lieutenant General Thomas F. Metz's III Corps in charge of tactical operations and giving Combined Joint Task Force 7 commander Sanchez responsibility for strategic operations. On 15 May 2004 this division of responsibility was made official when Sanchez became the first commander of Multi National Force–Iraq. General Metz became the new commander of Multi National Corps–Iraq. The Marine Corps area of responsibility subsequently became Multi National Force–West. Less than two months later, on 1 July, Army General George W. Casey Jr. relieved General Sanchez of command of Multi National Force–Iraq, and thus became the commander of the overall Coalition effort in Iraq.

The combat forces of I MEF concentrated on security and stability operations, keeping the routes clear, and then turning to the major problem of training more reliable Iraqi security forces. The Iraqi security forces had failed to fight effectively in too many instances, not only in the I MEF sectors but also in face of the al-Sadr revolt, where more than 1,000 members of the Iraqi Civil Defense Corps at Karbala and an-Najaf had deserted. The construction of the India Base near Camp Fallujah for Iraqi forces allowed Regimental Combat Team 1 to begin training in earnest. On 5 June, it opened to the initial class of Iraqi Civil Defense Corps under the direction of the regimental operations staff. With the turnover of sovereignty from the Coalition Provisional Authority to the Iraqi Interim Government at the end of June, the Iraqi Civil Defense Corps converted to the Iraqi National Guard. In addition, the regiment undertook the training of the new Shahwani Special Forces, establishing a camp for their initial training at Camp Fallujah under the direction of Company A, 3d Assault Amphibian Vehicle Battalion. In July the 1st Marine Division convened two-week courses for National Guard officers and non-commissioned officers at Camp Ramadi, using embedded Army and Marine Corps non-commissioned officers to mentor and to train them.

In Area of Operations Raleigh, Regimental Combat Team 1 ran constant patrols of the main supply routes thanks to the help of the Army 112th Military Police Battalion. As the last of the reinforcing units from Regimental Combat Team 7 units departed Area of Operations Raleigh in early May, Colonel Toolan divided the area into three sectors. The 2d Battalion, 1st Marines, oriented its efforts to the northwest of Fallujah along Route E1 and the town of Saqlawiyah.

From Camp Abu Ghraib, the 1st Battalion, 5th Marines, were positioned north of Fallujah toward al-Karmah, and 2d Battalion, 2d Marines, established a presence to the south of Camp Fallujah at the Euphrates River. Engineers removed the Marine defensive positions in the southern and northern edges of the city, now in the hands of the Fallujah Brigade and the Iraqi National Guard. As the Marine battalions expanded their presence in the surrounding villages, they began to mount combat patrols to attack insurgents attempting ambushes, laying explosive devices, or setting up rocket or mortar attacks.

No end came to the insurgent challenges at Fallujah. On 24 June, they launched coordinated attacks on Route E1 and Traffic Control Point 1. The fighting began early in the morning and lasted throughout the day. Marines of Company G, 2d Battalion, 1st Marines, effectively defended the position with a variety of direct fire weapons and air support. Tanks fired on buildings being used as insurgent bases while a section of helicopters engaged other targets as AV-8B Harrier attack aircraft circled overhead.

A volley of handheld rockets damaged one of the AH-1W Cobra attack helicopters. Multiple Harrier sections dropped laser-guided bombs on buildings from which insurgents continued to engage the Marine positions. The fighting eventually subsided as Iraqi security forces eventually responded and established control in the area.

The opportunity to focus all of Regimental Combat Team 1's efforts on the Fallujah situation soon faded, however. The initial suppression of the al-Sadr revolt allowed the Army to resume the redeployment of 1st Armored Division back to home stations, and the responsibility for northern Babil Province once again reverted to I MEF beginning 27 June. Marines of 2d Battalion, 2d Marines, returned to their base camp at Al Mahumdiyah. The soldiers of 1st Battalion, 32d Infantry, returned to Colonel Toolan's control and to their base—Forward Operating Base Chosin—near Iskandariyah. The Regimental Combat Team 1 area of operations doubled in size. Consequently, the need for more forces, including Iraqi units, became more apparent.

In the west, Regimental Combat Team 7 reestablished its presence in the main population centers of Area of Operations Denver. Although the improvised dispositions managed to keep the Haditha-Hit zone fairly stable, the 3d Battalion, 7th Marines, fought several fierce actions in and around al-Qaim and Husaybah, the contentious border town. Insurgents tried several ambushes of Marine reconnaissance and security probes, and explosive devices detonated daily against Marine patrols. Finally, a series of pitched fights led the battalion commander, Lieutenant Colonel Matthew A. Lopez, to personally lead a task force in a two-day assault and clearing operation of Husaybah using two of his rifle companies, the weapons company, and a detachment of 1st Force Reconnaissance Company to cordon and sweep the town. The fighting intensified, and battalion mortars and helicopter close air support added to the firepower that killed an estimated 120 insurgents amid considerable mayhem.

A newly constructed operations center greeted Regimental Combat Team 7's commander Colonel Tucker upon his return to al-Asad Air Base. On 7 May, 220 combat replacements arrived at the base for the 1st Marine Division, an indicator of the changed circumstances of occupation duty in al-Anbar Province. With the return of 3d Battalion, 4th Marines, from its duty with Regimental Combat Team 1, beginning on 13 May the regiment could begin the planning of new initiatives. From this planning emerged Operation Rawah II.

The 1st Light Armored Reconnaissance Battalion moved on 1 June into blocking positions to the north of Rawah. The 3d Battalion, 4th Marines, set up a staging area at Haditha Dam from where it planned to take its objective by road. At the same time, the battalion's L Company would be airlifted by helicopter from al-Asad Air Base. The supporting unit, 3d Battalion, 7th Marines, closed the borders and provided blocking force. Twenty-four aircraft flew in support over the small town, which had not seen Marine operations in over five weeks. An EC-130 Compass Call electronic-warfare aircraft first over flew the town to detonate explosive devices, followed by an electronic snooper Lockheed EP-3 Orion. As the light armored reconnaissance battalion units moved south toward Rawah, multiple sections of AV-8Bs orbited for surveillance and on-call close air support. Finally, an AC-130 checked in for support as the main effort moved out of Haditha toward Rawah. Company L boarded its CH-53E Super Stallion helicopters at al-Asad Air Base to be inserted at four different blocking positions simultaneously under cover of a section of AH-1Ws. An additional section stood on the ground in ready alert. Two CH-46Es Sea Knights carried the Regimental Combat Team 7 reserve platoon, intended to land as Airborne Vehicle Check Points to catch insurgents. Although Regimental Combat Team 7 had scheduled an EA-6B Prowler electronic-warfare aircraft to jam and perform electronic surveillance, it did not appear because of aircraft carrier difficulties.

This raid netted six of the top-25 high-value target persons on Regimental Combat Team 7 lists while the companies of 3d Battalion, 4th Marines, remained in the town exploiting the movement's success. The operation proved the last for this battalion; its relief unit, 1st Battalion, 8th Marines, began the turnover process on 29 June, the first of the mid-deployment rotations. General Mattis had detailed the outline of these operations at the time the Fallujah situation came to a standstill:

Following recent offensive operations the enemy has fallen back and resorted to small scale actions intended to inflict maximum casualties on our forces with minimal risk to his own. The key to maintaining the initiative is patient, persistent presence throughout the zone. This is best accomplished by dismounted troops aggressively patrolling their area of operations, gaining information from the populace and ambushing the enemy on his own ground. Episodic vehicular forays from our firm bases do nothing more than reveal our intentions, make us easy targets and incur severe handicaps. When he is weak, as he is now, he will implant improvised explosive devices along the main service routes in periods of darkness in our absence to strike our convoys. When he comes out to operate like this—we must be in ambush to meet and kill him. Through intelligence preparation of the battlefield, that identifies his likely avenues of approach and likely improvised explosive device sites, we must anticipate his next operation. We must think, move and adapt faster than he can and less overtly than we have to date. When we can keep the enemy at bay in an area, we must exploit the opportunity we have to conduct more aggressive civil military operations and reinvigorate our programs to select trustworthy members for training the Iraqi security forces.

The 11th, 24th, and 31st Marine Expeditionary Units Deploy to Iraq

Part of the solution to the challenges I MEF encountered in the expansion of its battle zone to the east came in the timely appearance of three Marine expeditionary units (MEUs) from the United States. A combination of early sorties and extended deployments made these important reinforcements available from July 2004 through the end of the year. On 4 May, the 24th Marine Expeditionary Force (24th MEU) under Colonel R. J. Johnson received its alert to pre-pare to deploy to Iraq from 15 June 2004 to 15 February 2005, instead of from 17 August 2004 to 17 February 2005 as originally planned. By deleting its special operations capable exercises and certification, the unit accelerated its preparations, loaded equipment on board USS *Kearsarge* (LHD 3) and USNS *Charleston* (T-LKA 113) in early June and began its airlift to Kuwait on 26 June. The expeditionary unit's ground combat element, the 1st Battalion, 2d Marines (Reinforced), completed the required pre-deployment training before beginning its airlift on 3 July. Assembling in Kuwait during early July, Johnson's organization reported to 1st Marine Division for operations on 24 July and accepted responsibility for northern Babil Province from Regimental Combat Team 1 on 1 August 2004. Johnson took operational control of 2d Battalion, 2d Marines, and relieved the Army's 1st Battalion, 32d Infantry, with his own 1st Battalion, 2d Marines. Johnson's unit then began security and stabilization operations on the essential main service route south of Baghdad while asserting a continuous presence in several key towns. His aviation combat element, Medium Helicopter Squadron 263, only had its normal inventory of CH-46E Sea Knights on board the *Kearsarge*, and upon arrival at al-Taqaddum, drew additional light-attack and heavy-lift helicopters from 3d Marine Aircraft Wing.

The acceleration of Colonel Anthony M. Haslam's 11th Marine Expeditionary Unit (11th MEU [SOC]) in its deployment came after it had completed its special operations certification. It departed San Diego on 27 May 2004 instead of the planned departure date of 17 June, embarking aboard three ships of Amphibious Squadron 5. It comprised part of Expeditionary Strike Group 3, commanded by Brigadier General Joseph V. Medina.

The initial assignment for 11th MEU was the smoldering city of an-Najaf. After unloading from its shipping at Kuwait, Haslam sent his aviation element, Medium Helicopter Squadron 166, to al-Asad Air Base while awaiting the preparation of Forward Operating Base Duke. The MEU's battalion landing team, 1st Battalion, 4th Marines, and its attachments under the command of Lieutenant Colonel John L. Mayer, used Forward Operating Base Hotel, which was three kilometers north of the city's center. The Marines and sailors of the 11th MEU moved into an-Najaf Province on 16 July. Five days later, the unit reported for operations to Major General Andrzej Ekiert, Polish Army, the commander the Multi National Division Center–South, and on 31 July they relieved the small battalion task force Dragon of the 1st Infantry Division. At this point, the 2,165 Marines and sailors of Colonel

Haslam's command held sole responsibility for the 16,000 square miles of the provinces of an-Najaf and Qadisiyah.

The nominal mission received from Ekiert consisted of conducting "offensive operations to defeat remaining non-compliant forces and neutralize destabilizing influences in an-Najaf Province" and to create a secure environment, supported by the usual stability and humanitarian operations. In effect, 11th MEU shouldered the responsibility of mopping up the remnants of the al-Sadr revolt following the departure of major U.S. Army forces that had destroyed most of the Mahdi Militia of al-Sadr during May and June.

In an-Najaf, the al-Sadr Militia had overwhelmed both the Iraqi security forces and General Ekiert's international military forces and occupied key positions, including the governor's compound and the two highly significant Shi'a religious sites, Kufa Mosque and the Imam Ali Shrine. Successive attacks by part of the 2d Brigade, 1st Armored Division, and elements of 2d Armored Cavalry Regiment in April and May recovered most of the city except for exclusion zones of one kilometer established around the two Shi'a holy sites, including the Old City and cemetery adjacent to the Imam Ali Shrine. The governor announced on 4 June that the Iraqi security forces would take responsibility for the exclusion zones, but the Mahdi Militia never laid down arms nor left the holy sites. Upon departing on 17 June, the 2d Armored Cavalry Regiment staff estimated that about 100 hard core fighters remained in each zone, along with an undetermined number of untrained insurgents.

Haslam reported on the day he took responsibility for the scene that "I anticipate aggressive surveillance and incidents from Mahdi Militia in the near term to test our reactions and resolve. The 11th MEU (SOC) stands at the ready." New outbreaks of fighting soon dispelled any illusion that simply training local security forces could accomplish the mission. Most of Colonel Mayer's battalion fought an inconclusive engagement with the Mahdi Militia around the cemetery and governor's compound on 5-6 August, supported by attack helicopters by day and an AC-130 Spectre gunship at night. General Metz, the deputy commander of the overall effort in Iraq, assigned an Army cavalry squadron to reinforce the 11th MEU after the first day. On 7 August, 1st Battalion, 5th Cavalry Regiment, reported to Haslam with the 1st Company, 227th Aviation Battalion's AH-56A Apache attack helicopters in direct support.

On 9 August, Iraqi and U.S. military leaders met at the governor's compound to discuss future operations. This group included an-Najaf Governor Arufi, Iraqi Prime Minister Ayad Allawi, General Casey, General Metz, and General Conway and his deputy, Brigadier General Dennis J. Hejlik. General Metz transferred the responsibility for the area to General Conway and assigned another Army squadron from Task Force Baghdad, the 1st Cavalry Division, to Colonel Haslam's control. After a brief interlude of fruitless negotiations between Allawi and al-Sadr's representatives, the Iraqi government finally authorized military force to settle the insurgency in an-Najaf.

General Hejlik oversaw the process with a small staff and Colonel Haslam received his reinforcements and planned the battle yet to come. As the reinforcements arrived, they applied a steady pressure against the al-Sadr militiamen with raids, probes, and skirmishes designed to determine their positions and exhaust their resources. The Iraqi National Guard's 404th Battalion operated under Haslam's control since the 31 July 2004 transfer of authority as the local garrison. The 2d Battalion, 7th Cavalry Regiment, the additional unit from 1st Cavalry Division, reported on 10 August. The 36th Commando Battalion, veterans of the Fallujah battle, joined on 13 August, and the 2d and 4th Battalions, 1st Iraq Army Brigade, arrived during the operation, remaining under the tactical control of I MEF. Several units of special operations forces operated in and around the city as well.

The final attack into the al-Sadr center of resistance came with Haslam's order of 16 August for a three-phase operation by U.S. and Iraqi forces to "clear Imam Ali Mosque Complex, to defeat Mahdi Militia, and capture or kill Muqtada al-Sadr to facilitate the return of the Imam Ali Mosque to proper Iraqi authorities." The first phase consisted of preliminary operations in which the two cavalry squadrons (1st Squadron, 5th Cavalry; 2d Squadron, 7th Cavalry) launched limited attacks to occupy the cemetery and the old city zone south of the Medina. The 1st Battalion, 4th Marines, would attack in the vicinity of Kufah and the remaining area of an-Najaf. This was followed with penetration operations in which the cavalry squadrons would fix the insurgents from the north and southeast while Mayer's 1st Battalion, 4th Marines, would push through from the northwest to encircle the shrine, bringing the Iraqi 36th Commando Battalion in assault amphibians to its final assault position. A third phase would entail decisive operations. The 36th Commando troops would assault and secure the shrine, which would then be occupied and secured by follow-on troops of the 1st Iraq Army Brigade.

After a final 22 August confirmation briefing to General Metz, General Conway, and the Iraqi defense minister, the attack began. Beginning late the night of 24 August, Marines and cavalrymen battled through the streets and buildings through the following day, culminating with Marines encircling the shrine at a distance of 100 meters by the end of the 25th. Amid heavy fighting, the issue never came into doubt. Under fire support from artillery, mortars, attack helicopters and AC-130 aircraft, the infantry, tanks, and other fighting vehicles cleared all opposition. For the next 24 hours, while the Iraqi commandos prepared to capture the shrine, mostly sniper engagements occurred in the area.

The al-Sadr Militia suffered terrible losses and resistance ended. The occupants of the Imam Ali Shrine had no hope of escape; their supporters fell back, broken and depleted. In the end, the intervention of Grand Ayatollah Sistani eliminated the need to assault the shine and to continue the action against the Kufah mosque. On 27 August, he brokered a truce on behalf of the Iraqi government. The Mahdi Militia agreed to surrender its weapons and to leave the Old City, including the Imam Ali Shrine. In addition, the militia agreed to relinquish the entire Najaf-Kufah area over to the Iraqi government, specifically the Iraqi police and the Iraqi National Guard. From this point onward, al-Sadr turned to peaceful and political options.

The 24 days of action in an-Najaf cost 11th MEU seven killed in action and 94 wounded; the Army cavalry units lost two men. Iraqi force casualties also included one American advisor killed and a significant number of Iraqi soldiers killed and wounded. These numbers paled in comparison to those inflicted on the Mahdi Militia. The 11th MEU estimated 1,500 of al-Sadr's fighters were killed and an undetermined number wounded, most likely in the thousands. A positive aspect was the steady performance of the Iraqi security forces at an-Najaf, as the Iraqi local police, 405th, and 36th Battalions all fought well and steadily, well-served by their embedded advisors. At an-Najaf, Marine Corps and Army units demonstrated an ability to maneuver and to reinforce a deteriorating situation even better than at the first battle of Fallujah.

The scarcity of capable Iraqi forces meant that Coalition security efforts remained under strength and under manned. To compensate for the shortage of forces, General Abizaid deployed a third Marine expeditionary unit to Iraq, the 31st MEU. As with the 24th MEU, the 31st MEU dispensed with its special operations capability requirement so that it could speed up its deployment.

The 31st MEU had operated in the western Pacific since January 2004, landing 2d Battalion, 3d Marines, for training in the Marianas followed by routine exercises in Korea, Okinawa, and Thailand. As deployment orders to Iraq came, it replaced its ground combat element with the 1st Battalion, 3d Marines, and attachments on Okinawa and then embarked with Amphibious Squadron 11 for training in the Marianas from 10 July to 4 August before going to Kuwait. When it arrived at the end of the month, its estimated deployment of 120 days (through 9 October) seemed half over, but its Marines and sailors would follow the experience of 11th MEU beginning in October.

In the midst of combat operations, the need to execute the scheduled turnover of forces in August and September remained. In certain cases, this had already begun, such as with the arrival of the 1st Battalion, 8th Marines, in western al-Anbar Province on 29 June. As specified in General Hagee's original decisions from November 2003, combat units would serve a six to seven-month deployment in Iraq while the personnel of I MEF's other organizations and staffs would be replenished with fresh groups flown in from their home bases.

The force turnover in I MEF took place over a three-month period. In addition, in September the

Table 4-1: Ground Combat Turnover, July–October 2004

Initial Deployment	Replacement Unit	Area of Operations	Transfer of Authority
3d Bn, 4th Mar	1st Bn, 8th Mar	Denver	14 July
1st Bn, 5th Mar	3d Bn, 1st Mar	Raleigh	17 July
1st LAR Bn	3d LAR Bn	Topeka	16 September
2d Bn, 7th Mar	1st Bn, 23d Mar	Denver	18 September
3d Bn, 7th Mar	1st Bn, 7th Mar	Denver	22 September
2d Bn, 4th Mar	2d Bn, 5th Mar	Topeka	26 September
1st Recon Bn (-)	2d Recon Bn (-)	Raleigh	27 September
3d Bn, 11th Mar	2d Bn, 11th Mar	Topeka	29 September
3d Bn, 24th Mar	2d Bn, 10th Mar	Taqaddum AB	4 October
2d Bn, 1st Mar	3d Bn, 5th Mar	Raleigh	8 October
2d Bn, 2d Mar	2d Bn, 24th Mar	Raleigh	11 October

Table 4-2: Aviation Turnover, August–September 2004

Initial Deployment	Replacement	Base	Relief in Place
VMU-2	VMU-1	Taqaddum	14 August
VMA-214	VMFA(AW)-242	al-Asad	17 August
HMLA-167	HMLA-169	al-Asad	23 August
HMM-261	HMM-365	al-Asad	27 August
HMH-466	HMH-361	al-Asad	2 September
HMLA-775	HMLA-367	al-Asad	7 September
VMGR-352/234	VMGR-352/452	Taqaddum	7 September
HMM-161	HMM-268	Taqaddum	8 September
HMM-764	HMM-774	al-Asad	19 September

Army replaced the 1st Brigade, 1st Infantry Division, with the 2d Brigade, 2d Infantry Division, commanded by Colonel Gary Patton. The 1st Marine Division exchanged artillery batteries and force reconnaissance, tank, combat engineer, and assault amphibian companies with fresh units. The I MEF intelligence service based in Ramadi also rotated battalions, as 2d Radio Battalion relieved 3d Radio Battalion and 1st Intelligence Battalion replaced 2d Intelligence Battalion.

As of 31 July 2004, 29,129 Marines and sailors were in Iraq with I MEF forces, with 190 more Marines stationed in Iraq with other organizations. Provided by Marine Corps Reserve Forces, 10,929 Marine reservists were on duty worldwide alongside their active component brethren, more than one-fourth the total reserve structure. Casualties to date in Iraq since March 2004 were 97 killed and 1,064 wounded in action, of which 780 of the latter had returned to duty in theater. With the situation in Fallujah yet to be resolved and persistent spikes in combat and violence still occupying in Ramadi, western al-Anbar Province was still untamed.

Chapter 5

The Second Al-Fallujah Battle

Following the first battle of al-Fallujah in April 2004, the Marines turned their efforts toward the pacification of the surrounding areas. Many insurgents had fled Fallujah before the fighting began and sought to establish themselves in new safe havens. The withdrawal of the reinforcements, provided by Regimental Combat Team 7, to western al-Anbar Province and Regimental Combat Team 1's continuing operations around Fallujah left the city itself in the hands of a desultory assembly of Iraqi police, Civil Defense Corps, and Fallujah Brigade "troops." In the ensuing month and a half, an uneasy peace settled on the city with few incidents reported. As a result, 1st Marine Division resumed civil affairs and humanitarian actions to reconstruct the city's infrastructure and support self-government. The division commander, Major General James N. Mattis, entered the city twice on well-armed "Fallujah patrols" to meet with city officials, and the Marines of 3d Civil Affairs Group resumed their efforts to identify and fund reconstruction projects.

Fallujah in Repose

Marines continued to man traffic control points in the outer cordon, while the police, Civil Defense Corps, and Fallujah Brigade assembled and prepared to patrol the city itself. Marines of Regimental Combat Team 7 and the Fallujah Brigade drove a demonstration convoy through the city on Route 10, halting briefly at the municipal government center. At no time, however, did the local security forces turn over usable weapons or insurgent prisoners taken from the city.

General Mattis saw some positive aspects of the event:

Today's successful joint patrol with the Fallujah Brigade represents the smallest of "baby steps" and should in no way be considered an opening of the city. Fallujah is still closed and a very dangerous place with large sections a "no man's land" controlled by jihadists, foreign fighters, and terrorists. In fact, an improvised explosive device was, without explanation, detonated at 0530, we think during emplacement and generally where the convoy principals dismounted

to meet with the mayor. The convoy was planned and executed as a combat patrol with two powerful quick reaction forces waiting just off stage ready to respond, supported by significant rotary and fixed wing close air support. The good news is the general population, while still openly hostile towards the Coalition, is reportedly tired of the fighting and disruption and willing to allow civil affairs money to flow into the city. They see the cease-fire, as well as today's events, as a continuation of their victory over the Coalition.

On 20 May, I MEF commander Lieutenant General James T. Conway expressed his satisfaction with the relative calm in the entire province and prepared to leave all Fallujah checkpoints in the hands of Iraqi security forces, except for the cloverleaf intersection of Routes 10 and E1 east of the city. More good news came with the arrival of air reinforcement: 20 AV-8B Harriers of Marine Attack Squadron 214, as requested by Major General James F. Amos. He noted that day that:

these aircraft with their third generation targeting forward looking infrared [system], the Litening II pod, equipped with a digital downlink capability, will give the Marines on the ground, in places such as Fallujah and Ramadi, the ability to see "real-time" what is going on around them. The Harriers will then be able to deliver ordnance as required, confident that what they are attacking is exactly what our ground forces want attacked.

Marine commanders judged sporadic but increasing attacks on Coalition forces in late May in opposition to the upcoming transfer of sovereignty to the Iraqi interim government. Thus, on 31 May, the Army's 112th Military Police Battalion departed I MEF control and returned to the 1st Cavalry Division after two months' service in al-Anbar Province.

The summer of 2004 saw the scheduled relief of the commanders of I MEF's major units. General Amos turned over command of the 3d Marine Aircraft Wing on 29 May to Major General Keith J.

Photo by LCpl William L. DuBose III, Defense Imagery, VIRIN: 041205-M-9529D-002

The summer of 2004 saw the scheduled relief of most of I Marine Expeditionary Force's commanders. MajGen Keith J. Stalder (above) relieved MajGen James F. Amos as commander of 3d Marine Aircraft Wing in May.

Stalder and departed to assume command of II Marine Expeditionary Force (II MEF) at Camp Lejeune. Major General Mattis relinquished command on 29 August to Brigadier General Richard F. Natonski and assumed command of the Marine Corps Combat Development Command at Quantico. Both departing officers were promoted to lieutenant general in their new commands and Brigadier General Natonski was promoted to major general. Finally, on 12 September, Lieutenant General John F. Sattler relieved General Conway as commander of I MEF. General Conway subsequently departed to serve as the new Director of Operations for the Joint Staff at the Pentagon. These new commanders would undertake the resolution of the Fallujah problem in the months that followed.

The eruption of coordinated attacks against Marine positions around Fallujah on 24 June marked what intelligence analysts considered spikes in insurgent activities. Reports of internecine fighting among tribal and extremist factions added to the frustrations of trying to assess progress in Fallujah. Al-

though the U.S. leadership hoped that these internal rifts reduced the effectiveness of the anti-Coalition insurgency, intimidation campaigns against Iraqis seeking to work for the Coalition or in Iraqi security forces continued to increase with deleterious effects upon the local security forces. An assessment of the Fallujah Brigade by the commander of Multi National Corps–Iraq, Lieutenant General Thomas F. Metz's strategic political-military staff in early July noted that the brigade had expanded to an overall strength of 2,075, including 23 general and 375 other officers. Although capable of limited city patrols and maintaining liaison with I MEF representatives, the brigade had not attained control over the city. In the view of the analysts, the Fallujah Brigade was a failure. At best, it could be converted into an Iraqi Army unit.

An ominous development surfaced with the continuing attacks upon 3d Marine Aircraft Wing helicopters flying in the Fallujah zone. The downing of an AH-1W Super Cobra attack helicopter during the 24 June attack was the second helicopter loss of the campaign and the second one in the vicinity of Fallujah.

Following the downing of the Super Cobra on 5 July, small arms fire northwest of Fallujah damaged a CH-46E Sea Knight transport helicopter of Marine Medium Helicopter Squadron 161. The aircraft came under fire soon after lifting off from its al-Taqaddum base and both pilots were wounded by the attack. The co-pilot, First Lieutenant Steven M. Clifton, assumed command of the aircraft. Ignoring his own injuries, he directed first aid efforts in the cockpit while flying evasive maneuvers and returned to base safely as the aircraft suffered electrical failures, a flash fire, and degrading flight controls. There were two other incidents where helicopters were damaged or destroyed by small arms fire, killing one pilot in one incident and wounding four crewmen in the other.

Unfortunately, the command seemed reluctant to face these trends. For example, the I MEF situation report for 9 September began with the following: "The overall number of attacks across the area of operations remains at decreased levels from the recent surge . . . However, a section of helicopters flying south of Fallujah received small arms fire and RPG fire and one helicopter was forced to land . . . Multi National Force–West will continue to closely monitor this emerging threat to Multi National Force–West air assets."

The decision process leading to the final assault on Fallujah and the eradication of the extremist and insurgent nests that it sheltered remained complex and diffuse. Prime Minister Ayad Allawi and the new

Iraqi political and military leadership had to be convinced of the benefits of the operation and that U.S. and Coalition support could and would be mobilized for the humanitarian relief and eventual reconstruction of the damaged city. The ability of U.S. forces to limit and ameliorate damage remained a contentious matter.

In September, the U.S. and Coalition military command authorized initial planning and the early concept of operations began to emerge in the I MEF staff. A briefing in the first week of that month characterized "Fallujah Clearing Operations" as a pending task where, on order, the I MEF and Iraqi security forces would conduct "clearing operations in the vicinity of Fallujah proper, to defeat extremist forces in Fallujah when ordered." Shortly thereafter, a staff paper identified the initial concept for shaping the upcoming battle.

In sum, the I MEF staff believed that the preparation of the battlefield required a steady tempo of attrition operations sustainable "until time for decisive action; mid-November." It characterized Fallujah as a safe haven for foreign fighters, terrorists, and insurgents, "a 'cancer' on the rest of al-Anbar Province." Among the operations necessary to prepare the city for the final assault were precision air strikes against leading insurgent operatives and foreign fighter groups. Continued pressure in the form of traffic control points limited but did not stop movement into the city. Marine attacks around the city limits could increase pressure and instill uncertainty in the insurgents. By 23 September, 1st Marine Division planners had produced a concept of operations for Fallujah, doubtlessly reflecting the time spent on the same problem in mid-April, when elements of both Regimental Combat Teams 1 and 7 stood in position around the city and the staff had prepared a final, decisive attack.

The division's plans called for building a target list that included assessments of the secondary and tertiary impact of each type of strike. Typical targets included safe houses, meeting places, weapon and ammunition caches, heavy equipment, insurgent patrols, crew-served weapons, indirect fire weapons, fortifications (both surface and underground), and communications. The plans proposed building pressure on the insurgents through selective strikes and using deception operations to uncover communications and movement routes in the city and discredit and humble the insurgent groups. After sufficient command nodes, and unfortified and fortified positions had been reduced, the Marines and soldiers would have accomplished the preliminary objectives required before the "decisive operations" or the assault phase.

Continuing Operations in the Province

As important as the Fallujah situation became, the rest of al-Anbar Province remained unsettled, and ar-Ramadi frequently flared with new violence. Colonel Craig A. Tucker's Regimental Combat Team 7 conducted meetings with regional sheiks and town councils to determine their degree of support for recruiting local security forces and making arrangements for their training in Iraqi and U.S. camps. The return of troops to the Haditha-Hit corridor and ar-Rutbah led to renewed counterinsurgency operations in both locations. Road sweeps and road improvements were also a priority effort while battalions conducted their reliefs in place. Because of the heavy fighting experienced in Husaybah and al-Qaim by 3d Battalion, 7th Marines, Colonel Tucker also reviewed the situation there. The Husaybah camp, now renamed Camp Gannon in memory of Captain Richard J. Gannon, the late commander of Company L, received special attention because its new occupants, 1st Battalion, 7th Marines, would also stand in relative isolation there and at al-Qaim during the renewed battle at Fallujah.

As Regimental Combat Team 7 prepared to reinforce Regimental Combat Team 1 at Fallujah, Tucker's Marines executed a flurry of disruption actions in Operation Rodeo (26–28 September). The Regimental Combat Team 7 forces executed 17 raids and cordon operations within 48 hours: six in Haditha, ten in Husaybah, and one in ar-Rutbah. On 27 September, Colonel Tucker began a command tour of Area of Operations Denver accompanied by Colonel W. Lee

In August, MajGen Richard F. Natonski relieved MajGen James N. Mattis as commander of 1st Marine Division.
Photo by LCpl Bryan J. Nealy, Defense Imagery VIRIN 030526-M-5455N-003

Photo by LCpl James J. Voorist, VIRIN 050222-M-8205V-037.

In September, LtGen John F. Sattler relieved LtGen James T. Conway as commander of I Marine Expeditionary Force.

Miller, commander of the 31st Marine Expeditionary Unit (31st MEU), who would assume responsibility for the area after Regimental Combat Team 7 departed for Fallujah.

At ar-Ramadi, the 1st Brigade, 1st Infantry Division, and its relieving unit, the 2d Stryker Brigade, 2d Infantry Division, conducted a continuing series of raids, cordons, and other actions to maintain a rough balance against the insurgents (Table 5-1).

Colonel Gary S. Patton's newly arrived 2d Brigade proved as well prepared as the 1st Brigade in meeting the challenges posed by Ramadi and its surrounding area. Patton's force was composed of two motorized and one mechanized infantry battalions, an artillery battalion (half employed as motor infantry), a combat engineer battalion, and Lieutenant Colonel Randy Newman's 2d Battalion, 5th Marines. The weapon systems in the brigade included 28 M1A1 Abrams tanks, 44 Bradley fighting vehicles, and six M109A6 Paladin self-propelled howitzers.

Amid stabilization operations and counterinsurgency strikes, more mundane missions also required the attention of Marines and soldiers in al-Anbar Province. To help rebuild local infrastructure, the

Rocket Attack on 1st Marines Headquarters

One characteristic of the Iraq War was that there were no true front lines. All Coalition soldiers, sailors, and Marines were vulnerable to insurgent assaults. This is clearly illustrated by the experience of the 1st Marines (Regimental Combat Team 1) in September 2004. On 14 September Colonel John Toolan relinquished command of Regimental Combat Team 1 to Colonel Lawrence D. Nicholson. That evening, Colonel Nicholson was discussing future operations with Regimental Combat Team 1's communications officer, Major Kevin M. Shea, when a 122mm rocket struck the Colonel's office. The explosion killed Major Shea and severely wounded Colonel Nicholson. Major Keith A. Forkin, Regimental Combat Team 1's Staff Judge Advocate, was near the blast and also injured. Despite suffering concussive effects from the explosion, Major Forkin provided life saving aid to Colonel Nicholson.

Colonel Nicholson was taken to Bethesda Naval Hospital for treatment. In December, just months after the attack, he returned to Iraq to serve as the Operations Officer for 1st Marine Division and eventually took command of the 5th Marines. On September 15, Colonel Michael A. Shupp took command of Regimental Combat Team 1.

Col Lawrence D. Nicholson (left) in October 2006.

Photo by Sgt. Chad Simon, Defense Imagery VIRIN: 061001-M-8299S-009

Table 5-1: Al Anbar Province Operations, 2004

Date	Operation
15 July	1st Brigade Operations Yellow Cab II and Speed Bump III.
17 July	1st Brigade Operation Black Rock.
23 July	1st Brigade Operation Cowboys.
3 Aug	1st Brigade Operation Traveler (with RCT-1).
11 Sep	2d Brigade Operation Pointer.
26 Sep	2d Brigade Operation Longhorn.
8 Oct	2d Brigade Operation Mountaineer.
12 Oct	2d Brigade Operation Seminole.

United States procured several large generators for power plants in Iraq, replacing destroyed or obsolete equipment. Immediately christened the "mother of all generators" by Marines and soldiers, these huge and expensive machines originated in Jordan and were eventually installed in Baghdad power stations. Six or seven combined heavy-lift vehicles moved each General Electric Frame 9E generator, weighing more than 250 tons. A convoy for a single generator comprised 15 heavy-lift vehicles accompanied by 10 private security vehicles. Civilian engineers preceded each convoy to lift or cut power lines, remove fences and guardrails, and make other minor improvements necessary for passage.

An even larger generator, the Siemens V94, was moved to the city of Taza using similar arrangements. These slow-moving (6 kph) convoys received the highest priority protection during weeks of transit through the various areas of operations. The two missions conducted to transport these generators were called Terrapin I and Terrapin II respectively. In each case, a security detachment of 2d Battalion, 11th Marines, remained with the generator all the way to its final destination. Thus, amid the smoke and dust of constant stability operations and the preparations for the major battle of Fallujah, Operations Terrapin I and II wound slowly across the I MEF battle space from 24 September to 12 October.

Assembling the Fallujah Assault Force

The 1st Marine Division began detailed preparations for an urban battle of proportions not seen by the Marine Corps since the Vietnam Battle of Hue City in 1968. As in that battle, Marines would share a significant part of the fight with comrades of the U.S. Army. The basic concept reprised some of the planning from mid-April, drawing as many forces as possible from two Marine regimental combat teams. In this case, each of them would conduct an assault on the city, working from north to south. Reinforcements from Multi National Force–Iraq would add both Army

and Iraqi combat units to the Marine assault regiments as well as additional forces to establish an effective cordon of the battle space surrounding Fallujah.

The first of these reinforcements, the 1st Battalion of the British "Black Watch" Regiment, reported to the 1st Marine Division on 27 October. The unit reported to Colonel Johnson's 24th MEU to assist in securing northern Babel Province and the vital main service routes running south of Baghdad.

On 31 October, six battalion-sized Iraqi units were attached to the division for the operation, now called Operation Phantom Fury. Previously assigned to the U.S. 1st Cavalry and 1st Infantry Divisions, these Iraqi units appeared likely to perform their missions better than the Iraqi troops fighting alongside Marines in April. Following their arrival and assembly in Camp Fallujah, they received U.S. liaison teams and fell under the operational control of the commanders of Regimental Combat Team 1, Regimental Combat Team 7, and the incoming 2d Brigade Combat Team, the Blackjack Brigade of the 1st Cavalry Division. A mechanized task force from the Army's 1st Infantry Division, the 2d Battalion, 2d Infantry, arrived for duty on 31 October. Heavily equipped with armor, mechanized infantry, engineers, cavalry, and self-propelled artillery components, it added considerable power to

As the Coalition prepared for a second assault on Fallujah, they made sure not to repeat mistakes committed during the first battle. Among these measures was ensuring the Coalition assault would receive the backing and support of the Iraqi Interim Government, then under the leadership of Prime Minister Ayad Allawi (below).

Photo by SrA Jorge A. Rodriguez, USAF, Defense Imagery VIRIN: 040614-F-4441R-016.

The combat zone facing Marines in Fallujah in November 2004 was an urban setting of densely packed, low-level buildings and a number of mosques.

Colonel Tucker's Regimental Combat Team 7. In like fashion, Regimental Combat Team 1, now commanded by Colonel Michael A. Shupp, received another powerful battalion task force that day, the 2d Squadron, 7th Cavalry, bringing more armor and mechanized infantry to the fight.

The vital mission performed by the Army's Blackjack Brigade, commanded by Colonel Michael Formica, consisted of taking over the entire battle space outside Fallujah, thus freeing both Marine Corps regimental combat teams for their assault roles. Upon the deployment of the brigade, the Marine assault units assembled in Camps Fallujah, Baharia, and Abu Ghraib for dispersal, rehearsals, and final preparations. Initially, the Iraqi battalions would operate in support of the attacking Marine Corps and Army battalions. Their essential missions eventually would include securing every building and position of the city.

Perhaps the most demanding reinforcement mission sent to the 1st Marine Division fell to the 31st Marine Expeditionary Unit. During 18 September–2 October, the Marines of Colonel Miller's command trained ashore in Kuwait at the Udairi Range to prepare for combat. On 3 October, Central Command head General Abizaid relinquished control of 31st MEU to General Sattler for operations with I MEF. The

key roles envisioned for the 31st MEU included reinforcing the Fallujah assault and relieving Colonel Tucker's Regimental Combat Team 7 of his responsibility for western al-Anbar Province during Operation Phantom Fury. Accordingly, 31st MEU passed to the operational control of Major General Natonski on 14 October and began moving to al-Anbar Province. Its ground combat element, 1st Battalion, 3d Marines (commanded by Lieutenant Colonel Michael R. Ramos) reported on 24 October to Colonel Tucker's Regimental Combat Team 7, where it provided additional infantry, armored vehicle, and artillery to the assault force. Lieutenant Colonel James A. Vohr's MEU Service Support Group 31 (MSSG-31) provided direct logistics support to Regimental Combat Team 7 during the operation with augmentation from Combat Service Support Battalion 7 (CSSB-7). The 31st MEU command and aviation combat elements flew and convoyed to al-Asad Air Base, from where Colonel Miller would take command of forces in Area of Operations Denver on 20 October. The 31st MEU's aviation combat element, Lieutenant Colonel Matthew G. Glavy's Marine Medium Helicopter Squadron 265, then joined the 3d Marine Aircraft Wing.

During the second battle of Fallujah, the 31st MEU would maintain the stability of Area of Operations

Denver, continue civil affairs operations, and support the Iraqi security forces. After the departure of Regimental Combat Team 7 and the other units assigned to Operation Phantom Fury, Colonel Miller reallocated the Denver battle space. The 1st Battalion, 7th Marines, now covered the Euphrates River Valley from the Syrian border to a boundary about 20 kilometers short of Haditha while 1st Battalion, 23d Marines, assumed responsibility to the eastern boundary of Area of Operations Denver. Ar-Rutbah and the extreme western sector became the responsibility of Task Force Naha, built around reduced companies from 3d Light Armored Reconnaissance Battalion, 1st Battalion, 23d Marines, and Battery S, 5th Battalion, 10th Marines, a provisional rifle company.

Target Fallujah

The pause between the first and second battles of Fallujah had permitted the insurgency to improve their defenses, which Marines had penetrated with comparative ease during the April battle. Intelligence reports estimated that between 3,000 and 4,000 insurgents had taken up positions in the city, thus exceeding the numbers Marines had faced in April. These sources also predicted insurgent leaders planned to hinder any I MEF assault on Fallujah by attacking external areas and routes, and cities such as Ramadi and Husaybah. The reported departure of many insurgents before the assault on Fallujah gave credence to this prediction.

Satellite and other forms of aerial surveillance revealed that the city had several lines of obstacles and fortified positions. The monitoring of insurgent responses to the Marine's preliminary operations also revealed the insurgents' defensive points. The relative densities of these apparent insurgent lines of resistance suggested the insurgents feared an attack from the east, especially from the much contested cloverleaf and zones north and south of Route 10, the location of the largest concentrations of roadblocks, berms, fighting positions, sniper holes, and checkpoints. A secondary concentration of positions on the southeast edge of the city showed attention paid to the Shuhada (Martyrs) District. Analysts also discerned likely positions prepared for later use by indirect fire weapons and small arms. The successive positions showed a willingness to fight in depth along Route 10 as well as much preparation for fighting in all directions from the strongholds of Jolan, Sook, and Muallimeen Districts. Planners presumed all routes into and within the city were armed with bombs and other types of booby traps.

After the Coalition forces began their attacks and pushed the insurgents out of their initial line of resistance, analysts assumed the insurgents would move in small elements into the interior positions. Four- to eight-man teams would fight a delaying battle back to strong points where up to platoon-sized elements would form to resist and even counterattack any Coalition troops that could be isolated in small numbers. The enemy would remain mobile and exploit any operational pause offered by Coalition forces. The enemy fighters would move through a series of caches and engagement areas built around major intersections and public buildings such as schools, mosques, civic buildings, and parking garages. Marine Corps and Army leaders expected the enemy to continually attempt to re-enter areas already cleared and to interdict supply lines after combat units penetrated the city. Some insurgent teams would stay behind hoping that the assault troops would bypass them, leaving them free to surface later and to cut Coalition lines or even to escape from the city. While insurgents favored improvised explosive devices, they also intended to fire mortars and rockets into Coalition positions within range after the attack of the city began. Infiltration routes, especially along the Euphrates River, could be used for resupply or for withdrawal as needed.

I MEF anticipated Fallujah insurgent groups would attempt to rally international opinion and mobilize propaganda to interfere with the planned assault, with the ultimate aim of disrupting it and causing a suspension of offensive operations. This time, however, the Iraqi interim government was involved almost from the beginning, and the Coalition planned a large-scale information operation to complement the planned battle and counter the worst charges of enemy propaganda. In short, the disadvantages encountered in the impromptu conduct of the first battle of Fallujah would not likely reappear in the more deliberately planned second battle for the city.

The Assault Plan and Aviation Support

Although directed tactically by Major General Richard F. Natonski and his 1st Marine Division command, Operation Phantom Fury required the participation of the entire I MEF organization and vital Army and Coalition reinforcements. During the battle, the stability operations of the 31st and 24th MEUs in the western and eastern extremes of I MEF's zone of responsibility and the operations by the U.S. Army's 2d Brigade, 2d Infantry Division, at Ramadi ensured that the operations in Fallujah took place without interference by the enemy in those areas. The full array of 3d

Marine Aircraft Wing capabilities was engaged in the action as well as the resources of the 1st Force Service Support Group.

As early as 24 September, Colonel Shupp and Colonel Tucker, the respective commanders of Regimental Combat Teams 1 and 7, had planned the assault operation with only four Marine infantry battalions (two from each regiment) with additional Iraqi forces. As commanders realized the extent of the problems they would be confronting, planners began to augment the force, and the forces allocated quickly grew. The final plan emerged by the beginning of October and passed through successive analysis and wargaming until the commanders had settled upon the details.

The objective of the attack remained as desired in April: to occupy the entire city, defeating all opposition, and clearing any caches or other resources that might sustain the insurgency. General Sattler's mission statement to I MEF set the tone:

> On order, Multi National Force–West attacks to destroy the Anti-Iraqi forces and insurgent forces in Fallujah-Ramadi to deny the use of Fallujah-Ramadi as their safe haven and to facilitate the restoration of legitimate governance, security, and reconstruction.

The operational plan to retake Fallujah consisted of five phases. The first would last from September to October and entailed what planners described as "limited shaping operations." These are actions conducted to collect intelligence, disrupt, isolate, and reduce the enemy while securing key infrastructure and routes. Information operations would highlight enemy failures and atrocities. Leaflets and broadcasts encouraged the citizens of Fallujah to leave the city. At the last moment, the information campaign would notify inhabitants to take cover in cellars and remain away from any fighting.

Planners described Phase II, or D-day, as "enhanced shaping" operations. These included "violent" action over a short period of time (approximately 24 hours) and the positioning of I MEF forces to attack Fallujah. Phase III, or D+1, would entail "decisive operations" to destroy the insurgents in Fallujah and to seize control of the city and to deny the use of Fallujah as a safe-haven. The "transition to an interim emergency government" would be Phase IV of the operation. Combined Multi National Force–West and Iraqi forces operations and reconstruction projects in Fallujah would help build the legitimacy of the Iraqi Interim Government in the eyes of the citizens. Multi National Force–West forces would provide security to facilitate reconstruction projects and establishing an

A Marine F/A-18D Hornet fighter-bomber of All-Weather Fighter/Attack Squadron 332 blasts away in full afterburner from al-Asad Air Base. Hornets provided close air support throughout the second battle of Fallujah.

Photo by LCpl Sheila M. Brooks, Defense Imagery, VIRIN: 051025-M-7404B-455

Photo by SFC Johan Charles Van Boers USA, Defense Imagery VIRIN: 041109-A-1067B-011

Soldiers from the 2d Brigade Combat Team, 1st Cavalry Division, prepare to enter and clear a building in southern Fallujah in the early stages of Operation al-Fajr.

Iraqi government and police force. The operation would be completed with Phase V, the transition to permanent, local government and security.

Little difference remained between "limited" and "violent" shaping operations in the vicinity of a dangerous place such as Fallujah. The shaping operations of Phase I were typified by an air strike called on 9 September, just after midnight, by special operations forces against a house being used as an insurgent headquarters. An Air Force F-15E Strike Eagle fighter-bomber destroyed the house with two 500-pound guided bombs with minimal collateral damage to adjacent buildings. Two days earlier, the 2d Battalion, 1st Marines, conducted a typical feint using tanks, LAV-25 light armored vehicles, and armored Humvees against the southeast corner of the city. This set the pattern of seemingly endless forays of various sorts against the insurgent positions, all aimed at disguising the true intentions of the attack, its location, and its timing.

Apart from shaping operations, Operation Phantom Fury began with the deployment of the 2d Blackjack Brigade, 1st Cavalry Division, directly from its Baghdad bases to relieve Regimental Combat Teams 1 and 7 of their positions so that they could regroup and re-

hearse their battle plans at Camps Fallujah and Bahariah. As the brigade relieved the two regiments, it received tactical control of the 2d Reconnaissance Battalion and the Iraqi 6th Battalion, 3d Brigade. The planned positioning of the Army brigade at the last minute gave minimal alert to the insurgents that a major alteration of the balance of forces had been accomplished.

Within hours of the establishment of the Blackjack Brigade around Fallujah's outskirts, the plan called for Task Force 3d Light Armored Reconnaissance Battalion to advance on D-day. The force included headquarters, one light armored reconnaissance company, one rifle company, a mechanized company and engineer platoon from the 2d Striker Brigade, 2d Infantry Division, and the Iraqi 36th Commando Battalion. The plan called for the task force to maneuver the length of the peninsula formed by the Euphrates River to the the west of the city. By securing the peninsula, the Coalition would prevent the hospital there from being used by insurgents as either a sanctuary or battle position. In the last hours of D-day, initially scheduled for 5 November, but changed to 7 November, the attack battalions moved through the night from their base camps and occupied attack positions along the northern outskirts of Fallujah, attacking at "A-hour" (for stage A of Phase III, Offensive Operations) of 1900 on D+1, or 8 November. During D-day, the assault battalions of Regimental Combat Teams 1 and 7 moved into covered locations beyond the railroad station and rail lines that constituted the first barriers guarding entry into the city from the north.

The division planned the assault to begin on D+1, whereupon both regimental combat teams would launch penetration attacks to prevent insurgent forces from evading U.S. forces and escaping the city. The leading assault battalions had the mission of overcoming obstacles and defeating insurgents wherever encountered. Any buildings or areas not cleared in the initial assault had to be cleared and secured by additional battalions fighting in trace, using the support of the Iraqi battalions assigned to each regiment. The division plan assigned the main effort to Regimental Combat Team 1, which would attack from north to south through the familiar Jolan district. The regiment would then continue until the northwestern quarter of the city had been searched and cleared. The eastern half of the city fell to Regimental Combat Team 7 to assault and clear in like fashion. Jolan Park and the Government Center became division objectives one and two, respectively, for the two regiments. At this point, the plan called for Regimental Combat Team 1 to consolidate and mop up in its sector, securing Route 10 for use in supporting the remainder of the operation. Iraqi troops were to take the forefront of the mop-up in an attempt to demonstrate Iraqi sovereignty. The assault battalions of Regimental Combat Team 7 would continue south and southwest, clearing and securing the rest of Fallujah, south of Route 10. At the conclusion of the mop-up of remaining resistance and the clearing of all enemy materiel and personnel, conditions for Phase IV would be met and the forces would turn to the stabilization and recovery of the city.

Logistics preparations initially centered on stockpiling the forward bases with the required materiel

A Marine from Company B, 1st Battalion, 3d Marines, mans a rooftop security post during Operation al-Fajr. The buildings in Fallujah were relatively low, and most of the roofs were enclosed by a low wall that created an easily defensible firing position for insurgents and Marines alike.

Photo by LCpl Jeremy W. Ferguson, Defense Imagery VIRIN: 041117-M-2353F-013

A Marine from 1st Battalion, 8th Marines, fires a MK153 Shoulder-launched Multipurpose Assault Weapon round at an insurgent stronghold during the opening phase of Operation al-Fajr.

and supplies in what came to be known as the "Iron Mountain." Marine planners had noted the largely unsuccessful attempts by insurgents to interdict routes and supply lines during the April Fallujah operations. This time, the 1st Force Service Support Group provided forward operating bases a minimum 15 days of supply in advance of the operation. Because of problems with civilian contractors, the group also mobilized the I MEF Engineering Group on short notice to build camps for the Iraqi Army battalions that had to move into the Fallujah camp complex before the operation.

The 3d Marine Aircraft Wing designed an aviation integration plan for Operation Phantom Fury after studying the after-action reports from the first battle of Fallujah and the battle of an-Najaf. During Operation Vigilant Resolve in April, the air observers and forward air controllers had to coordinate through two levels of air command and control systems before connecting the attacking aircraft to the terminal controller. The lack of a common grid reference system made for very long times from target acquisition and engagement for both fixed and rotary wing aircraft. After studying these and other lessons from April, the air plan established a "high density air control zone" and devised a "keyhole template" inside it. These tactical control measures emerged from a U.S. Central Command tactics review board held in July. In it, representatives from I MEF's division and aircraft wing

briefed the command on the airspace requirements and the need for unity of command to support the forward air controllers. The density of the airspace and the proximity of ground forces made the keyhole template a good solution to achieve the safety, unity of command, and integration of fires required by the urban operation.

For airspace management, two temporary flight restrictions established templates over both Ramadi and Fallujah. Each city had a 15 nautical mile radius and shared a center cap. After evaluating the many variables to include the size of the cities, weapon release parameters, Litening pod capabilities, ranges of insurgent weapons, safe release, egress maneuver room, and drone employment, a five-nautical-mile radius was chosen for this inner ring. This template essentially required aircraft to hold between the contact point and the initial point. The outer ring of 15 nautical miles served as that contact point and the 5-nautical-mile ring served as the initial point for the use of forward air controllers. This area needed to be defined carefully to minimize interference with neighboring air patrols. Two semi-cardinal lines extending out of the city center point defined each air patrol or sector. The airplane holding technique remained at the discretion of the pilots as long they remained within the lateral limits of the sector and altitude assigned.

The altitudes assigned for aircraft loiter and holding in the keyhole template also reflected the parameters of target acquisition, insurgent weapons, and the need to stack multiple sections of different types of aircraft in each sector. In the case of the Fallujah keyhole, the east sector, placed over the friendly bases of Baharia, Camp Fallujah, and Abu Ghraib, allowed a primary altitude of 13,000–15,000 feet and a secondary altitude of 18,000–20,000 feet. This arrangement also allowed fixed wing aircraft on the east and west to drop simultaneously. The 3d Marine Aircraft Wing planners added procedures for the use of odd-numbered "time over target" for Regimental Combat Team 1 and even ones for Regimental Combat Team 7 for fixed-wing aircraft. A poor weather scheme changed the sector altitudes for a "high war," "low war," or "split war," based upon cloud layers.

Considering combined arms needs, the plan incorporated the maximum elevation for artillery ordnance required to shoot across the city from proposed battery locations. This measure set the minimum operating altitude of the inner ring so that aircraft remained above 9,000 feet while inside, permitting artillery and mortar fire to a maximum elevation of 8,500 feet. Outside the ring, artillery could fire up to 11,000 feet. In both cases, no need remained to clear aircraft before firing artillery mis-

sions. If artillery required higher elevations for their missions, standard clearance procedures would be used.

The plan held rotary-wing aircraft in battle positions around the city at no closer than 1 kilometer from the city edge. Planners selected positions from which helicopters could fire an AGM-114 Hellfire missile against any target in the city. Operating at altitudes from the surface to 1,500 feet, no coordination would be required to clear their operations.

The planners recognized the need to operate unmanned aerial vehicles over the city but also acknowledged the risk of UAVs colliding with aircraft. They used a "little UAV, big sky" approach, hoping for a low probability of collisions because of the small size of the UAVs. Planners anticipated using four to five drones in the inner ring at anytime. North and south tracks for the drones permitted a certain measure of control such that they could be moved to a known track if necessary. The altitudes used depended on the characteristics of the three main drones employed: Predator, Pioneer, and Scan Eagle.

The aviation support plan specified standard loads for each aircraft type: AH-1W Super Cobras would be armed with four Hellfire antitank missiles, two Tube-launched, Optically-tracked, Wire-guided

GySgt Ryan P. Shane (center) is hit amid heavy enemy sniper fire as he and an unidentified Marine, both from Company B, 1st Battalion, 8th Marines, try to pull a fatally wounded comrade to safety during Operation al-Fajr. The second battle of Fallujah was among the fiercest in the history of the Marine Corps.

Photo by Cpl Joel A. Chaverri, Defense Imagery VIRIN: 041109-M-2789C-016

Photo by SSgt Jonathon C. Knauth, Defense Imagery VIRIN: 041110-M-5191K-035

Marines from Regimental Combat Team 7 are deployed along a roadway in Fallujah during Operation al-Fajr. The regiment's drive into the city's western districts provided important support for the main thrust conducted to the east by Regimental Combat Team 1.

(TOW) antitank missiles, a rocket pod, and 300 to 400 rounds of 20mm cannon ammunition. F/A-18 Hornet fighter-bombers were equipped with one GBU-38, 500-pound JDAM (Joint Direct Attack Munition) bomb, two GBU-12 500-pound laser guided bombs, or one GBU-12 and one laser-guided Maverick air-ground missile. The F/A-18 airborne controller replaced one of the weapons noted above with four 5-inch Zuni rockets. AV-8B Harriers were armed with one GBU-12 or Maverick.

The Marine fixed-wing aircraft all carried a Litening targeting pod. Mounted externally, the system provided an infrared detector, video camera, laser rangefinder, and laser designator in a single unit. Four of these pods were downlink-capable to the RQ-2B Pioneer drone system operated by the Marine Unmanned Aerial Vehicle Squadrons 1 and 2. The Army also furnished continuous coverage with two AH-64 Apache helicopters in a direct support role of the Blackjack Brigade

The air plan used a single "gridded reference graphic" based upon the target reference points,

phase lines, and building naming conventions of the two assault regiments. The graphic was designed for both cockpit and ground use and was made readable in red lighting, which is used to preserve night vision. The 1:7,500 scale image included overlays with the grid lines, phase lines, and target references. The image was further subdivided into 250 meter increments and labeled for eight-digit grid coordinates to facilitate quick target acquisition. A 1:5,000 scale version was also available. An additional overlay of approximately 700 buildings with accompanying coordinates and designated city blocks outlined for ground combat use was provided. All units received these aids through the military secure internet about four weeks before Operation Phantom Fury began.

Each regiment was assigned an AC-130 gunship, with both aircraft given the call sign "Basher." These would operate at night at altitudes of 9,000–11,000 feet initially with slightly overlapping tracks. While hesitant about operating two aircraft inside the five-nautical-mile ring, the Air Force crews practiced this procedure before the commencement of Phantom

Fury and executed it without error or mishap. During Operation Vigilant Resolve, AC-130s often ran out of ammunition, but 3d Marine Aircraft Wing succeeded in having the aircraft "floor loaded" with additional 40mm and 25mm ammunition for the second battle.

Having prepared command and control measures in great detail for the operation, schedulers had to line up the required aircraft. The fixed-wing aircraft would be "pushed" from bases to provide two sections of aircraft continuously overhead for a 17-hour period. With AC-130s on station at night, the requirement dropped to a single section of fixed-wing aircraft as augmentation. 3d Marine Aircraft Wing's KC-130 refueling planes provided around the clock coverage to prevent fuel exhaustion limiting ordnance delivery. The usual procedure of strip alert, quick fueling, and rearming also would be used so that tempo, not fuel, drove the fight. In short, the airmen wanted to respond to the tactical situation without concerns for logistical needs.

Additional AV-8B Harrier aircraft deployed to Iraq for this battle in addition to the first squadron ordered in after Operation Vigilant Resolve, Marine Attack Squadron (VMA) 214, which had arrived on 20 May. By the time the battle began, the 3d Marine Aircraft Wing wielded a "super-squadron" of AV-8Bs built around VMA-542, supplemented with planes and pilots from VMA-214, a detachment from the 31st MEU's VMA-211, and a detachment from VMA-311. The relief squadron for VMA-214 arrived at al-Asad Air Base on 17 August and Marine All Weather Fighter-Attack Squadron (VMFA[AW]) 242, operated its two-seat F/A-18D Hornets to good effect. The rotary-wing plan used the scheme of "pull" in that a two-section presence with two more available in alert status would be maintained for about 17 hours a day. The attack helicopters planned to fly from 0900–0200 daily, thus providing overlap of the AC-130 by several hours to attack targets on the outer edges of the city, to support additional ground units, and exploit their night combat capabilities.

The Seizure of Fallujah (7–19 November 2004)

At the urging of the Iraqi Interim Government,

A Marine from 1st Battalion, 8th Marines, Regimental Combat Team 7, uses his helmet to draw insurgent fire from atop a Fallujah roof during the early phase of Operation al-Fajr.

Photo by LCpl Joel A. Chaverri, Defense Imagery VIRIN: 041110-M-2789C-005

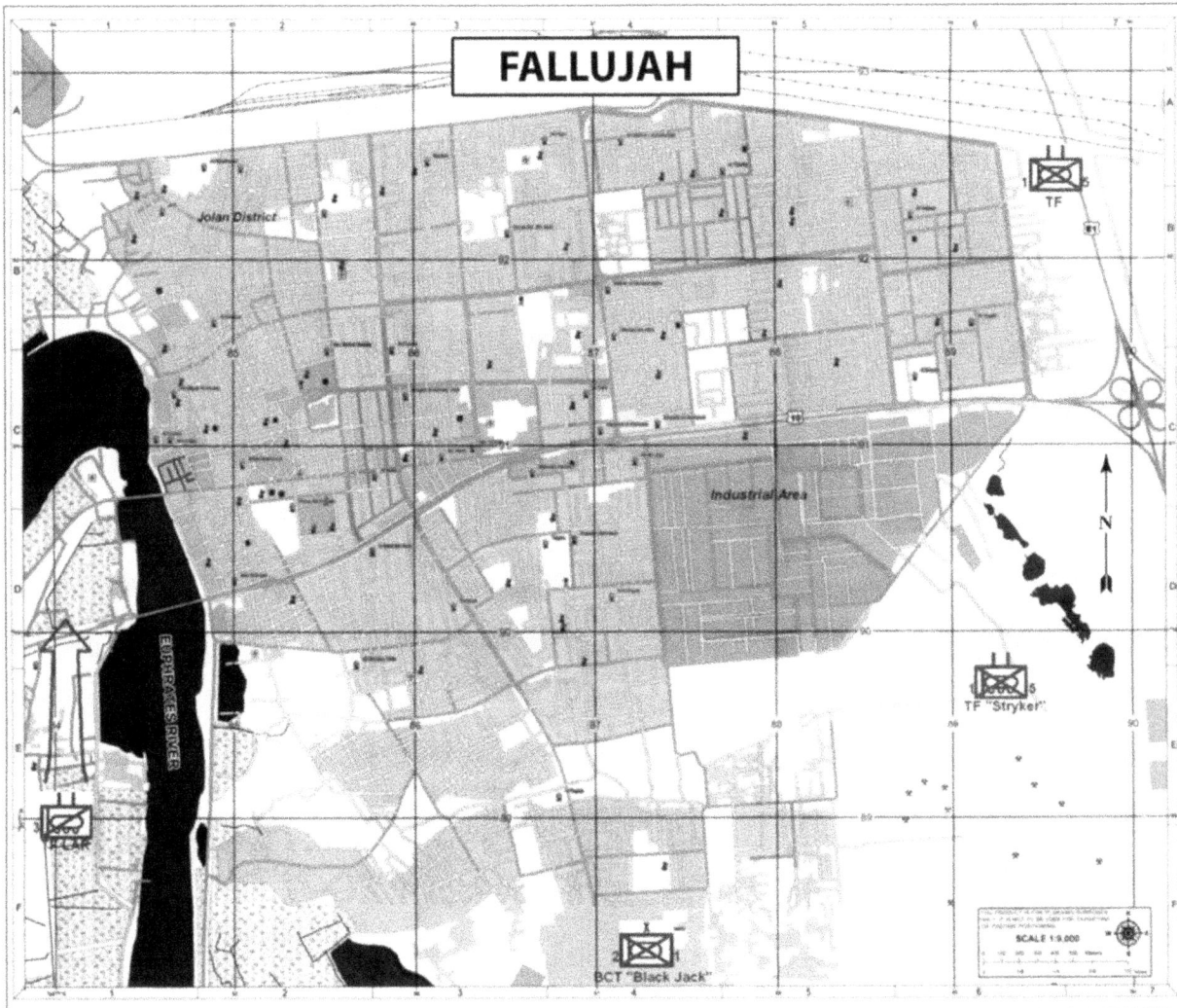

FALLUJAH

2d Topographic Platoon Map, Adapted by History Division

The al-Fajr plan called for Task Force LAR and supporting Iraqi units to seize and secure the hospital located west of Fallujah on 7 November. Meanwhile, Army mechanized infantry and cavalry units would set up cordons to the east and south of the city in order to prevent insurgents from escaping the city.

the U.S. military command renamed Operation Phantom Fury Operation al-Fajr (Dawn). Hours before the assault, Major General Natonski visited Army, Marine Corps, and Iraqi units in their attack positions outside the city. The Iraqi Interim Government invoked emergency powers and instituted a curfew in the Fallujah/Ramadi area. I MEF expected a surge in insurgent violence when the operation commenced. Commanders initiated curfews throughout the I MEF area of operations as engineers prepared to cut the city's power supply.

These final measures reflected the political preparations deemed necessary by the Coalition military commanders for successful operations in Fallujah. Leading up to the decisive assault, the Iraqi Interim Government announced the upcoming joint opera-

tions by the Coalition to re-establish Iraqi governmental control of Fallujah and to liberate the citizens from the insurgents. The Iraqi Interim Government appointed an ambassador to make political overtures of inclusion and reconciliation to the people of Fallujah but in the meantime declared a state of emergency. Iraq closed its borders with Syria and Jordan (although the Jordanian crossing was only partially closed) and made available the Iraqi security forces necessary to support the operation, including Iraqi Army, National Guard, and police units.

D-Day and D+1 (7–8 November)

On 7 November, the Iraqi 36th Commando Battalion and 3d Light Armored Reconnaissance Battalion task force seized the Fallujah Hospital on the penin-

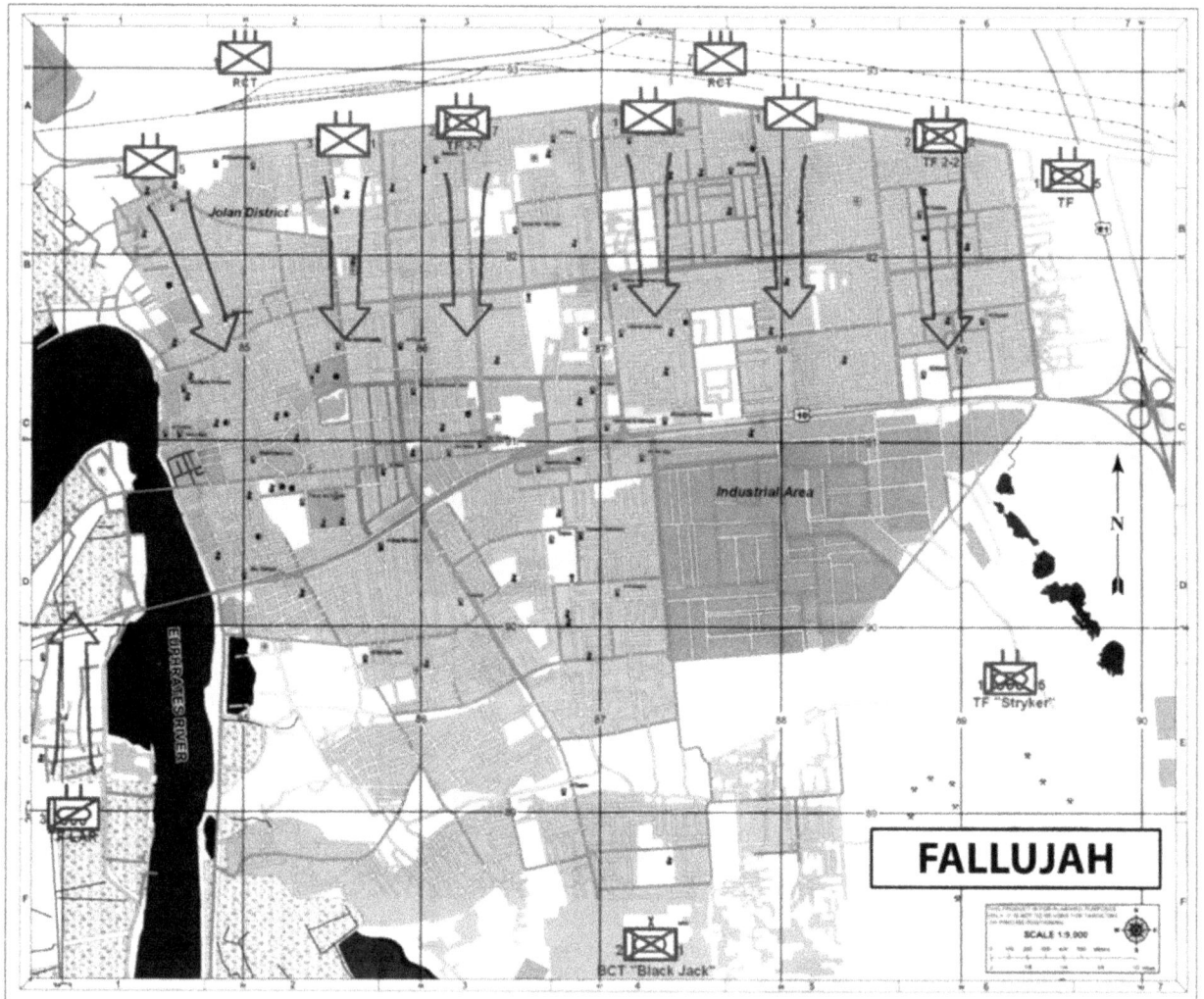

2d Topographic Platoon Map, Adapted by History Division

The second day of the assault on Fallujah was 8 November. With the hospital to the city's west secure and escape routes to the east and south cut off by U.S. Army forces, Marine Corps and Army battalions attacked the city from the north, clearing the city of insurgents as they methodically advanced south.

sula at 2207. The reconnaissance battalion secured the bridges from the peninsula to Fallujah at 0005 on 8 November and established three vehicle checkpoints. By 1045, Marines of 4th Civil Affairs Group completed their survey of the hospital and unloaded medical and humanitarian assistance supplies for its use.

The units of Regimental Combat Team 1 and Regimental Combat Team 7 moved to attack positions during the night of 7-8 November. The 3d Battalion, 5th Marines, attacked at 1052 on 8 November to clear an apartment complex northwest of Fallujah and completed its seizure of the area at 1255 with only light resistance. The 3d Battalion, 1st Marines, prepared to seize the train station east of the apartment complex. The A-hour of 1900 approached for the as-

sault battalions, beginning the vital clearing of the lines of departure of remaining obstacles and explosive devices. To breach the railroad tracks at the planned penetration point, four F/A-18Ds of VMFA(AW)-242, one flown by wing commander Major General Stalder, dropped eight GBU-31 2,000-pound guided bombs on the berms and tracks at 1420 when 3d Battalion, 1st Marines, assaulted the station to effect the breach. As a final step, a team of Navy Seabees and 4th Civil Affairs Group Marines entered the power substation just west of the apartment complex and cut Fallujah's electricity supply at 1800. The Marines hit the train station at 1859, taking sporadic small arms and rocket launcher fire. They secured the station by 2034 and began the hasty clearing of the breach area. The lead companies of 3d

Photo by LCpl J.A. Chaverri, Defense Imagery, VIRIN 041111-M-2789C-038

In contrast to the first battle of Fallujah, during Operation al-Fajr the Iraqi forces trained and assigned to 1st Marine Division did not desert, and fought alongside Coalition troops throughout the battle.

Battalion, 5th Marines, jumped off from their positions at the apartment complex at 1926, with tanks leading through their breach lanes, joining the tanks supporting 3d Battalion, 1st Marines, as they engaged insurgent antitank teams.

The engineers began their breach operations at 2200, and the advance elements of 2d Squadron, 7th Cavalry, began to cross at 0014, 9 November. The cavalrymen judged the breach as insufficient for their wheeled vehicles, however, so the engineer efforts continued. The 3d Battalion, 1st Marines, passed through the breach between 0503–0538, and 2d Squadron pushed its lead armor elements forward in sufficient strength to protect the left flank of the main effort by that Marine battalion as it thrust south into the heart of Jolan. By 0636, 3d Battalion, 5th Marines, neared its limit of advance for the first day, having cleared the Jolan Cemetery, and the cavalry squadron began to occupy strong points along its axis of advance. The Iraqi follow-on forces began to cross into the city in trace of the assault battalions at 0852, and began to secure cleared areas and guard some of the numerous weapons caches uncovered in the assault.

The small craft company, placed under Colonel Shupp's Regimental Combat Team 1 for the operation, began to fire and move at 1114 against insurgents trying to flee the city along the bank of the Euphrates where it rounds the peninsula.

The assault of Regimental Combat Team 7 into its zone of action began at A-hour using three reinforced battalions line-abreast, attacking to penetrate the city and clear an area to Route 10, seizing the Government Center (Division Objective 2) and supporting Regimental Combat Team 1's attack. Colonel Tucker assigned his main effort to 1st Battalion, 8th Marines, commanded by Lieutenant Colonel Gareth F. Brandl, on his right flank, moving somewhat east of the boundary with Regimental Combat Team 1, designated Phase Line George, but angling to the west to seize the Government Center and coordinating with Colonel Shupp's regiment via the 2d Squadron, 7th Cavalry. The center unit, 1st Battalion 3d Marines, attacked in zone at the center, and the U.S. Army 2d Battalion, 2d Infantry, attacked on the left flank of Colonel Tucker's force.

On 9 November, accompanied by Iraqi Special

Forces, the 1st Battalion, 8th Marines, penetrated along Phase Line Ethan and took the regimental objective, Hadrah Mosque, at 0900 . The Army mechanized infantry battalion moved rapidly along the left edge of the city, all the way to Route 10, killing approximately 48 enemy and then sending indirect fire into insurgent targets. The 1st Battalion, 3d Marines, experienced difficulty clearing its penetration point and instead moved its vehicles through the Army battalion, continuing to move south afterward with little further difficulty.

Leading the attack, Lieutenant Jeffrey T. Lee (Company A, 1st Battalion, 8th Marines) aggressively directed his tank platoon through major firefights. Initially operating continuously for over 12 hours, he ran the risk of low fuel while continuing to destroy insurgent resistance, enabling the battalion to reach its objectives. Days later, while leading Company A in its drive south, he was shot through his right arm yet refused to leave his unit and instead advanced two blocks further south, reaching the assigned battalion phase line. Surrounded by enemy insurgents, he supported the Marine riflemen taking positions in nearby buildings, eliminating more insurgents who attempted to attack the position. His aggressiveness and bravery contributed to the breaking of enemy resistance.

D+2 to D+3 (9–10 November)

While the Army cavalrymen of the 2d Squadron, 7th Cavalry, continued south on their thrust along the boulevard of Phase Line Henry, the 3d Battalion, 5th Marines, cleared its zone in the northern half of the Jolan District. The regiment's other Marine assault battalion cleared areas in the cavalry squadron's rear. The intense fight for the heart of Jolan District by the 3d Battalion, 1st Marines, took the rest of 9 November and culminated in a turn to the west in preparation to complete clearing operations to the river's edge. The 2d Squadron, 7th Cavalry, reached Route 10 (Phase Line Fran) at 2200 and controlled the streets to the east and west of its attack route. The accompanying Iraqi 4th Battalion continued to clear buildings along Phase Line Henry, which had armor strong points now posted along its entire length north of Route 10. The insurgents could do little against the firepower and armor of the cavalry squadron, and any who resisted were quickly eliminated. Fire from tanks and 25mm automatic cannon fire from armored vehicles destroyed many of the improvised explosive devices and car bombs arrayed along the routes, with little effect on the attacking forces. The cavalrymen took Jolan Park (Division Objective 1) at the end of the day, well ahead of the attack plan schedule. The 3d Battalion, 1st Marines, began its attack to the west at 1305 on 10 November to clear the remaining unoccupied part of Fallujah north of Route 10 to the river's edge. On its left flank, the cavalrymen of 2d Squadron attacked along Route 10 to secure the two highway bridges from the east at 1424 . The 3d Light Armored Reconnaissance Battalion already held the western sections. By the

A Marine from Company B, 1st Battalion, 3d Marines, watches the smoke rise as a building in Fallujah burns in the distance.

Photo by LCpl Jeremy W. Ferguson, Defense Imagery: 041112-M-2353F-002

end of 10 November, Colonel Shupp's regiment had captured the entire northwest quadrant of Fallujah with a classic cavalry screen established on the eastern edge of his zone and the two Marine battalions poised to mop up the interior and continue the attack south of Route 10.

In Regimental Combat Team 7's zone of operations to the west, the 1st Battalion, 8th Marines, began its movement at 0100 on 10 November south from the Hadrah Mosque area with two rifle companies. At 0400 it launched Company A, mounted in amphibious assault vehicles and escorted by tanks and light armored vehicles. The mounted company seized the Government Center at noon, but the other companies fought for several more hours to overcome snipers and pockets of resistance before securing their sections of Route 10. Two rifle platoons, however, had to return to the Hadrah Mosque that night to prevent insurgent reoccupation of the site.

As 1st Battalion, 3d Marines, joined the rest of Regimental Combat Team 7 on the Route 10 line, several changes to the planning took place on 10 November. The rapid advance of both regiments to Route 10 (Phase Line Fran) had eliminated any need for Regimental Combat Team 7 to undertake the clearing of southern Fallujah alone. Instead, each regiment would continue south following the extended traces of the same boundaries and phase lines already in use. The securing of the northern part of the city, however, already taxed the Iraqi forces in the operation even though they had performed well supporting the assault battalions. Command and control of Iraqi units remained problematic, and Marine battalions would remain behind in each regimental zone to complete the mopping up phase. Therefore, 3d Battalion, 5th Marines, and 1st Battalion, 3d Marines, were assigned to secure the northern half of Fallujah within their respective regimental sectors while the assault to the south ensued.

Sergeant Jeffrey L. Kirk led his 1st Squad, 3d Platoon, K Company, 3d Battalion, 5th Marines, in successive assaults of a fortified building and courtyard, eliminating insurgents and a machine gun position personally with rifle fire and grenades. Although wounded, he refused medical attention and led a third assault. Nearby, K Company's Private First Class Christopher S. Adelsperger executed a series of single-man attacks, clearing houses, rescuing wounded Marines, and leading the charge into a courtyard after an assault amphibious vehicle crashed through its wall. Although he did not survive his wounds, Adelsperger used amazing courage and energy in destroying the last strongpoint in the Jolan district.

The broadcast by loudspeakers of the Marines' Hymn over Fallujah by B Company, 9th Psychological Operations Battalion, took place in the early evening of 10 November as units set in for the night. The observation of the Marine Corps birthday varied throughout the zone, and most units celebrated in small groups during the early morning hours. Observing the date allowed Marines to revel in their cherished traditions at a time of great danger.

D+4 to D+13 (11–20 November)

Regimental Combat Team 1 continued the attack into southern Fallujah, sending 2d Squadron, 7th Cavalry, south along Phase Line Henry to act once again as the supporting effort beginning at 1900. The armor company leading the thrust encountered a complex obstacle that required close air support and AC-130 fire to reduce. The armored attack continued south to the assigned limit of advance for the day, some 1,200 meters south of Route 10, by 0300 on 12 November. Supporting arms suppressed enemy fire, and the mechanized infantry company, following in trace, established a screen. Operating several hundred meters to the east, 3d Battalion, 1st Marines, began its main attack at 1600 on 11 November, undertaking the mission of clearing the entire zone between the cavalry advance and the river's edge.

During the daylight hours of the 11th, the insurgents in front of Regimental Combat Team 1 had retreated south and attempted to regroup and reorganize what men they could for their defenses. Marines and soldiers moved into the night, not making much contact. The cavalry screen anchored the regiment's left, with a section of either M2 Bradley fighting vehicles or M1A1 Abrams tanks at every major intersection. True to form, as the sun came up on 12 November, the enemy came out to fight.

At 1030, Marines of 3d Battalion, 1st Marines, reported strong insurgent contact, receiving mortar and small arms fire about 500 meters south of Route 10 near the cavalry advance. A Pioneer drone showed eight to 10 men fighting along rooftops of four houses. Although the battalion reported two companies were running low on fuel and ammunition, one of these companies had reached the limits of south Fallujah by 1640.

The last major contact by Regimental Combat Team 1 with organized resistance came the next day (13 November) at 1017, when Marines of 3d Battalion, 1st Marines, fought squad-sized enemy elements. Several Marines fell wounded in one house and six insurgents in the upper floor prevented four of the Marines from being evacuated. First Sergeant Bradley

A. Kasal ran forward from the unit providing cover for the endangered Marines and joined a squad making a fresh assault inside the house. Killing one insurgent at close quarters, he was struck down by rifle fire and fell with another Marine. He shielded the wounded Marine with his body from hand grenade fragments and then refused evacuation until all other Marines had been removed. He shouted encouragement to all concerned as more Marines cleared the house. Inside the house, Corporal Robert J. Mitchell Jr., leading the squad Kasal had joined, charged through rifle fire and grenades to reach a critically wounded Marine and begin first aid treatment. His covering fire permitted a corpsman to join him, and Mitchell was then hit while crossing the lower room to assist other casualties. At close quarters, he killed an insurgent with his combat knife and then turned to assist in the evacuation of the wounded. After they had been rescued, a Marine tossed in a satchel charge, which brought the house down and finished the last insurgent resistors.

At the end of 12 November, Colonel Shupp signaled that Regimental Combat Team 1 had completed its initial assault through the west side of Fallujah:

The soldiers of 2-7 [Cavalry] demonstrated ex-traordinary courage in the face of the enemy. Their firepower and can-do spirit has saved Marine lives. 3/5 [3d Bn, 5th Mar] conducted detailed house-to-house searches and have uncovered tens of thousands of unexploded ordnance, which they are systematically destroying to ensure the safety of the Jolan. 3/1 [3d Bn, 1st Mar] successfully seized the southern portion of the Regimental Combat Team 1 zone. Without regard for their own safety, the Marines and sailors of 3/1 made great gains despite running into some of the stiffest resistance since the fighting began. Resistance included suicide attacks by suspected foreign fighters.

On the other hand the continued clearing of Fallujah proved difficult. Enemy contact was heavy during the early afternoon of 13 November and continued at lesser levels through the night and into the morning of 14 November.

Marines and soldiers of Regimental Combat Team 1 now entered an even more dangerous period in the operation. An increasingly desperate and tenacious enemy used suicide attacks, snipers, and booby-trapped buildings to inflict more casualties. The assault troops, however, continued to dominate

Marines from 3d Battalion, 5th Marines, guard captured Iraqis after a December 2004 cordon-and-knock operation in Fallujah.

Photo by LCpl James J. Vooris, Defense Imagery VIRIN: 041206-M-8205V-016

what they already termed the "ten-second firefight" and effectively applied combined arms to eradicate resistance at every encounter.

As his regiment continued clearing its zone, Colonel Shupp crossed the south bridge over the Euphrates on 15 November, officially opening it for military traffic. Navy Seabees assessed the north bridge as being in good condition, and it opened shortly thereafter. The next day, shortly after noon, the 3d Battalion, 1st Marines, reported that its sweep of the south bridge with dogs and explosives ordnance disposal teams had uncovered six bombs. The removal of these came just before the symbolic crossing of the bridge by General Casey, accompanied by Colonel Shupp, and led by Lieutenant Colonel Willard Buhl, the commander of 3d Battalion, 1st Marines.

On the eastern side of Fallujah, Colonel Tucker resumed his advance with the Army's 2d Battalion, 2d Infantry, pushing armor south of Route 10 at 1900, 11 November, along the eastern fringes of the city. 1st Battalion, 8th Marines, operated further to the west in the zone. The Marine battalion crossed Route 10 in the attack at 1500 with two companies on line, tanks in the lead, and assault amphibious vehicles following in trace. Here they encountered their heaviest resistance in the entire operation. Marines crossed the highway, and insurgents responded with automatic gunfire and antitank rockets. In three hours of fighting, both companies battled their way 250 meters to the south and stopped in some buildings at dusk. They advanced another 250 meters under the cover of darkness beginning at 0001 on 12 November without incident and again set into defensive positions. Iraqi troops joined later in the morning and cleared a mosque with no resistance. At 1800, another move south and west, under the cover of darkness, brought the lead companies of the battalion to the vicinity of Regimental Combat Team 1's 2d Squadron, 7th Cavalry, screen without incident.

Although the Army mechanized task force encountered some heavy resistance in the southeast corner of Fallujah, Colonel Tucker's regiment effectively switched from its attack phase on 15 November and commenced mopping up in the interior of the city.

Combat operations did not cease with the occupation of the city. Hard pockets of resistance continued even as most insurgents sought to flee the city. The reports of the two assault regiments for 20 November showed each using two Marine infantry battalions in clearing operations, encountering some defended houses, especially in the southern sectors.

The Army's 2d Battalion, 2d Infantry, continued house clearing as well, and 2d Squadron, 7th Cavalry, continued occupying strong points on the boundary between the regiments. Of the assault battalions, the Army mechanized battalion task force became the first to depart Fallujah, leaving on 21 November for its parent organization.

Phase IV Operations in Fallujah (21 November–23 December 2004)

There was no clear-cut distinction between combat and stabilization operations following the successful assault on the city. The assault battalions occupied assigned sectors of the city and crossed and re-crossed them in sweeps and house-clearing operations, using the attached Iraqi battalions to the extent that their abilities permitted.

Colonel Shupp's Regimental Combat Team 1 reports noted increasing humanitarian assistance efforts and civil-military operations in the last third of the month. Colonel Tucker's Regimental Combat Team 7 reported the same by 27 November and the regiment began rotating Marines by platoon back to base camps for 24-hour rest periods beginning on 29 November. The 2d Squadron, 7th Cavalry, completed its withdrawal to Camp Fallujah on 23 November. Continuing discoveries of arms caches plagued the operation in its final weeks, creating security problems and also permitting renewed attacks in the city by surviving insurgents. The total number of caches uncovered reached 370 at the end of the month.

Throughout the last weeks of November and the first two weeks of December, the 4th Civil Affairs Group staff worked with a variety of higher commands and the Interim Iraqi Government to develop a return and reconstruction plan for the city that would allow its residents to return to their homes but, at the same time, preclude insurgents from returning to the city. A new scheme of internal movement control came into practice, making use of biometric identification technology, a variety of scanners, and a new series of movement control points. The city's water, sewage, and electrical systems were repaired as the more than 200,000 residents of Fallujah began to return and restore the city to some sense of normalcy. I MEF's staff created an inter-ministerial coordination group, located in the civil-military operations center that coordinated all Iraqi and Marine stabilization operations in Fallujah.

On 23 December 2004, the shift from assault to recovery operations in Operation al-Fajr occurred. It was the first day that Fallujah's inhabitants began to return to the city as 600 civilians returned to the al-

Andalus District. In other respects, the day was little different from previous ones as Marine rifle companies with attached Iraqi troops continued to conduct security patrols. The 3d Battalion, 5th Marines, fought 10 to 15 insurgents in northern Fallujah. Its Marines employed tanks and air strikes to destroy buildings occupied by the combatants. Three Marines were killed in action, and five more suffered wounds. Sergeant Jarrett A. Kraft led three assault squads on three separate instances to repel insurgents and clear houses. Despite receiving repeated blast effects from grenades and being knocked down stairwells, he continued to lead his Marines with courage and spirit. At the same time, another squad leader in the same platoon, Corporal Jeremiah W. Workman, led his Marines into several buildings, rescued wounded Marines, and then personally covered them with his fire after receiving fragment wounds in his arms and legs. He led his Marines in one more assault before reinforcements arrived to complete the action.

The Phase IV (stability operations) plan used by I MEF and the 1st Marine Division aimed at establishing competent Iraqi security forces in the city that would require only minimal backup from U.S. forces. Civil affairs group teams and detachments from 1st Force Service Support Group operated with every battalion in the Fallujah operation, assessed damage, and sought to protect infrastructure wherever possible. In the aftermath of combat operations, the priorities for Marine commanders in restoring the city's operation were public health, public works and utilities (water, food, electricity, medical), infrastructure (communications and transportation), the economic infrastructure, emergency services, and finally the reevaluation of projects previously begun that might prove salvageable. During 14–16 December, the Army's 2d Blackjack Brigade, 1st Cavalry Division, departed 1st Marine Division, transferring responsibility for the area outlying Fallujah to Regimental Combat Team 7. The latter regiment left Fallujah on 10 December, leaving 1st Battalion, 3d Marines, under the tactical control of Colonel Shupp's Regimental Combat Team 1, which now conducted the occupation and stabilization of the city proper.

Colonel Shupp's instructions to Regimental Combat Team 1 conveyed the complexity of the change in mission:

Our operational success depends on our efforts in this phase. At no time is the phrase "No better friend, no worse enemy" more applicable. This phase however, will be complicated with no clear beginning and probably starting as

areas of Fallujah are cleared of enemy activity. Identified forces must roll into these tasks on the heels of our advance. We must keep the citizens of Fallujah informed through creative info ops that readily offer aid and assistance. We must reach out to the citizens to reduce their human suffering and quickly restore daily operations. We must introduce the Interim Iraqi Government as soon as possible and steadily transition to their control and operations. The citizens must be impressed with the power of Iraq's legitimate authorities and identify with the government as their benefactor and hope for the future. We must destroy any ties to criminal elements and seek the assistance of the people. Maintaining security is paramount to enabling all other operations, but it must not consume our focus.

As the troops of Regimental Combat Team 1 began to occupy the "secured" eastern half of Fallujah, some surprises occurred. Although combat also continued in the western half, where 3d Battalion, 1st Marines, held security and stabilization responsibilities, most engagements and many cache discoveries occurred in the eastern side after 10 December. The 3d Battalion, 5th Marines, and 1st Battalion, 3d Marines, combined to fight and kill approximately 35 insurgents on 12 December using tank fire and close air support. Another engagement on the following day saw seven bombs dropped and more tank fire used to kill five insurgents. Assistant division commander, Brigadier General Joseph F. Dunford, told the division that more clearing and reclearing operations would be required even as the city was returned to a more peaceful state.

As in all combat operations conducted in Iraq, the civil affairs teams accompanying the assault troops included payment teams compensating owners for battle damage to property and paying death claims to families who lost members during the battle. As soon as feasible, labor and construction contracting would employ local workers and provide basic items (wheelbarrows, shovels, etc.) to clear and repair roads and streets. Humanitarian assistance measures sought to provide essential services (initially water, food, and fuel distribution) to mosques and 1st Force Service Support Group operated humanitarian service centers. Depending upon the Iraqi government actions, the civil-military teams (Marine Corps and U.S. diplomatic) sought to once again establish a civil-military operations center with the local government in the downtown government center capable of coordinating military assistance.

As stabilization operations came to a close, Iraqi forces were given responsibility for maintaining security in the city (Phase V). Meanwhile, U.S. quick reaction forces were maintained to support subsequent security and civil military operations.

Assessing Operation al-Fajr/Phantom Fury

The second battle of Fallujah defined I MEF's campaign of 2004–05. Marines and soldiers fought through the city at close quarters, frequently engaging in point-blank firefights and hand-to-hand fighting. No enemy tactic or procedure sufficed to repel the ferocity and effectiveness of squads, teams, and even individual Marines and soldiers. Caught in their defensive maze, the insurgents fought to the death, surrendered, or fled, the latter move becoming increasingly difficult as the assault forces cleared the city.

An exchange monitored between two insurgents demonstrated the decisive blow of the battle:

A: Where is this shooting?
B: Everywhere. In every area.
A: What is it, artillery?
B: Artillery, mortars and tanks everywhere.
A: Where are you?
B: By the flour mill.
A: They are attacking the flour mill?
B: Yes, and they are attacking us too. The artillery is destroying us. All of Fallujah is in ruins. Not a house is left standing. What can stand? The tanks come down every street with artillery falling ahead of them.
A: Get out of there!
B: Where? How? If I go in the streets I get shot. If I stay inside I get shelled. And let's not forget the mortars and the aircraft and the snipers!
A: But . . . They said the Americans had withdrawn!
B: The Americans are everywhere.
A: They said Nazl was still safe . . .
B: Nazaal is a warzone.
A: Where is A_____?
B: No one knows.
A: Try to make it somewhere . . .
B: Even if I go in the yard I will be attacked.
A: What about Shuhada?
B: Just bombing there, they have not entered yet.
A: Listen, on the streets, it's just tanks right? Nobody on foot . . .
B: Yes but you see, a tank is roughly as big as a house . . . You can hit it with a rocket and it doesn't blow up.

A: What about Jolan?
B: War zone.
A: They said Mujahideen reinforcements were arriving.
B: Well they haven't arrived yet. There are still Mujahideen in Askeri, only because they regrouped there from Souq and crossed over the new road. Fallujah is finished. It is the attack of all attacks. All the sheikhs have left us and are happily organizing demonstrations and protests in other parts.
A: How can you say the sheikhs have left?
B: They fled with the families from Jolan and elsewhere. They may still be leaving; they are still getting families out somehow. Today a family of a woman and children had a house fall down around them. They got them out and took them to Jubeil or somewhere . . .
A: Look, call me if anything develops. I don't care what time you call. Try to find A____.
B: I'll do what I can. We did burn one tank.
A: That's good at least.
B: Yes, but if you burn one tank they send three more. It's useless.
A: Two aircraft were brought down. Hang in there.

The tactical surprise accomplished at the second battle of Fallujah ranks as one of several remarkable accomplishments of I MEF and the 1st Marine Division during a highly complex battle. The attack disoriented the insurgent defenses at the outset, and they never recovered their balance. Although the Jolan district contained the heart of Fallujah's insurgency, the rapid penetration into it forced insurgents from their positions and prevented a sustained defense. After the operation Coalition soldiers and Marines discovered the majority of safe houses and other insurgent sanctuaries in the area. In the south, specifically in Nazl and Shuhada, the assault units found the most formidable defenses, including foxholes, spiderholes, and tunnels inside and between fortified houses and insurgent billeting areas. Considerable caches of ordnance were found throughout the city.

The enemy typically fought in small groups of four to 12 individuals, armed with small arms and RPG-type rocket launchers, who generally chose to fight from inside buildings rather than out in the streets. In general, the insurgents chose not to fight at night. Although these groups tended to congregate in houses, which were close to one another, they fought as individual groups rather than establishing a mutually supporting series of positions. Although Marines sustained some casualties from rooftop shootings, most casualties occurred inside buildings where the enemy waited

Photo by Cpl Theresa M. Medina, **Defense** Imagery, VIRIN: 041202-M-2583M-007

Maj M. Naomi Hawkins, the public affairs officer of the 4th Civil Affairs Group, is interviewed by an Arab television news crew in front of the Dr. Talib Al-Janabi Hospital in Fallujah. The foreign media toured the city in December 2004 to view ongoing reconstruction efforts by multi national forces in the wake of the November battle of Fallujah.

for assault troops to come to him. These tactics were probably a result of dominant U.S. firepower on the streets and rooftops. The enemy usually opened fire on Marines as the latter were entering a house or ascending the stairwell. The insurgents often used rifles and grenades to initiate the engagements and would usually continue to fight until killed. Fighting to the death does not mean, however, that Marines fought a suicidal enemy. In many instances, insurgents attempted to escape by throwing down their weapons and either trying to evade U.S. units or approaching them pretending to be civilians. By all accounts, however, the enemy that Marines encountered in Fallujah proved more willing to stand and to fight to the death than any enemy forces met elsewhere in al-Anbar Province.

As noteworthy as the ground assault of 1st Marine Division and its reinforcements was, the employment of the aviation support of the Coalition and 3d Marine Aircraft Wing and the various artillery batteries pro-

vided supporting arms fire. The operating altitudes changed to the poor weather plan on D+1. The fixed-wing aircraft loitering for close air support came to the 10,000 to 12,000 or 11,000 to 13,000 feet blocks many times due to the weather. In the following days, these lower blocks continued in use even when the weather was good. Lower altitudes enhanced targetting ability by reducing slant range for sensor acquisition and had very limited effect on the clearance of artillery fires. Although insurgent antiaircraft missiles were always a concern, the airmen accepted the risk of low-altitude flight needed to retain the accuracy demanded in this complex environment. Many times fixed-wing aircraft would use the lower block to find or verify the target location and then exit the ring and come in at a higher altitude for release of guided bombs. Several times during the battle multiple aircraft in multiple sectors worked on targets both inside and outside the 5-nautical-mile ring.

The staging of multiple aircraft in the keyhole pat-

Table 5-2: Artillery Missions Fired during Second Fallujah Battle

	7–8 Nov	8–9 Nov	9–10 Nov	10–11 Nov	11–12 Nov
Call for Fire	47	53	37	35	45
Counter Fire	22	15	10	21	11
	12–13 Nov	13–14 Nov	14–15 Nov	15–16 Nov	16–17 Nov
Call for Fire	28	31	24	7	7
Counter Fire	9	8	23	22	4
	17–18 Nov	18–19 Nov	19–20 Nov	20–21 Nov	21–22 Nov
Call for Fire	2	1	0	0	0
Counter Fire	10	3	5	4	4

155mm High-explosive Ammunition Expenditure

Expended 7–22 Nov	Daily Rate	Daily Avg. Call for Fire Rate, per mission	Daily Avg. Counterfire Rate, per mission
5685	379	21.1	11.4

terns served to maximize the response time and tempo of air support. Often a section of aircraft performed target acquisition in the ring at 16,000 to 18,000 feet for one assault regiment while another aircraft section circled at 13,000 to 15,000 feet delivering ordnance for the other regiment. These aircraft shared their space with five to seven drones while six to eight battalions engaged insurgent forces on the ground. A thorough knowledge of the plan and good situational awareness allowed these operations with minimal risks. No friendly fire of any kind occurred at the second battle of Fallujah as the result of supporting arms fire.

Many times rotary wing aircraft flew up to 3,000 to 4,000 feet to avoid the high volume of small arms fire and to improve pilot visibility. Drone and manned surveillance aircraft flights over the city averaged seven at night and four to five during the day. Although more than anticipated, the keyhole system template accommodated them well.

The employment of laser-guided Maverick and gun attacks required more coordination. The keyhole template was designed for efficiency and speed, and when aircraft used such flat trajectory weapons, the controllers moved the drones and restricted the maximum elevation of artillery and mortar fire. The pilots and forward

Table 5-3: Second Fallujah Battle Casualties

Unit	KIA	WIA	RTD	NBD	NBI
Fallujah Assault Force:					
HQ RCT-1		5	5		
3d Bn, 1st Mar	22	206	123		8
3d Bn, 5th Mar	8	56	39		4
3d LAR Bn	1	36	11		5
HQ RCT-7		15	14		1
1st Bn, 8th Mar	16	102	51		16
1st Bn, 3d Mar	10	79	45		11
Army Units					
2d Bn, 2d Inf	5	24	16		1
2d Sqdn, 7th Cav	1	12	5	1	
Rest of al-Anbar Province:					
2d Bde, 2d Inf Div		9	6		1
2d Bn, 11th Mar		1			1
31st MEU		2			1
2d LAR Bn*		7	5		
2d Recon Bn*	1				
2d Tk Bn*		3	5		2
2d Asslt Amph Bn*	1	12	7		3
Total	65	582	339	1	54

air controllers modified the delivery parameters to accomplish the Laser Maverick and gun attacks. While these required more coordination, only minutes were required to move the drones and to coordinate other fires.

During Operation al-Fajr, aviation expended approximately 318 precision bombs, 391 rockets and missiles, and 93,000 machine gun or cannon rounds. The artillery consumption demonstrated the relative intensity of the ground fighting during the battle.

The overall Marine Corps casualties for the operation, according to summaries of the Manpower Department, Marine Corps Headquarters, totaled 70 Marines killed in action, 651 wounded in action (394 returned to duty), with another three non-battle deaths and five deaths from wounds received in action.

The brunt of these losses fell upon the 1st Marine Division and its attachments.

Among the immediate results of the second battle of Fallujah, non-combatants fled the fighting in large numbers before the operation, and many insurgents left the city by hiding among the non-combatant populace departing Fallujah. The attempts at organizing sympathetic uprisings in other parts of the province failed. The surviving insurgents could only seek to rearm and reorganize, waiting for a return of civilians to the city.

In the immediate aftermath, the insurgent operational capacity seemed severely impaired as indicated by the notable drop in indirect fire attacks on Coalition bases and camps. These indications directly encouraged I MEF and the staff of Multi National Force–Iraq to set conditions for some form of exploitation operations.

Chapter 6

Optimism and Doubt

During the last phases of Operation al-Fajr, Marines began to pursue those forces no longer capable of offering effective resistance. These operations would continue into 2005 and would comprise part of the military operations conducted in support of the 30 January elections. In the al-Anbar Province insurgency, however, the multifaceted and numerous enemy factions and elements had simply melted into the network of hiding places, sanctuaries, and training areas. Bringing them to battle remained difficult. Making contact proved typically elusive.

Operations outside Fallujah

Pursuit operations began with Operation Plymouth Rock, conducted by the 24th Marine Expeditionary Unit (24th MEU) in northern Babil Province between 24 and 27 November 2004. A complicated series of targeted raids on known and suspected insurgent sites by 1st Battalion, 2d Marines was combined with maneuvers by the British Black Watch Battalion and 2d Battalion, 24th Marines, with Iraqi units in blocking positions. These raids and maneuvers were intended to keep the enemy off balance and away from the vital Route 8 linking Baghdad to Kuwait. The two-stage Operation Lightning Bolt (28–30 November, 3–19 December) saw the 2d Blackjack Brigade first isolate and clear Amariyah, with the Black Watch Battalion blocking from the south, and then execute a similar operation on the opposite side of al-Fallujah against Al Khalidiyah and Karmah, while cooperating with 2d Brigade, 2d Infantry Division, to clear Saqlawiyah. A second Plymouth Rock operation (22-23 December) repeated raids in northern Babil Province as the 24th MEU sought to capitalize on the resulting enemy movement away from the Army brigades in Area of Operations Raleigh. At this last juncture, however, the responsibility for northern Babil Province and tactical control of the 24th MEU had already (6 December) moved to the 1st Cavalry Division, another regional modification undertaken as the Coalition commanders shifted priorities toward Baghdad and the January election. From 4–5 December, the Black Watch Battalion began its return to southern Iraq, having sustained five soldiers killed in action while serving with I MEF. At that point, all the non-Marine Corps reinforcements previously detailed for Operation al-Fajr had departed.

As 2005 began, I MEF planners focused on the 30 January national election, defeating the insurgency, preparing Iraqi security forces, and repopulating Fallujah. The expected arrival of II Marine Expeditionary Force (II MEF) in February and March instilled thoughts of a smooth turnover and departure by the sailors and Marines for their home stations. For the election to succeed, its security and the smooth functioning of the electoral process had to be guaranteed by military authorities throughout Iraq. Soldiers and Marines carried out numerous operations in Areas of Operations Raleigh, Topeka, and Denver, aimed at upsetting insurgent regrouping, destroying arms caches, and, where feasible, supporting Iraqi security and government entities, however disparate they might be in their nascent state. The border stations with Syria remained closed, and Jordanian access was limited to authorized commercial traffic.

In the eastern part of al-Anbar Province, 1st Cavalry Division's responsibilities and the Baghdad political center of gravity led to the turnover of all of an-Najaf and Karbala Provinces to I MEF. Given the number of units already transferred out of the Fallujah operation, the additional area had to be taken over by Colonel Haslam and his 11th MEU, a logical choice in light of the unit's success in stabilizing an-Najaf the previous summer. All the Marine expeditionary units sent to Iraq, however, now required relief and return to home stations in the very near future. An Army brigade would arrive in February and relieve both the 11th MEU and 24th MEU of their responsibilities in a combined Area of Operations South, operating under the tactical control of the I MEF commander, Lieutenant General Sattler. For the time being, however, Colonel Johnson's 24th MEU continued to operate with the cavalry division, which even took tactical control of 2d Battalion, 24th Marines, on 27 December to support its operations securing Route 8. Meanwhile, 1st Battalion, 2d Marines, continued to cover Taheer Firm Base, Eskan Patrol Base, Haswah Police Station, and patrols in zone. Only on the first day of February did 24th MEU return to I MEF tactical control, when it began relief in place activities with elements of the U.S. Army 155th Brigade Combat Team. On 6 February, 1st Bat-

Photo by LCpl Zachary R. Frank, VIRIN: 041201-M-5901F-010

In the aftermath of the second battle of Fallujah, Marines from I MEF conducted a series of pursuit operations to destroy insurgent forces that had fled the city. Here, Marines from Company B, Battalion Landing Team, 1st Battalion, 2d Marines, 24th Marine Expeditionary Unit, fire at enemy insurgents in Jurf as Sakhr, during Operation Plymouth Rock, a counterinsurgency operation conducted in November and December 2004.

talion, 155th Infantry, and 2d Squadron, 11th Armored Cavalry Regiment, relieved 1st Battalion, 2d Marines.

The 2d Brigade, 1st Cavalry Division, handed over responsibility for Karbala Province to 11th MEU on 22 December, bringing it not only extensive territorial responsibilities but also new Iraqi police and military units for its Marines to train, direct, and mentor. With very little interference from insurgents and criminal elements, the 11th MEU ended its first campaign in Iraq with major success in stability operations and in facilitating the elections in Karbala and an-Najaf. On 14 February, Colonel Haslam transferred authority of his vast area of responsibility to the 155th Brigade and the next day his organization joined the departure movements to Kuwait and local air bases. By this point, the newly arrived 15th MEU under Colonel Thomas C. Greenwood offloaded in Kuwait and as of 20 January was the Central Command operational reserve.

Security for the 30 January Elections

The Iraqi elections directly affected the pace of operations in al-Anbar Province, as well as the efforts to plan and to conduct the repopulation of Fallujah. It was hoped that the displaced inhabitants could return in time to participate in the elections and at the same time they could receive humanitarian relief and begin the reconstruction of their city.

The efforts of Regimental Combat Team 1 Marines and sailors produced one significant benchmark when the notorious Jolan District opened on 30 December to receive citizens. The openings of specific districts continued until 14 January, when all of them stood ready to receive their residents. Civil-military operations at this point focused on resettling Fallujah, rendering humanitarian assistance, and re-establishing Fallujah and al-Anbar Province's governance at all levels.

The bulk of election support actions centered on the key cities of ar-Ramadi, Fallujah, Karbala, and an-Najaf. In mid-January, the Independent Election Commission of Iraq (IEC-I) requested that Coalition military forces provide "life support" (meaning shelter and subsistence), transport election materials, and support Iraqi forces as they provided security at polling sites. Anticipating these needs, the Marine commanders had begun preparations for election support by surveying and determining the most suitable voting sites.

Photo by GSgt Kevin W. Williams, Defense Imagery, VIRIN: 050130-M-9015W-005

Providing a secure and stable environment for elections on 30 January 2005 was a critical mission objective for I MEF. Here, an Iraqi translator attached to 1st Battalion, 23d Marine Regiment, prepares to submit his vote at Haqlaniyah.

Operationally, the Coalition plan for securing the elections involved controlling borders, securing Baghdad, neutralizing insurgents in selected key cities, and supporting the election process. Dubbed Operation Citadel II, the Coalition military election support countered insurgent activities, selected offensive actions against known targets, erected multiple cordons of security for voting sites, and organized the logistical support for the election process.

Marines and sailors of the 1st Force Service Support Group (1st FSSG) and the MEF Engineer Group (MEG) hardened the polling sites with field fortification and highway barrier materials. They also received and transported election materials and life support sets to the sites for the workers and the Independent Election Commission personnel who would train and supervise the workers. Most workers and IEC-I personnel arrived in al-Anbar Province on board C-130 flights of the 3d Marine Aircraft Wing, which transported some 2,300 of these passengers between 26 and 29 January.

At Fallujah, units of Regimental Combat Team 1 cooperated with Iraqi security forces and provided outer cordon security for voting centers. Citywide, they enforced election curfews and operated the entry checkpoints and humanitarian assistance missions. The infantry battalions also screened the city perimeter to prevent infiltration by insurgents, encountering light enemy contact. A raid conducted on the peninsula captured 17 men suspected of insurgent activity.

In the area surrounding the city, Regimental Combat Team 7 provided similar security at its polling centers while enforcing election day curfew, driving, and weapons restrictions. The 2d Reconnaissance Battalion patrolled Zaidon with the Iraqi 2d Battalion, Muthanna Brigade, during which the troops discovered weapons caches near Nasr Wa Salam and Abu Ghraib.

In and around ar-Ramadi, the U.S. Army 2d Brigade enforced curfews, provided the outer cordon at election sites, and conducted patrols, random checkpoints, and raids. The insurgents launched nu-

On 26 January 2005, a CH-53E Super Stallion from Marine Heavy Helicopter Squadron 361 (similar to the one pictured here) crashed in a sandstorm in western al-Anbar province. Thirty Marines and a Navy corpsman died in the crash.

Photo by LCpl William L. Dubose III, Defense Imagery VIRIN: 041213-M-9529D-01

merous small attacks, several of which targeted polling centers or troops guarding them. Marines of 2d Battalion, 5th Marines, guarded the government center and conducted security patrols along Route 10. In western al-Anbar Province, the battalions of 31st MEU stretched to counter numerous attacks with rockets, mortars, and improvised explosive devices. It was during these operations that a CH-53E crashed 26 January in a sand storm near ar-Rutbar, killing the four-man crew from Marine Heavy Helicopter Squadron 361 and the 26 Marines and a Navy corpsman from 1st Battalion, 3d Marines. As of mid-2010, this event remained the deadliest single incident suffered by U.S. forces during the Iraq War.

In considering the results of the 30 January election, the deep sectarian division within the Iraqi population was apparent. In the mixed and Shi'a dominant provinces of Karbala and An-Najaf, an estimated 90 percent of eligible voters turned out at 431 polling centers, with women representing more than half that number. In Sunni-dominated al-Anbar Province, the Sunni election boycott prevailed and only 16,682 voters entered the 49 polls. The exception came at Fallujah, where 7,679 persons, believed

Photo by MSgt Dave Ahlschwede, USAF, Defense Imagery, VIRIN: 050130-f-1631A-029

Fingers stained with purple ink became the symbol of the 30 January 2005 Iraqi elections. An Iraqi citizen in Baghdad proudly displays proof that he voted.

to number one-third to one-half of the eligible voters present, cast their ballots. This first of several elections in 2005-06 created a 275-seat transitional National Assembly, a provincial assembly in each of the 18 provinces, and a Kurdistan regional assembly. The election system used proportional representation with voters indicating a preference for a list of candidates posted by a specific party or other political entity.

Conducting a fair and secure election remained the primary objective of the I MEF commanders. Despite the Sunni boycott, I MEF met those objectives. The insurgents made considerable efforts to disrupt voting, making 38 separate attacks on 16 sites during 28–30 January. No voters were harmed. The Marines and soldiers remained alert after the polls closed and until all workers and their election materials had left the sites. On 31 January, border crossings reopened and on 2 February, the Iraqi security details returned to their garrisons.

The results of the January election became known about two weeks later, and the clear winners emerged among the Shi'ite United Iraqi Alliance, Kurds, and a few secular parties. Sunni Arabs won only 17 national assembly seats spread over several lists and very few seats on the provincial assemblies.

Table 6-1: Polling Sites Established in I MEF Area of Operations, January 2005

MSE	Area	No. Polling Centers	Alt. Polling Centers
2 BCT	Ramadi	10	4
	Tammin	2	0
	Khalidyah	1	1
	Habbaniyah	1	1
RCT-7	Karmah	1	0
	Nasser Wa Salem	2	3
RCT-1	Fallujah	3	6
31 MEU	Hit	1	2
	Hadithah	2	1
	Al Qa'im	1	1
	Trebil	1	0
	Baghdadi	1	1
	Akashat	1	0
	Waleed	1	0
	Rutbah	1	0
2/11	Nukhayb	1	0
	Musayib	0	1
	Ar Ar	0	1
Total		27	22

Photo by TSgt Cherie A. Thurlby, USAF, Defense Imagery VIRIN: 050412-F-7203T-453

Jalal Talabani, who was elected President of Iraq on 30 January 2005, listens to a question during a Baghdad press conference.

After the first tumultuous sessions of the national assembly, a somewhat balanced government formed with some Sunni representation, including the assembly speaker, one of two deputy presidents, one of three deputy prime ministers, and six cabinet ministers. The presidency went to Kurdish leader Jalal Talabani while the Shi'a leader Ibrahim al-Jafari became prime minister.

Resettling Fallujah

Despite U.S. efforts to limit collateral damage, Fallujah's residences, mosques, city services, and businesses all received varying degrees of damage in the course of Operation al-Fajr. Of the city's more than 200 mosques, about 60 were destroyed in the fighting. An estimated 7,000 to 10,000 of approximately 50,000 residences were destroyed, and a large portion of the remainder was damaged. Of the nearly 350,000 inhabitants, up to 200,000 were likely displaced as a result of the two battles for the city.

Fallujah's repopulation began only after returnees received biometric identification and new identity cards. Residents of Fallujah continued to return to the city and evaluate their holdings and life support means, often departing again to displaced persons camps. An increasing number gradually remained in the city and sought to re-establish their lives. Businesses began to reopen, and the Marines and sailors patrolling the city and operating the humanitarian assistance sites detected a sense of purpose. The Iraqis displayed an open friendliness toward the Americans, and in many cases assisted Marines by showing them hidden weapons caches and unexploded ordnance. A new newspaper hit the streets in February, *Al Fajr*, published by Regimental Combat Team 1. It found an accepting audience, especially because it contained information on security rules governing the city, reconstruction programs, and how to make damage claims and obtain medical treatment. On 12 February, Fallujah traffic police began routine patrols of the city streets.

By 25 February, the pace of resettlement indicated genuine progress. On that single day, almost 15,000 civilians entered the city with over 2,000 vehicles. In addition, 466 contractors and 1,117 government workers came through the entry control points. By that date, over 87,000 individuals had visited the humanitarian assistance sites, and 32,546 claims payments totaling over $6.5 million had been paid. A shattered city showed signs of mending. An estimated 30 percent of the population had returned by the end of March.

Post-Election Return to Normal Operations in Al-Anbar Province

The increasing stabilization in Fallujah and the pending turnover to units of the incoming II MEF led to the redeployment of I MEF organizations to their original bases. The departure of Regimental Combat Team 7 from Camp Baharia to Area of Operations Denver began on 1 February. The final turnover of Area of Operations Raleigh to Regimental Combat Team 1 was conducted on 5 February. Regimental Combat Team 7 commander Colonel Tucker's immediate task, the relief of 31st MEU, had to be accomplished rather quickly in December. The U.S. Joint Chiefs of Staff had approved the extension of 31st MEU's deployment in December for another 45 days, but the expeditionary unit had to first recover all its component units before moving to Kuwait and embarking in amphibious shipping in time to exit the U.S. Central Command theater by 15 March. The turnover came promptly at al-Asad Air Base on 7 February. The 1st Battalion, 3d Marines, had returned from Fallujah in late January and Medium Helicopter Squadron 265 flew its last combat mission for Regimental Combat Team 7 units at Camp Korean Village in support of Task Force Naha on 7 February. The

An Iraqi woman and boy walk toward the female and children search tent at the edge of Fallujah in January 2005. Residents began to return to the city in December 2004, and by the end of March, about 30 percent of the city's pre-battle population had resettled in the city.

squadron returned to al-Asad Air Base the following day and rejoined the 31st MEU. Colonel Miller then began the retrograde movements of his reunited organization back to Kuwait, using both ground convoys and aircraft of 3d Marine Aircraft Wing. The embarkation on USS *Essex* (LHD 2) and accompanying ships of Amphibious Squadron 11 began on 26 February, and the force sailed for Okinawa on 6 March 2004.

The reconstitution of Regimental Combat Team 7 in Area of Operations Denver during February culminated in the launch of Operation River Blitz (20 February–6 March), the last major operation conducted by 1st Marine Division before its rotation to home bases. Centered in the western Euphrates River Valley, the operation assigned Regimental Combat Team 7 and the Army 2d Brigade, 2d Infantry, to a series of counterinsurgency operations against major sanctuaries and logistical routes to prevent any interference with the pending turnover of forces with the 2d Marine Division. The staffs of both divisions participated in the planning and execution of River Blitz with 2d Marine Division taking over the operation under the

successor name, Operation River Bridge (10–25 March). The transfer of authority between the two divisions took place on 17 March, and the second campaign of I MEF in Iraq ended on 27 March. At that point, 307 Marines had died in action and 3,456 were wounded. Added to the 2003 campaign losses, I MEF had sustained 365 killed and 3,740 wounded in action since the Iraq War began. Of the wounded, 2,203 had returned to duty. Furthermore, there were 90 non-combat deaths and 145 non-combat injuries in I MEF.

In the aftermath of the Fallujah Campaign, Marines of the outgoing I MEF saw the tide apparently turning against the Iraqi insurgency. The operational reporting emphasized nearing success, and I MEF planning forecast the pending establishment of Iraqi regional control.

Considerable doubt remained, however, that favorable conditions had been achieved. During December, as the Army reinforcements sent to participate in the second battle of Fallujah began to withdraw from Area of Operations Raleigh, Lieutenant Colonel Jeffrey R. Chessani, the operations officer of

Regimental Combat Team 1, sent a poignant memo to his commander, Colonel Shupp:

I spoke with the [division] G-3 this evening and he indicated that the chain of events that are eventually going to happen is going to happen sooner than we like, but when we expected it. The G-3 indicated that Blackjack Brigade would be folding up shop and heading out on 15 Dec, which means there will be a relief in place beginning on or about 12 Dec between Regimental Combat Team 7 and Blackjack Brigade. Regimental Combat Team 7 will take 1/8 [1st Battalion, 8th Marines] out of the city with them to relieve Blackjack Brigade. Regimental Combat Team 7 will have 1/8 and 2d Recon Bn to run area Raleigh. As you know 1/8 and 3/1 are slated to go home on time and currently have a latest available date of 13 January. If they were to execute this, 3/1 would need to leave Fallu-jah in December so they could embark and prepare for redeployment. Exactly when would be up to you. However, their initial cut for being relieved in place is 15 Dec. Not sure they need an entire month to get ready to redeploy. It can be done in less time. . . . But why would higher headquarters want to create a vacuum like this after successfully crushing an insurgency that has been a thorn for more than a year? I understand there are other fish to fry in Iraq, that we are not the only show. What I do not understand is why higher headquarters would not want to ensure there was some semblance of stability in Fallujah before they walked away from Fallujah. Higher headquarters got what it wanted . . . a destroyed insurgency in Fallujah or so it would appear. They are going to walk away thinking they did their part and the smoldering heap of rubble that is Fallujah is going to start sparking again because higher headquar-

A Marine MK48/18A1 Series Logistics Vehicle System delivers humanitarian aid to the Jolan District of Fallu-jah in December 2004.

Photo by Cpl Theresa M. Media, Defense Imagery VIRIN: 041211-M-2583M-082

ters failed to follow though with the resources we need to smother the embers. Then they are going to ask us why we let the embers become a fire again.

I sincerely believe . . . our immediate headquarters is going to contribute to snatching defeat from the jaws of victory. By forcing division to move Regimental Combat Team 7 and 1/8 out of Fallujah before the conditions are right, Multi National Force–Iraq will in effect contribute directly to the destabilization of a situation that is currently under control. I am not sure they have even thought about let alone considered the 2d, 3d and 4th order effects of simply moving Blackjack Brigade out of area Raleigh. This is not a hard one to read, but they seem to be missing the effects and the situation they will create by re-deploying the Blackjack Brigade.

The first stabilization campaign of I MEF ended with the recapture of Fallujah. A large number of local insurgent fighters were killed and a surging Sunni rebellion had been defeated. The level of destruction achieved in the Fallujah battles, however, almost prohibited repetition by the Iraqi-U.S. leadership. The costs and efforts required to repopulate and rebuild the city would in fact tie down enormous resources when the rest of al-Anbar Province remained outside of Coalition control. The battle did not engage the insurgents decisively, for their leadership and many non-local insurgents had likely fled before the November assault, leaving mostly local militants behind. Much work remained, therefore, for the incoming II Marine Expeditionary Force.

Chapter 7

The Mission Continues

Following the national elections in 2005 and the creation of a national assembly, the Iraqi Interim Government (IIG) was replaced by the Iraqi Transitional Government. The government ministries already bore the responsibility for governing at regional and local level as well as the administration and control of Iraqi security forces. U.S. forces in Iraq would no longer control the pay and formation of these forces. For the foreseeable future, the Iraqi Civil Defense Corps and new Iraqi Army would remain under the operational control of the Commander, Multi National Corps–Iraq, who also took the responsibility to equip, train, and mentor them in the field. Regardless the outcome of these ambitious plans for Iraq's future, the Multi National Force–Iraq staff forecast that a force totaling 17 U.S. or Coalition brigades would be required to meet the security mission for the ensuing 12 to18 months.

The Multi National Corps–Iraq staff also undertook a new campaign plan because the scope of the existing one had extended only to the transition to Iraqi sovereignty. Thus, effective from that point, the new mission called for:

full spectrum counter-insurgency operations in support of the Interim Government, and in partnership with the Iraqi security Forces, to provide a safe and secure environment; enabling the functioning of legitimate governance and allowing the restoration and development of Essential Services and the Economy; to assist Iraq in rebuilding itself as a stable and responsible sovereign state and to permit the redeployment of Coalition Forces.

In the summer of 2004, Headquarters Marine Corps began planning for a series of deployments to replace I Marine Expeditionary Force (I MEF) in early 2005. Marine Corps Commandant General Michael W. Hagee, promulgated his guidance for the relief deployment, tentatively termed "Operation Iraqi Freedom III" by the Joint Chiefs of Staff in early July. Based upon initial planning conducted since the requirement had first been identified in February 2004, the Commandant published the task organization agreed to by mid-summer:

II Marine Expeditionary Force (Forward)
2d Marine Division
Regimental Combat Team 8–three infantry battalions, a company each of light armored reconnaissance, tanks, assault amphibious vehicles, artillery and combat engineers.
Regimental Combat Team 5–three infantry battalions, a company each of light armored reconnaissance, tanks, assault amphibious vehicles, and combat engineers.
2d Marine Aircraft Wing (Forward)
Marine Aircraft Group 26–three light attack, three medium transport and two heavy helicopter squadrons, plus one fighter or attack squadron and an aerial refueler detachment.
Ground support units and a squadron of unmanned aerial vehicles.
2d Force Service Support Group–six support battalions of various types.

As with the previous guidance given for the deployment of I MEF, the plan included the authority to draw upon normally scheduled deployments of ground and aviation units of III Marine Expeditionary Force (III MEF) on Okinawa. Planning anticipated the assignment of an Army brigade to the force, with the required capability of supporting an additional Army brigade for surge operations. The secretary of defense approved the planning on 21 June. Because the new Multi National Corps–Iraq organization placed a lieutenant general in overall command of the forces, a major general would now head the Marine Corps contingent. Considerable thought was given to assigning the commanding general, 2d Marine Division, to a dual position as the commander of II MEF (Forward), but in the end the force structure included separate commanders and staffs. Marine Corps doctrine prevailed amid the inevitable bureaucratic infighting in the Iraq military command structure, and Major General Stephen T. Johnson, the deputy II MEF commander, led the new contingent relieving Lieutenant General Sattler's I MEF.

The assignment of only three battalions from the 1st Marine Division to the 5th Marines to create Regimental Combat Team 5 in the June force plan did not survive long, probably reflecting uncertainties

Photo by Kayli Olinde, Defense Imagery, VIRIN: 031001-M-1527O-016

The creation of the Multi National Corps–Iraq meant that the most senior Marine in Iraq from 2005 on would be a two-star general. In 2005, II Marine Expeditionary Force (Forward) deployed under the command of the MEF's deputy commanding general, MajGen Stephen T. Johnson (pictured in 2003).

about the readiness of 2d Marine Division forces to handle all competing global requirements. By August, the 2d Marine Regiment had been selected as the second regimental combat team headquarters in the task organization, and was assigned only two infantry battalions normally assigned to the 1st Marine Division. The staff officers of II MEF and subordinate commands developed the details of the deployment including the final organization and the identity of almost all units during August and September. Given the ongoing campaign of the two battles for Fallujah then being waged by I MEF, the studies and planning ranged widely.

The planning guidance's initial assessment of Area of Operations Atlanta highlighted the persistent unrest that II MEF would be facing:

> As the provincial capital Ramadi will be the focus of Anti-Iraqi Forces attacks, Anti-Coalition Forces will continue standoff attacks, assassinations and coercion of IIG leaders, Coalition

Forces and perceived collaborators in an attempt to disrupt election preparations and delegitimize the Iraqi Interim Government. Anti-Coalition Forces may increase the level of attacks or attempt a "spectacular" attack prior to the elections to prevent popular support of the Iraqi Interim Government and promote instability throughout the area of operations. There are indications that the rift between competing agendas of different Anti-Coalition Forces is widening and Coalition Forces information operations may be able to exploit it. Developing credible Iraqi security forces and performing successful civil military operations will help win the information operations war during this pivotal period. The potential for violence hinges on success or failure of these efforts.

The two regiments of Major General Richard A. Huck's 2d Marine Division brought six infantry, one reconnaissance, and one light armored reconnaissance battalion to Iraq. The force was smaller than the one sent the previous year, lacking the two infantry battalions and a provisional military police battalion that had been deployed a year earlier with 1st Marine Division. In theory, the more robust Iraqi security forces now present in the province would compensate for such a shortfall in ground combat power. However, that Iraqi security presence had proven illusory in 2004 and remained to be proven in 2005.

Though the deployment of II MEF varied considerably from I MEF, there was wide agreement on the exchange of equipment and like Marine Corps units replaced each other in all cases. For the renamed "Operation Iraqi Freedom 04-06.1" (a new Joint Chiefs of Staff term reflecting the fiscal year and sequencing of the deployment) strategic deployment by II MEF, little sealift took part although the presence of prepositioned shipping in Kuwait ports served to provide fresh ground and aviation support equipment as required. A single roll-on, roll-off ship, USNS *Cape Hudson* (T-AKR 5066), supported the II MEF movement. The scheduled air transport movements of civilian charter and military aircraft moved the more than 22,000 Marines and sailors of II MEF in approximately eleven weeks during the period 9 January to 30 March. This comparatively unforced pace of the relief of I MEF by II MEF permitted sequential relief of battalions with key areas such as al-Fallujah and Area of Operations Topeka first in the cycle. It also allowed for a generous overlap in forces

Table 7-1: Typical Monthly Aircraft Usage Data, early 2005

Type	Avg. Missions Flown, each	Normal Planning Utilization*
AH-1W	36.6	18.3
UH-1N	41.6	18.8
CH-46E	46.9	18.2
CH-53E	40.3	17.6
KC-130	53.3	36.9
FA-18D	85.8	30.8
AV-8B	59.2	23.2
EA-6B	57.6	29.9

*Weapons Systems Planning Document (WSPD) Standard

such that no vulnerability could develop before the transfer of authority took place. For instance the percentage of I MEF departures to II MEF arrivals on 10 February stood at 11:26 and on 24 February was 24:55. On 8 March, 45 percent of I MEF personnel had departed while 75 percent of the II MEF manpower had arrived.

One difference in the deployment of II MEF compared to I MEF was the much-abbreviated Reception, Staging, Onward movement, and Integration of forces phase, which proved mostly unnecessary because of the pre-deployment training of II MEF forces in the United States and the convenience of relieving like forces in theater. For example, 3d Battalion, 25th Marines of the Marine Corps Reserve, 4th Marine Division, mobilized at eight home stations in January and deployed to the Air-Ground Training Center, Twentynine Palms, California, on 10 January, where it conducted combat training through the end of the month. In February, the battalion completed its combined arms exercise and conducted a stability and security operations exercise at March Air Force Base, California. On 19 February its advance party departed for Iraq, and the remainder of the battalion flew on 1 March to Kuwait, spending only a day there to change mode of transport to C-130 aircraft for the final arrival at al-Asad Air Base. It conducted a transfer of authority with 1st Battalion, 23d Marines, on 15 March.

Some equipment concerns in Iraq had begun to surface before the arrival of II MEF. The high usage rate for ground vehicles and aircraft of all types in just months was the equivalent of years of peacetime use. Almost predictably, the tracked armored fighting vehicles showed signs of deterioration first. The 2d Assault Amphibian Battalion dispatched a team of 90 Marines to Fallujah in early January 2005 as a "reconstitution detachment" built around the battalion's A Company. A six-week effort refurbished or replaced a total of 84 AAV7A1 amphibious assault vehicles, including 42 brought from Camp Lejeune in North Carolina. After six weeks, the equipment in the hands of I MEF, with few exceptions, showed readiness in the 80–95 percent range. An equivalent effort in the following month swapped the tanks and tank recovery vehicles of the two tank companies with vehicles drawn from the maritime prepositioned shipping.

Aviation also suffered from heavy use, and serious concerns surfaced in particular with the readiness of light attack and heavy lift helicopters. The entire aviation complement of I MEF had operated consistently at high tempo, as shown in the typical 30-day cycle ending on 9 March (see table 7-1).

One particular aspect of materiel readiness troubled II MEF considerably less than its predecessor. The various armor enhancement programs for the wheeled tactical vehicle fleet had reached fruition by February 2005. The Maintenance Center, Marine Corps Logistics Command, Albany, Georgia, had

The 2d Marine Division under MajGen Richard A. Huck (center) relieved MajGen Natonski's 1st Marine Division in 2005.

Photo by LCpl Matthew Hutchison, Defense Imagery: VIRIN: 050418-M-9470H-007

The major commanders of Multi National Force–West units in June 2005 included (from left): BGen Robert E. Milstead Jr, commanding general, 2d Marine Aircraft Wing (Forward); Army BGen Yves J. Fontaine, commanding general, 1st Corps Support Command; BGen Ronald S. Coleman, outgoing commander, 2d Force Service Support Group (Forward); BGen John E. Wissler, incoming commander, 2d Force Service Support Group (Forward); LtGen James F. Amos, commanding general, II Marine Expeditionary Force; MajGen Stephen T. Johnson, commanding general, II Marine Expeditionary Force (Forward); and Army BGen Augustus L. Collins, commanding general, 155th Brigade Combat Team.

served as the primary producer of Marine Corps armor for the program, both in the form of kits and armor plates. This effort included fabrication of the 3/16-inch and 3/8-inch plates for the Marine armor kit as well as explosive resistant coating processes. Later in the year, the equivalent facility at Barstow, California, became an armor producer. Additional armor components for undercarriage, tailgate, back plates, and gunner's shields also entered production during 2004. In that year, the Logistics Command processed some 5,000 tons of steel to produce armor for 5,000 vehicles, including 1,000 delivered to the Army.

The next objective was upgrading the force with uparmored and armor-kit Humvees and fitting all seven-ton trucks with their specific armor systems. The Albany armor installation team arriving at Camp Taqaddum in late February was ordered to begin installation in March, building to a capacity of 200 units per month. The parallel seven-ton truck armor installation began in May at 40 per month. By 30 April, II MEF reported the processing of 276 Humvees by the Marine armor installation site.

Initial Employment of II Marine Expeditionary Force

Colonel Stephen W. Davis, commanding Regimental Combat Team 2, deployed his three battalions to Iraq during 24 February–1 March from Camp Lejeune. He conducted his relief with Regimental Combat Team 7 in Area of Operations Denver. From 10–17 March, Regimental Combat Team 7, followed by Regimental Combat Team 2 from 17–25 March, conducted Operation River Bridge, interdiction operations to disrupt and defeat enemy elements that might endanger the relief as well as countering enemy infiltration in the area. On 17 March, Regimental Combat Team 2 effected its transfer of authority at al-Asad Air Base. As an indicator of the new look hoped for in future operations, the battalion commander of the 503d Iraqi National Guard Battalion, operating out of Camp Hit, attended the ceremony. During this phase, 3d Battalion, 2d Marines, replaced 1st Battalion, 7th Marines, at al-Qaim, and 3d Battalion, 25th Marines, relieved 1st Battalion, 23d Marines, at Hit and Haditha. The 2d Light Armored Reconnaissance Battalion initially operated with two line companies and K Battery, 3d Battalion, 10th Marines, attached as a provisional rifle company as it relieved 3d Light Armored Reconnaissance Battalion at Camp Korean Village. Each infantry battalion gave up a rifle company to the security force assigned to al-Asad Air Base. The remaining attachments clustered with the Regimental Combat Team 2 headquarters at al-Asad Air Base for operations as required in Area of Operations Denver: 1st Force Reconnaissance Company; Company A, 2d Tank Battalion; Company A, 4th Combat Engineer Battalion; and Company A, 4th Assault Amphibian Battalion.

Units of Regimental Combat Team 2 continued their tasks under Operation River Bridge. This operation remained focused on interdicting insurgent logistical routes east of the Euphrates River between Hit and Haditha. Tactics included small unit raids, vehicle checkpoints, cordon and knock, and cordon and search. In addition, specialized teams conducted raids in search of high value individuals to kill or capture. The regiment's main effort centered on Task Force 3d Battalion, 25th Marines, operating in Hit and along the Hit-Haditha corridor with direct support from 1st Force Reconnaissance Company. The other battalions conducted tasks in their zones, contributing to the operation.

Regimental Combat Team 8, commanded by Colonel Charles M. Gurganus, conducted its transfer of authority with Regimental Combat Team 1 slightly later than Regimental Combat Team 2. Two of its battalions had deployed considerably earlier in the II MEF deployment schedule to relieve battalions covering Fallujah, where they operated under Regimental Combat Team 1 until the transfer of authority. The 3d Battalion, 8th Marines, departed home station on 14 January and relieved 1st Battalion, 8th Marines, at Fallujah on 20 January. The battalion immediately commenced its operations in support of the Iraqi elections. It provided security of polling sites as well as participating in training and integrating Iraqi forces into the operation. On 30 January, a rocket attack wounded 11 Marines from the 3d Battalion, 8th Marines, just south of al-Karmah. The attack was a precursor to what awaited the rest of the II MEF forces.

On 9 January 2005, the 3d Battalion, 4th Marines, left its California base and arrived at Camp Abu Ghraib on the 17th. Three days later, the battalion conducted its transfer of authority with 1st Battalion, 3d Marines. Thus began 3d Battalion, 4th Marines' third deployment to Operation Iraqi Freedom, coming only five months after it had returned from Iraq following the first battle of Fallujah. The battalion as-

sumed responsibility for the southern half of Fallujah and for operating entry control point 1, the primary entrance route into the city of Fallujah for contractors, government officials, and vehicles carrying cattle and produce. The battalion also relieved Company A, 2d Light Armored Reconnaissance Battalion, on 13 February and assumed responsibility for the battle space west of Fallujah, known as the Peninsula.

The remainder of Regimental Combat Team 8 mostly deployed with the main body of II MEF from its bases during 5–15 March. It immediately began relief of Regimental Combat Team 1 until assuming sole responsibility for Area of Operations Raleigh on 21 March, with a final transfer of authority on 27 March. The leading battalions already in place, Colonel Gurganus assigned 2d Reconnaissance Battalion to the Zaidon area and 1st Battalion, 6th Marines, to Camp Bahariah, east of Fallujah. An additional battalion deployed with the regiment, but 1st Battalion, 5th Marines, actually traveled independently from its Camp Pendleton home station and replaced 2d Battalion, 5th Marines, at Camp Hurricane Point, operating under the Army 2d Brigade task organization and missions on 17 March after an 11-day transfer of authority process. The regiment's combat support attachments settled into Camp Fallujah before beginning their supporting missions in Area of Operations Raleigh: Battery A, 1st Battalion, 10th Marines; Company A, 2d Combat Engineer Battalion;

Maj Todd C. Waldemar, assigned to 3d Battalion, 25th Marines, practices his Arabic with Iraqi children while on patrol in Haditha during Operation River Bridge. Throughout 2005, Marines from II MEF (Fwd) conducted a range of operations focused on establishing a military presence in the towns and cities along the Euphrates River Valley.

Photo by Cpl Neill A. Seveluist, Defense Imagery VIRIN: 050318-M-2819S-027

Photo by Cpl Robert R. Attebury, VIRIN: 050629-M-3301A-025

Marines from Company A, 1st Battalion, 6th Marines, prepare to raid a house occupied by suspected insurgents in Saqlawiyab. With cooperation between Marines and Iraqi forces a critical component of counterinsurgency operations in Iraq, the Marines are assisted in the June 2005 operation by Iraqi Security Forces (wearing green helmets).

Company B, 2d Tank Battalion; Anti-Tank Platoon, 2d Tank Battalion; Company B, 2d Assault Amphibian Battalion; and Scout Platoon, 8th Tank Battalion.

Regimental Combat Team 8 entered its first full month of operational control by holding Fallujah and striving to disrupt insurgent bands throughout the area. Operation White Feather began on 1 April with a mission to clear main supply roads of improvised explosives and other threats. Marines of 3d Battalion, 4th Marines, routinely screened Iraqi civilians, government officials, and contractors entering the city at entry control points 1, 4, 5, and 6. Elements of 1st

Battalion, 6th Marines, conducted equivalent searches at entry control points 2 and 3. Regimental Combat Team 8 and the 5th Civil Affairs Group also worked to improve the quality of life for the Fallujans and the inhabitants of the surrounding areas. The regiment experienced its first coordinated attack on 2 April, when the Abu Ghraib prison received an indirect fire and small arms insurgent attack.

Brigadier General Robert E. Milstead's 2d Marine Aircraft Wing (Forward) replaced the 3d Marine Aircraft Wing elements in detail, sending a light attack helicopter squadron detachment to al-Qaim; another

Table 7-2:Tactical Vehicles Operated by Marine Corps Forces in Iraq (February 2005)

	Level 1 UAH	Level 2 AOA	"Level 3 "Hardening"	No Protection		Total
				On Base	Off Base	
HMMWV	364	2683	12	196	0	3255
MTVR	0	940	0	31	0	971
LVS	0	236	0	0	0	236
5 Ton	0	179		8	0	187
TOTAL	364	4038	12	235	0	4649

Note: UAH: Up-Armored HMMWV, a new production item (M1114) AOA: Add-on Armor, armor kits, installed in theater. "Hardening": expedient or improvised of plating.

detachment to Camp Korean Village. General Milstead also deployed a light attack helicopter squadron, a medium helicopter squadron, and most of the unmanned aerial vehicles (UAVs) to al-Taqaddum. At al-Asad Air Base, Colonel Thomas M. Murray, commanding Marine Aircraft Group 26, exercised control over all aircraft squadrons at al-Asad Air Base, including a second light attack helicopter squadron, two medium helicopter squadrons, and one heavy helicopter squadron, as well as one squadron of F/A-18D Hornets, one AV-8B Harrier squadron, and a squadron of EA-6B Prowlers. The usual aerial refueler squadron detachment provided logistics support using the KC-130J. An Army air ambulance company was attached for casualty evacuations. At Fallujah, the air control squadron and a detachment of drones supported the immediate needs of the II MEF commander. The two aircraft wings conducted their transfer of authority on 1 March.

In June, command of II MEF (Fwd)'s support element, the 2d Force Service Support Group (Forward), changed from Brigadier General Ronald S. Coleman to Brigadier General John E. Wissler. The task-organized detachments deploying from the al-Taqaddum base reflected the new logistics doctrine under way in the Marine Corps. Combat Logistics Regiment 25 provided general support to the entire II MEF (Fwd) area of operations. Combat Logistics Battalion 2 supported the vast Area of Operations Denver from Camp al-Asad, while Combat Logistics Battalion 8 performed the same from Camp Fallujah in Areas of Operations Raleigh and Topeka. The supporting 22d Naval Construction Regiment based one battalion at Camp Fallujah and another in Ramadi. The Seabee regiment executed a transfer of authority with the I MEF Engineer Group on 11 March, and the two force service support groups transferred authority the following day.

The deployments of the 11th and 24th MEUs came to an end on 14 and 15 February, respectively. The Army's 155th Brigade Combat Team, deployed from Mississippi and other home stations, took responsibility for the northern Babil, Karbala, and an-Najaf Provinces, an area designated Area of Operations

Initial Deployment of II Marine Expeditionary Force (Forward) Units in al-Anbar Province, March 2005.

I MEF Briefing Map, Adapted by History Division

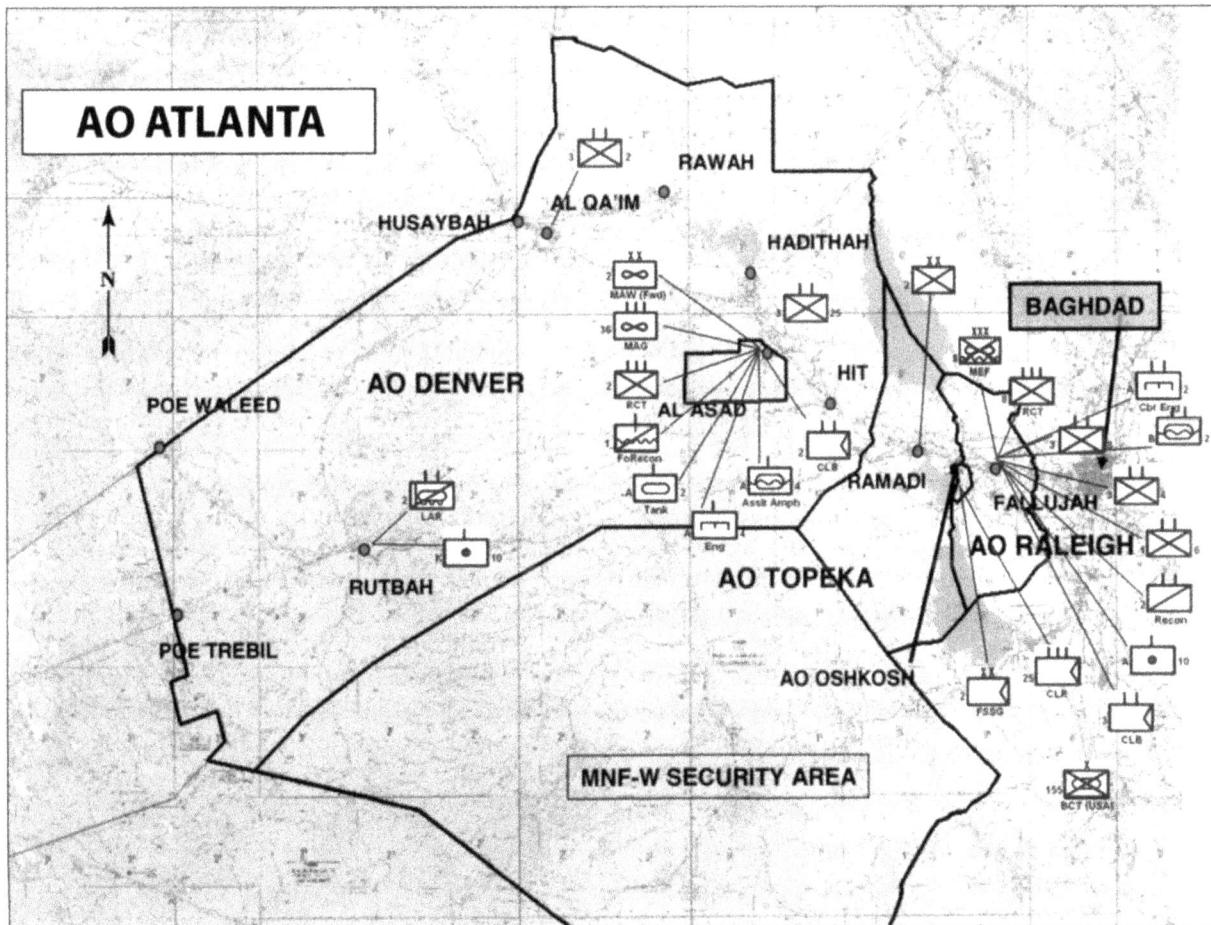

Biloxi. Unlike the previous command relationships, where Army brigades were under the operational control of the deployed Marine division, the 155th Brigade was under the tactical control of the commanding general, I MEF, with the commanding general, Multi National Corps–Iraq, retaining operational control. Although this arrangement spared the 1st and 2d Marine Division commanders the additional operational responsibilities, the Marine expeditionary force commanders and staffs had to work out the operating relationships, with special attention to air support and logistics responsibilities yet to be specified. With a battalion each of motorized infantry, armor, armored cavalry, combat engineers, and field artillery, the 155th Brigade, under Colonel (later Brigadier General) Augustus L. Collins, proved a capable partner in the campaign, operating under the tactical direction of the II MEF commander.

Almost unnoticed in the shuffling of the forces, the special operations capable 15th MEU operated in Iraq during the period 11 March–7 April, but only partially with I MEF and II MEF. Colonel Thomas C. Greenwood reported this organization for duty as the new Central Command theater reserve on 23 January, having conducted humanitarian operations in Sumatra and Sri Lanka for two weeks while en route from the United States. After a period of combat training in Kuwait, the 15th MEU moved to the southeastern edge of Baghdad, and on 11 March occupied Forward Operating Base Falcon, the former base of the 5th Brigade, 1st Cavalry Division. Now under the tactical control of the 3d Infantry Division, the Marines and sailors of the 15th MEU secured a portion of northern Babil province until the later arrival of the 3d Armored Cavalry Regiment the following month. The 15th MEU Marines stopped insurgent mortar and rocket attacks into the city from the south as the newly elected Iraqi parliament convened for the first time.

The aviation component of 15th MEU did report to I MEF tactical control, however, and Medium Helicopter Squadron 165 operated from al-Asad Air Base and al-Taqaddum bases with the 2d Marine Aircraft Wing, supporting I and II MEF activities during the deployment. From its Falcon base, the rest of Colonel Greenwood's command, especially 1st Battalion, 1st Marines, commanded by Lieutenant Colonel David J. Furness, worked for Army commanders while conducting mechanized patrols on National Route 8,

counter-rocket and counter-mortar sweeps, and the usual range of security patrols and cordon operations in its sector. MEU Service Support Group 15, under Lieutenant Colonel Jay L. Hatton, provided the usual logistical support for all 15th MEU operations from Falcon and carried out six humanitarian assistance operations at villages in the 15th MEU area. In addition, the MEU Service Support Group 15 Marines conducted a number of security missions to complement the efforts of the infantry battalion, including route security patrols, security for raids, and vehicle check points. For these missions, the Army Multi National Command–Iraq issued 15th MEU a large number of uparmored Humvees with radios and a few Blue Force tracker devices to perform these missions and to interface adequately with the Army command and control systems. After participating in Army directed Operations River Sweep, Iron Fist, Warning Track, and Strong Will, 15th MEU returned to Kuwait after having turned over its responsibilities to 3d Squadron, 3d Armored Cavalry Regiment, on 6 April. It left the theater on 22 April.

The 2d Marine Division executed its transfer of authority with 1st Marine Division on 17 March. Meanwhile, subordinate elements continued their own reliefs. This was an advantage of having major formations of the same service at hand, each containing units of the two U.S.-based Marine divisions. II MEF conducted its transfer of authority on 27 March and subsequently stood up as Multi National Force–West. Expeditionary force units continued to flow into theater until months' end, when 22,630 Marines and sailors of II MEF were in Iraq with 10,599 Army and Navy personnel attached with various units. Marine Corps forces in Iraq totaled 30,887, including 5,699 personnel of I MEF awaiting redeployment. At this point 12,997 Marine and Navy reservists of the Marine Corps Reserve were on active duty Marine Corps–wide, of whom 92.5 percent served in operating forces with 43 percent serving in Iraq.

The relief operation by the two Marine expeditionary forces required 325 inter-theater and 1,059 intra-theater airlift missions to transport some 52,010 Marine Corps and Navy personnel during 10 January–4 April 2005. This effort represented a significant level of achievement for Marine Corps operations but remained somewhat obscured by what was likely the largest troop rotation in U.S. military history.

Chapter 8

Into the Fray

To prevent insurgent cells from taking advantage of the transition from experienced to newly arriving units, forces from I Marine Expeditionary Force (I MEF) and II Marine Expeditionary Force (II MEF) conducted a series of operations intended to disrupt and damage insurgent cells. This reflected the overall strategy of U.S. forces in Iraq during the spring of 2005, as the Army conducted its own annual turnover of forces .

In al-Anbar Province, these operations differed little from most other major efforts mounted against insurgent enclaves and operating areas. The transfer presented insurgents with the opportunity to damage U.S. and Coalition troops and discredit their mission objectives. Consequently, stopping any enemy actions affecting or occurring during this period was imperative.

The 1st Marine Division's Operation River Blitz (20 February–5 March) began the series of offensive actions as II MEF forces began to arrive. Typically, it served as an overall directive that guided subordinate commands as they conducted operations to counter insurgent moves and deployments while accounting for local conditions and the views of local commanders.

1st Marine Division commander General Richard F. Natonski estimated likely results at the outset:

Operations at both ends of the Husaybah-Baghdad corridor preceded initiation of operation "River Blitz." We assess that the insurgents may perceive the [operations] to the north in Rawah and Regimental Combat Team 1's raids in Karmah and entry control pointss [established] around Nasr Wa Salam and Shahabi as part of Multi National Force's overall operation.

As yet, there is no reporting suggesting that insurgents are fleeing; they are waiting to determine the scope and duration of Multi National Force operations. The formal release in the media headlining "River Blitz" will further amplify the scale of the operation in insurgents' eyes. Arabic media agencies are providing sensationalized coverage; al Jazeera news carried a headline of troops "flooding" into Ramadi. Insurgents will begin to flow toward gaps around

Lake Tharthar, Akashat, and the Salafist seam south of Fallujah as Multi National Force make current safe havens untenable. Key insurgent leaders may flee.

In the far west, Regimental Combat Team 7 continued the division's program with Operation River Bridge (10–17 March). This was continued by Regimental Combat Team 2 (Regimental Combat Team 7's relieving unit) through 25 March. The operation consisted of interdiction efforts in Area of Operations Denver to disrupt and defeat insurgent elements, prevent infiltration of terrorist bands into Mosul and ar-Ramadi, and prevent enemy interference with the relief by Regimental Combat Team 2.

Operation River Bridge focused on interdicting insurgent logistical routes east of the Euphrates River between Hit and Haditha. In Haditha, Company L, 3d Battalion, 25th Marines, engaged insurgents, killing four by an aircraft delivering a GBU-38 500-pound JDAM bomb. In Haditha and Hit, the 3d Battalion, 25th Marines, operated with tank and assault amphibian support and were assisted by Iraqi National Guard troops.

As a result of Operations River Blitz and River Bridge, the enemy was unable to disrupt or capitalize on the transfer of authority. Some intelligence reporting indicated that the enemy did not know or suspect that a relief had occurred until it was completed. Further, the detention of nine insurgent leaders or collaborators and the killing of two more significantly decreased insurgent activity throughout Area of Operations Denver, especially in the Hit-Haditha corridor. The intelligence analysts suspected that insurgent higher-level leaders moved to alternate sanctuaries such as Rawah, Tikrit, and Mosul.

A more routine event took place shortly thereafter, with yet another transfer of a commercial generator for the Mosul power grid from Jordan. Dubbed Operation Terrapin III (22–31 March), the convoying of another "Mother of all Generators" through Area of Operations Denver occupied Regimental Combat Team 2 until it transferred the generator to the U.S. Army's 42d Infantry Division across the Euphrates for continued movement to Mosul. Elements of the 2d Light Armored Reconnaissance Battalion and 224th

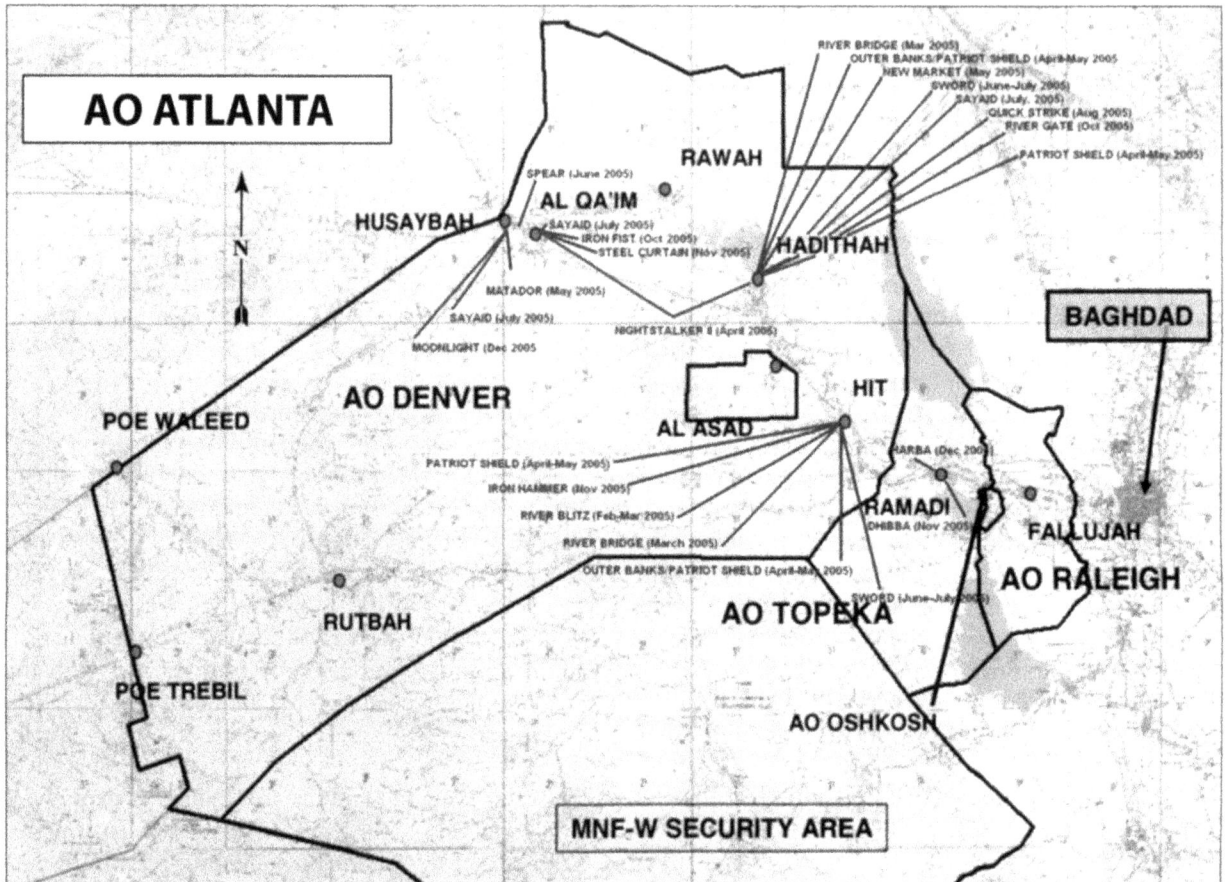

I MEF Briefing Map, Adapted by History Division

II Marine Expeditionary Force (Forward) Counterinsurgency Operations Conducted in 2005.

Engineer Battalion escorted the convoy without incident.

In a special effort against saboteurs, 1st Force Reconnaissance Company and 3d Battalion, 25th Marines, conducted Operation Nightstalker I. The first in a nearly continuous series of operations to kill insurgents placing mines and explosive devices on the main supply and auxiliary supply routes, the operation saw units deploying sniper teams and directing precision fires. This first operation focused on known areas of interest in the Hit-Haditha corridor.

Maintaining the Momentum

Operation Patriot Shield, covering April–May 2005, consisted of a series of tactical actions clearing the Hit-Haditha corridor. These locations included Barwanah, Baghdadi, Abu Hyat, Muhamadi, Kubaysah, the three train stations between Hit and Haditha and Haqlaniyah. Marines encountered small-arms engagements, mines, improvised explosive devices, and indirect fire attacks. They confiscated several small caches of weapons. Commanders estimated that the limited contact and low resistance to Coalition force

moves confirmed that the insurgents had not found alternate sanctuary in lesser population centers but simply had "gone to ground" in the major population centers or were displaced out of Area of Operations Denver. Sniper teams of 1st Force Reconnaissance Company and 3d Battalion, 25th Marines, combined efforts again for a repeat Operation Nightstalker II (1–10 April), between Haditha and Camp al-Qaim.

On 23 April, Regimental Combat Team 2, commanded by Colonel Stephen W. Davis, received its first Iraqi Army unit as a partner for combined operations. The 7th Reconnaissance Company, consisting of 34 soldiers, reported for operations. These soldiers had been former Iraqi Republican Guardsmen who then joined the Shahwani Special Forces, one of the first Iraqi units formed to fight for the new Iraq before the establishment of the new Iraqi Army. In eight-man squads, the Iraqi soldiers began to work with Marine Corps battalions throughout Area of Operations Denver. Regimental Combat Team 2 began to integrate the Iraqi National Guard units in its area of responsibility as well. The Iraqi government offered enlistment in the army only to the 503d and 504th Battalions. A total of 127 of these personnel agreed to continued service, whereupon they boarded buses for their movement from Hit to Kirkush Military Training Base for basic training.

During May, Colonel Davis shifted his focus to the far west of his regiment's zone of operations. With Operation Matador (8–14 May), he sought to sweep enemy sanctuaries north of the Euphrates. With only three battalions at his disposal in the vast Area of Operations Denver, he could concentrate forces only at the expense of drawing down security in the more populated areas, which also tended to be the insurgent objective areas. The key element in Matador, therefore, consisted of a very rapid assembly of designated units from the three battalions and an immediate maneuver through the objective area, using assault amphibian vehicles and helicopter mobility as available.

The enemy had attacked Camp Gannon the previous month in an unusually brazen and coordinated attack. Located on the Iraqi-Syrian border, Camp Gannon occupied an abandoned warehouse complex on the northwest corner of the town of Husbayah, located on the Syrian border. Considered the "mouth" of the insurgent logistical routes leading to Baghdad and points north, the Marine Corps presence there continued to attract attention from insurgents.

Beginning at 0815, 11 April 2005, insurgents fired mortars and launched three suicide vehicle bombs. They tried to pin down the camp guard with mortar and rocket fire while the three explosive-laden vehicles moved in succession to break through and destroy the base. The first vehicle blew up against Guard Post 2, but the defenders rallied and stopped the next two, a dump truck and a fire engine. The fire engine had a driver, a spotter, and a bulletproof windshield, and carried bottled gas containers filled with explosives.

The initial blast scattered fragments and debris, damaging a few structures including the detention facility and Post 2. Also, the lightweight counter-mortar radar was destroyed during the fighting that followed. One officer reported that the attack "demonstrates an extremely mature and capable insurgency. It showed its ability to mass a very complex attack very quickly."

The garrison, consisting of Company I, 3d Battalion, 2d Marines, deployed its quick reaction force and called for support. Enemy mortar and rocket launcher fire continued for an hour, but AH-1 helicopter gunship fire and F/A-18 air strikes turned the tide against the enemy. The small arms volume fire ceased around 0930, but some random shots continued for another

A Marine Corps M1A2 Abrams main battle tank attached to 3d Battalion, 2d Marines, patrols the streets of al-Ubaydi during Operation Matador in May 2005.

Photo by Cpl Neill A. Sevelius, Defense Imagery, VIRIN: 050512-M-2819S-036

Photo by Cpl Neill A. Sevelius, Defense Imagery, VIRIN: 050511-M-2819S-001

Marines from 3d Battalion, 2d Marines, provide security for a patrol as al-Ubaydi is secured during Operation Matador in May 2005.

10 hours. While the exact number of enemy killed in action or wounded remained unknown, commanders estimated that the Marines killed at least 16 enemy insurgents and wounded 15 during the 24-hour engagement. The enemy force, including support personnel, must have approached 100.

With Operation Matador, Regimental Combat Team 2 responded to insurgents in the 3d Battalion, 2d Marines, sector to eliminate their sanctuaries in the vicinity of Ramana. Several elements comprised Lieutenant Colonel Timothy S. Mundy's Task Force 3d Battalion, 2d Marines: Companies I and K, 3d Battalion, 2d Marines; Company L, 3d Battalion, 25th Marines; Company B, 2d Light Armored Reconnaissance Battalion; Combat Logistics Battalion 2; and the Army's 814th Bridge Company. The initial plan called for the deployment of two rifle companies, (Company L, 3d Battalion, 25th Marines; and Company K, 3d Battalion, 2d Marines) by helicopter using six CH-46E and four CH-53E helicopters in three waves. Intelligence received shortly before the operation, however, caused a shift from helicopters to assault amphibious vehicles, because the insurgents seemed to be reacting too well in advance. The tank and light armor sections secured the old Ramana Bridge site near Ubaydi, and tank sections and the Army bridge unit moved to place a temporary span across the Euphrates, permitting all Regimental Combat Team 2 vehicles to operate throughout the city. The assault amphibious

vehicles filled with the assault companies moved forward as well and prepared to sweep the objective area with mounted infantry and tanks, while the light armored reconnaissance company screened the northern flank. A vehicle accident and other difficulties with the bridging company, however, led to a 13-hour delay before the assault units crossed the river.

The operation produced some fierce fighting during the first 24 hours when both the blocking position at the Ramana Bridge and the bridge-crossing units became decisively engaged, leading to significant insurgent losses and the clearing of most of New Ubaydi, which had been considered calm after a recent civil-military operation. On the morning of 9 May, the amphibious vehicles crossed the river and the mounted infantry commenced clearing operations. By the evening of the ninth, the Army ribbon bridge became operational and with it Regimental Combat Team 2 established a secure line of communications on the north shore of the river. The Task Force cleared from Ramana to ar-Rabit. Once at ar-Rabit, the Marines scoured the suspected cave networks lining the dominating escarpment that bounded the river valley. As the task force withdrew to the south side of the river on 14 May, it attacked New Ubaydi prior to returning to base. All forces returned to al-Qaim by 1930 on 14 May.

At the Ramana Bridge position, Second Lieutenant Brian M. Stann led his mobile assault platoon of 3d

Battalion, 2d Marines Weapons Company, to seize the position and then defend it by traversing across four kilometers of urban terrain at New Ubaydi. Effectively employing air support with his heavy machine gun Humvees and attached tanks, Stann defeated every insurgent attack over a six-day period. The regiment's air officer made good use of ground-data links to the Litening system on board the supporting F/A-18D aircraft, which permitted him to see and then to direct strikes at the insurgents in the town. Enemy casualties included an estimated 144 killed and 40 prisoners. Ongoing intelligence collection confirmed the presence of foreign fighters.

During the operation six vehicles rigged with bombs were captured and destroyed along with a significant quantity of enemy weapons and bomb-making materials. Friendly casualties as a result of Operation Matador included nine killed and 39 wounded. Equipment losses consisted of two assault amphibious vehicles, one M1A1 tank, one M88A2 tank recovery vehicle, and four armored Humvees.

Ten days later, Haditha received the same treatment. On 24–30 May, Regimental Combat Team 2 conducted Operation New Market to neutralize and disrupt insurgents there. This operation was led by Lieutenant Colonel Lionel B. Urquhart's Task Force 3d Battalion, 25th Marines, reinforced with Company K, 3d Battalion, 2d Marines.

Company K, 3d Battalion, 25th Marines, made a helicopter assault on the left bank of the Euphrates, while two companies, Company K, 3d Battalion, 2d Marines, and Company L, 3d Battalion, 25th Marines, swept into town from the west, mounted in assault amphibians and accompanied by tanks and LAVs. The operation killed 11 insurgents, wounded eight, and produced 31 detainees. Over 300 82mm mortar rounds were seized and destroyed as were several other, smaller caches of ordnance. Friendly losses in Operation New Market included two killed, nine wounded, and the disabling of two assault amphibians.

During one of the 25 May sweeps by Company L, an insurgent ambush pinned down the command element. To overcome the enemy, Sergeant David N. Wimberg left his covered position and crossed enemy fire to scale a wall and enter a courtyard from which the fire originated. Opening the gate to the courtyard, he covered the entry of his fire team and then led the assault on the door of the house containing the insurgents. Breaking in, he came face-to-face with

LCpl Williams, radio operator with Company L, 3d Battalion, 25th Marines, carries the radio used by Capt Toland, the commanding officer of Company L's 3d Platoon, during Operation Matador.

Photo by Cpl Eric C. Ely

Col Stephen W. Davis, commanding officer of Regimental Combat Team 2, examines weapons captured from caches in Karbilah in June 2005 during Operation Spear.

four insurgents, fired his rifle until he was wounded, wounding one, but stunning the enemy. Corporal Jeff S. Hunter, stepped forward to assist Wimberg, firing his rifle at the four men as he pulled the sergeant out of the house. He then led a squad back into the house and killed the insurgents. Wimberg died but saved many lives by his selfless actions. Hunter virtually repeated the feat three days later, leading a squad in three repeated assaults, the last with tank support, to capture a house from which insurgents had ambushed another squad.

The 1st Force Reconnaissance Company conducted Operation Night Stalker III during 4–8 June. Snipers killed seven insurgents who were positively identified as they were digging and emplacing mines or bombs. Marines also uncovered bomb making materials that had been cached for use. This typical discovery included one 152mm round, four 130mm rounds, three 122mm rounds, a video camera, two Motorola receiver-transmitters, a cell phone, and a washing machine timer.

During 15–20 June, Regimental Combat Team 2 conducted Operation Spear in the vicinity of Karabilah, located on the south shore of the Euphrates midway between al-Qaim and the border town of

Husaybah. As in previous operations, it was a show of force drawing several units temporarily from nearby Regimental Combat Team 2, and aimed to disrupt insurgent refuges and kill or capture their leadership. This force consisted of the regimental command element, 3d Battalion, 2d Marines; Company L, 3d Battalion, 25th Marines; Company C, 2d Light Armored Reconnaissance Battalion; Company A tanks and assault amphibians, 1st Force Reconnaissance Company; Iraqi 7th Reconnaissance Company; and Iraqi 2d Battalion, 4th Brigade. After establishing blocking positions south and northeast of the town, Task Force 3d Battalion, 2d Marines, sent Company K, 3d Battalion, 2d Marines, and Company L, 3d Battalion, 25th Marines, to clear the town of Karabilah from south to north, beginning at 0300.

As they cleared the town, Marines fought numerous engagements with insurgents, and several buildings were destroyed by attack helicopter fire and fixed wing aircraft bombs to overcome resistance. The advancing riflemen found numerous caches of weapons and explosive materials, and a tank section discovered and eliminated more than two dozen vehicles, rigged with bombs, discovered in a parking lot.

All units withdrew from Karabilah to al-Qaim on 20 June. While disrupting this insurgent nest, Task Force 3d Battalion, 2d Marines, destroyed 24 vehicles rigged with bombs, two explosive devices, and numerous munitions caches. Marines killed an estimated 47 enemy fighters and detained one suspect. The Marines suffered one killed, six wounded, and eight non-combat injuries.

Operation Sword, conducted from 28 June to 6 July brought the Regimental Combat Team 2 clearing effort to the town of Hit.

The operation commenced with 1st Force Reconnaissance Company conducting a raid into the city aimed at capturing an insurgent leader while elements of Task Force 3d Battalion, 25th Marines, simultaneously moved into blocking positions to isolate Hit from the north, east, and west. For this operation, Company C, 1st Battalion, 9th Infantry; Company B, 2d Light Armored Reconnaissance Battalion; and two Iraqi companies reinforced 3d Battalion, 25th Marines. The raid detained two people while 3d Battalion, 25th Marines, moved through Hammadi and Company L, 3d Battalion, 25th Marines, and Company C, 1st Battalion, 9th Infantry, gained a foothold in their respective sectors in southern Hit. The light armored reconnaissance company drove by night from Rutbah and crossed the Euphrates Bridge and secured the far shore. The task force cleared Hit and established two "firm bases" intended for permanent occupancy in an abandoned school and a youth center. Hit thus became the first town in Area of Operations Denver per-

A Marine from Company L, 3d Battalion, 25th Marines, stands on lookout on a rooftop in the city of Hit during Operation Sword in June 2005. Hit was the first town permanently occupied by Regimental Combat Team 2 during the operation.

Photo by Eric C. Ely, VIRIN: 050628-M-8172E-039

manently occupied by Regimental Combat Team 2. Marines of Combat Logistics Battalion 2 provided Texas and Jersey barriers (usually made of concrete to separate traffic lanes or to stop vehicles) as it fortified both bases. They also set up generators and swamp coolers to improve living conditions. Explosive devices remained the most likely threat at Hit with 19 destroyed on 2 July alone.

Operation Sword ended on 5 July with the detachment of the Army and light armor companies. From 27 June to 5 July the battalion received Task Force Lionheart from the control of Colonel Davis. This task force swept the left bank of the Euphrates River for weapons caches with limited results. The battalion then received two infantry companies and a headquarters company from the 2d Battalion, 1st Brigade of the Iraqi Army. Each Iraqi infantry company was assigned to a firm base. Company I, 3d Battalion, 25th Marines, rejoined its battalion from al-Asad Air Base and conducted a relief in place at Firm Base 1 with Company L on 19 July. Company K remained at Firm Base 2. The battalion also transferred its main headquarters from Camp Haditha to Camp Hit on 15 July. The two rifle companies conducted joint combat patrols with their Iraqi partners daily. Engagements with the insurgents varied as the patrols encountered car bombs, explosive devices, and indirect and direct fire engagements. Task Force Lionheart returned in the middle of July and swept south of Hit, locating and destroying a large number of weapons caches.

In Area of Operations Topeka, 1st Battalion, 5th Marines, occupied the central core of Ramadi, between the Euphrates River and the canal, with 1st Battalion, 503d Parachute Infantry (motorized), covering the eastern quarter of the city and its approaches and the 1st Battalion, 9th Infantry, holding the sector extending south of the canal into farmland beyond. In its exclusively urban sector, 1st Battalion, 5th Marines, worked diligently to maintain patrol coverage and operated entry checkpoints, traffic control points, observation posts, and secured vital government facilities in the city. The continuous patrolling and constant pressure of raids kept the insurgents off balance. During 15–16 June the battalion saw its heaviest fighting, and simultaneous attacks against several of its positions confirmed that the enemy remained present and offensively oriented. The battalion responded with mandatory vehicle inspections at chokepoints, increased patrolling, and cordon and search operations of the more troublesome neighborhoods.

Checkpoint duty continually exposed the soldiers and Marines to perils. On 3 May, First Lieutenant David T. Russell oversaw his platoon's operation of an

A house is searched by Marines of Company B, 1st Battalion, 6th Marines, during Operation Khanjar at Lake Tharthar in June 2005. Khanjar was one of several dozen counterinsurgency operations conducted by Multi National Force–West units to clear al-Anbar Province of insurgent activity.

entry control point in Ramadi when 13 insurgents assaulted it with small arms, machine guns, and grenades. From his position on the second level of a building, he saw an insurgent manning the machine gun and killed him with a single shot. Ignoring the fire of six insurgents, he then crossed to a bunker where one of his Marines needed ammunition. While directing subsequent fire and maneuver, a rifle bullet hit his helmet, knocking him to the ground with head injuries. After recovering his wits, he crossed the kill zone several more times to direct his Marines and also retrieve a wounded Iraqi soldier. Only when ordered to receive medical treatment did he relinquish command at the scene.

Colonel Gurganus's Regimental Combat Team 8 commenced its portion of the 2d Marine Division's Operation Patriot Shield with Operation White Feather, conducted from 1–7 April. It focused on the main service roads in Area of Operations Raleigh and disrupting insurgent actions, especially those placing bombs. Battalions continued integrated patrols with their Iraqi counterparts throughout Fallujah and along nearby major routes. In addition, the 1st Battalion, 6th Marines, secured Jolan Park to support Operation Greenback, which was the extensive compensation

payment program for the people of Fallujah who had lost property during the November offensive. Third Reconnaissance Battalion commenced its Operation Zaidon Focus with offensive actions in the southern portion of Area of Operations Raleigh.

Operation Clear Decision, conducted from 30 April to 5 May, marked the beginning of Regimental Combat Team 8's efforts to clear towns that Coalition forces had not garrisoned. Colonel Gurganus deployed Lieutenant Colonel Stephen M. Neary's 3d Battalion, 8th Marines, to al-Karmah, reinforced by elements of 3d Reconnaissance Battalion, Company B tanks and assault amphibians, Company A engineers, Combat Logistics Battalion 8, and the Regimental Combat Team 8 command group with its security detachment. After establishing a cordon with the tank unit at 0300, a pair of CH-46E Sea Stallions dropped leaflets, and 3d Battalion, 8th Marines, began to clear the town at 0530, using cordon and knock techniques. The reconnaissance battalion scoured the countryside north of the town. Combat Logistics Battalion 8 and the regimental commander's security detachment took the normal posts of 3d Battalion, 8th Marines, during the operation.

Company L, 3d Battalion, 8th Marines, and the

Iraqi 2d Muthanna Battalion moved into the southern sector of al-Karmah. Marines reestablished old Camp Delta and established observation posts in and around the city. Scout-sniper teams dispersed to several locations to conduct surveillance and to prevent insurgents from escaping the cordon. Company B moved its assault amphibians into the city and secured the police station to facilitate its use by civil affairs and medical units. Company I, 3d Battalion, 8th Marines, and the 1st Company, 2d Muthanna Battalion, then moved into the northern sector of al-Karmah. By 2 May, al-Karmah was declared secure with no friendly casualties and only one civilian casualty from an escalation of force incident. Third Reconnaissance Battalion continued to find several weapons caches, including a large cache just inside the 3d Infantry Division's Baghdad area of operations. On 13 May, the town was turned over to the 2d Muthanna Battalion.

Team Brawler, comprising elements of Company B, 2d Tank Battalion, and Team Gator, similarly formed from Company B, 2d Assault Amphibian Battalion, moved into the regimental security sector north of Fallujah. Regimental Combat Team 8 subsequently began Operation Firm Control on 8 May, which lasted until the 16th. At 0300 on 8 May, Team Brawler commenced cordon and search tasks in the eastern portion of the northern regimental security area, while Team Gator worked the western half. Regimental Combat Team 8 established a joint combat operation center in the area. Simultaneously, 3d Reconnaissance Battalion conducted two raids in the Zaidon area in the southern portion of the regiment's

As the sun sets, Marines with 2d Squad, 1st Platoon, Military Police Company, Combat Logistics Regiment 25, 2d Force Service Support Group, mark improvised explosive devices in an up armored Humvee at al-Taqaddum.
Photo by LCpl Bobby J. Segovia, Defense Imagery: 050930-M-3717S-117

area of operations and 1st Battalion, 6th Marines, continued with its operations in northern Fallujah, as did 3d Battalion, 4th Marines, in the south. Third Battalion, 8th Marines, continued to maintain security in al-Karmah, Nassar Wa Salaam, and connecting routes.

The move north by Teams Brawler and Gator initiated a string of significant events for Regimental Combat Team 8. The first 24 hours produced two indirect fire attacks, five by small arms, and then the discovery of three explosive devices. Insurgents made several efforts to strike 3d Battalion, 8th Marines, in al-Karmah, and the tank and assault amphibian units continued to uncover significant caches of weapons and ordnance, including one uncovered on the last day near Lake Tharthar by Team Gator, which included 19 mortars and two rocket launchers.

June inaugurated 2d Marine Division's Operation Guardian Sword. Regimental Combat Team 8 contributed with Operation Dagger conducted from 1–21 June. Attacking as far as the Lake Tharthar resort to disrupt insurgent operations, Company B, 2d Assault Amphibian Battalion, and Company B, 2d Tank Battalion, surged into the northeast region to find enemy command and control, logistical, and training areas. Within hours of arriving in their zone, Marines of Team Gator discovered a cache containing 11 122mm rockets and 71 120mm mortar rounds. The team later found intelligence materials and military manuals near the northeast corner of the regimental security zone as well as several underground facilities and more weapons and ammunition caches. One house held insurgent materials and evidence of recent use. These discoveries by Regimental Combat Team 8 indicated that the insurgents used this area for training, equipment storage, and planning. Dust storms then pummeled Area of Operations Raleigh between 6 and 8 June, resulting in the early return of the teams from the northern regimental security area.

At 0330 on 18 June, Task Force 1st Battalion, 6th Marines, with supporting attachments (Company B, 2d Assault Amphibian Battalion, and B Company, 2d Tank Battalion) moved to the northern regimental security area to conduct the next stage of Operation Dagger. These units received support from elements of Combat Logistics Battalion 8, including a fully functional field surgical hospital.

U.S. Army forces located further north outside the II MEF area also operated to support the regiment, blocking insurgents from fleeing. The Army's 2d Brigade supported 1st Battalion, 6th Marines, providing mortar fire and blocking positions southwest of the Marine battalion. Aviation and fire support furnished key elements of the operation. Battery A, 1st Battalion, 10th Marines, moved two 155mm artillery pieces north to the 1st Battalion, 6th Marines, forward command post to provide on-call fire support for the task force. Marine and Coalition aviation units came to the fight, providing almost 20 hours of continual air support during the first day of task force actions. Company K, 3d Battalion, 8th Marines, reported for operations as Regimental Combat Team 8's reserve to the south.

The more detailed coverage of the zone by the infantry battalion uncovered caches of munitions that were confiscated and destroyed (Table 8-1):

These results remained typical throughout the campaign of 2004–2005 for that level of effort and indicated that a seemingly inexhaustible supply of munitions remained within easy reach of the insurgents and foreign fighters. Upon return of its units from Operation Dagger, Regimental Combat Team 8 had completed numerous major and minor operations since its assumption of the mission. Thus far, six of its Marines and sailors had died in action and 88 more were wounded. Still, the focus remained on maintaining control of Fallujah.

On the southern approaches to the city, a mobile patrol of Weapons Company, 3d Battalion, 4th Marines, ran into an ambush on 19 June when an estimated 50 insurgents triggered an explosive device and opened fire with small arms. The section leader on the scene, Corporal Wyatt L. Waldron, ordered his vehicles into the oncoming automatic weapons fire, gained fire superiority with vehicular weapons, and then called for a dismounted assault against the enemy flank. Waldron personally killed five insurgents and captured two of their fighting positions as the Marine assault broke the enemy's resistance. Waldron's team then remounted, pursued, and killed 16 and captured six more insurgents. Another six improvised explosive devices were found at the ambush site.

On 23 June a car bomb ambush in Fallujah killed the first female Marine during Operation Iraqi Freedom. The coordinated attack with small arms fire left five Marines and one sailor dead and more than 12 Marines wounded. The daily rituals at Camp Fallujah, however, continued with female Marines ready

Table 8-1: Munitions Confiscated and Destroyed

155mm shells	20
122mm shells	31
120mm mortar rounds	233
80mm mortar rounds	45
82mm mortar rounds	10
82mm fuzes	4
60mm mortar rounds	69
60mm fuzes	50
60mm mortar tubes	2
RPG warheads	15
RPG propellants	5
RPG boosters	4
Powder bags	5
Primers	8

to conduct searches of female Iraqis while continuing to provide basic security for Fallujah's inhabitants.

On 30 June, Regimental Combat Team 8 assumed control of Area of Operations Jackson from the 155th Brigade Combat Team. This measure expanded its area of operations another 1,000 square kilometers. Such boundary shifts in this area continued to ebb and flow throughout the Iraq campaign depending upon the priorities claimed for the Army forces operating in and around Baghdad.

II MEF headed into July and the pending rotation of its Army brigade after a highly active period in which U.S. forces and insurgents tested each other. With limited manpower, the regiments and brigade managed to extend their reach with operations outside urban boundaries, striking into the countryside to disrupt enemy sanctuaries. Inside the urban cores, they continued stability and security operations to deny easy movement to the insurgents, to assist the public with civil affairs and security measures, and to find insurgent cells with cordons and raids. The enemy replied with continued attacks by explosives, small arms, and indirect fire. An unsettling discovery, given the mission at hand, came with the unreliability of the Iraqi Security Forces, which were repeatedly formed and trained only to dissolve and necessitate reformation and retraining. The Iraqi government and its advisors had yet to develop an indigenous security force of any depth and reliability.

Chapter 9

Protecting Self-Rule

Assessing the Mission

Major General Stephen T. Johnson's campaign planning before the entry of II Marine Expeditionary Force (Forward) (II MEF) into al-Anbar Province recognized the essential need for Iraqi security forces to augment his forces and to take over local security. The campaign planning by the staff of Multi National Force–Iraq had set specific goals in this regard: local control in key cities by 30 December 2004; provincial authority established by 31 July 2005; and constitutional elections in mid-December. That ambitious plan, however, had already failed since local control in key cities remained an illusion to date.

Thus, the outlook for Marine Corps commanders in 2005 changed in the face of these and other realities. The establishment of local control could only be hoped for in Karbala and an-Najaf by mid-2005, and perhaps the ar-Ramadi–Abu Ghraib sector by mid-December and the elections. Expectations remained that local control might be established in all of al-Anbar Province by March 2006 and provincial control by 31 July.

The planned establishment of a division and two brigades of Iraqi security forces in al-Anbar Province remained key to these plans. Whether those forces proved capable or not, the political goal of conducting national elections in mid-December was an unalterable requirement for II MEF and the other U.S. forces in Iraq. With or without the recovery of Iraqi political and security authority at the local and provincial levels, the elections remained a paramount goal.

Coalition forces also adjusted the estimated enemy order of battle by adding a new sub-category of enemy: "Sunni Arab Rejectionists." This group, made up primarily of former regime loyalists, now posed the most significant threat to stability in Iraq. Although the Sunnis ranked statistically as an ethnic minority in Iraq, they had maintained political, economic, and military dominance over the country's other major ethnic groups for nearly 600 years. Given the Coalition objective of assisting Iraq in forming a democratic form of government, the Sunnis stood to lose considerable influence. As discussed in Chapter 1, the loss of political and economic power, a lack of security, and decisions made following the collapse of Saddam Hussein's regime acted as catalysts for this insurgency. While many Sunnis did not necessarily oppose a new form of government, the perceived injustices imposed on them since the collapse of their minority rule in 2003 created a level of distrust and animosity toward the Coalition and Iraq's Interim Government. This particular insurgency therefore sought to rouse Sunni anxieties and create a pool of recruits. Their motivations reflected a wide range of political objectives primarily driven by socio-economic concerns.

The II MEF campaign strategy for counterinsurgency centered on conducting five "Lines of Operation" simultaneously to improve local conditions and counter the discontent and chaos that fed the insurgencies: Security, "Operationalize" the Iraqi Security Forces, Governance, Economic development, and Influence. These concepts provided an operational

Table 9-1: Ground Combat Turnover, July–October 2005

Initial Deployment	Replacement Unit	Area of Operations	Transfer of Authority
3d Bn 4th Mar	2d Bn 7th Mar	Raleigh	23 July 2005
2d Bde 2d Div	2d Bde 28th Div	Topeka	28 July 2005
3d Bn 8th Mar	2d Bn 2d Mar	Raleigh	6 August 2005
3d Bn 2d Mar	3d Bn 6th Mar	Denver	10 September 2005
1st Bn 5th Mar	3d Bn 7th Mar	Topeka	20 September 2005
3d Bn 25th Mar	3d Bn 1st Mar	Denver	21 September 2005
2d LAR Bn (-)	1st LAR 6th Mar	Denver	24 September 2005
1st Bn 6th Mar	2d Bn 6th Mar	Raleigh	4 October 2005
3d Recon Bn (-)	1st Recon Bn (-)	Raleigh	7 October 2005

Photo by LCpl Vrian M. Henner, Defense Imagery VIRIN: 050220-M-9019H-048

One of the coalition's primary goals in 2005 was to stand up effective Iraqi military forces. Cpl Robert W. Johnson, from the 3d Battalion, 4th Marines, sights targets alongside an Iraqi soldier during marksmanship training in February 2005.

framework for applying the kinetic and non-kinetic actions necessary to change the environment, which alone could bring a separation of the insurgents from the Iraqi population of al-Anbar Province.

The plan provided specific definitions for each of the lines of operations:

Security. Create an environment in which insurgents are not allowed to intimidate or to cause fear among the people, to inhibit legitimate self-governance, or to prevent the development of Iraqi infrastructure.

Operationalizing the Iraqi Security Forces. The Iraqi Security Forces must be trained, equipped, supported, and mentored in a manner enabling their organizations to grow in size, confidence, and skill. The effectiveness of the Iraqi Security Forces must be developed so they can assume an increasingly greater role, allowing Multi National Force–West (II MEF) presence to be proportionally reduced.

Governance. Create an environment that allows elected officials to govern in an effective manner consistent with the expectations of the electorate. The Iraqi populace must perceive that its local elected officials can provide basic security and quality of life services such as electricity, water, and sanitation. Al-

leviating legitimate political grievances is an important element for a successful counterinsurgency.

Economic Development. Create an environment allowing jobs to be created, where people are free to earn a living and can procure or receive essential services fundamental to a decent quality of life, and where critical infrastructure exists to support economic growth.

Influence. Influence binds the other four lines of operation by affecting information content and flow in the area of operations, particularly into and out of its key population centers. This will involve affecting three distinct information audiences: anti-Iraqi forces, local and regional populations, and friendly forces.

II MEF and the 2d Marine Division sought to implement these lines of operation for the rest of the year following the transfer of authority from I MEF. After the March operations successfully protected the turnover between the two Marine expeditionary forces, the 2d Division ordered Operation Patriot Shield in April and May. As noted in the previous chapter, the two Marine regiments and the Army's 2d Brigade planned and conducted numerous local combat operations under Patriot Shield to interdict insurgent lines of communications from the border,

Table 9-2: Aviation Turnover, August–October 2005

Initial Deployment	Replacement Unit	Base	Relief in Place
VMFA-224	VMFA-332	al-Asad	1 August 2005
HMLA-269	HMLA-167	al-Asad	21 August 2005
VMGR-252(-)	VMGR-252(-)	Al-Asad	21 August 2005
HMM-264	HMM-266	Al-Asad	24 August 2005
VMFA-142	VMA-223	al-Asad	28 August 2005
HMM-364	HMM-161	Taqaddum	8 September 2005
HMH-465	HMH-466	al-Asad	27 September 2005
HMM-764	HMM-774	al-Asad	30 September 2005
HMLA-775	HMLA-369	Taqaddum	4 October 2005
VMU-2	VMU-1	Taqaddum	6 September 2005

to operationally shape the Ramadi sector by controlling access and establishing Iraqi security forces, and to protect the gains made in pacifying al-Fallujah by disrupting insurgent enclaves in the surrounding areas.

Under the overarching II MEF operation plan for 2005, Operation Sunrise, the Marines in al-Anbar Province conducted a wide range of operations. The Patriot Shield series ended on 30 May and gave way to Operation Guardian Sword, actually a series of operations conducted between 6 June and 15 August.

Here, the objectives called for neutralizing the insurgencies in Ramadi while covering the rotation of combat units and personnel in other units for the second half of the deployment, including the Army's rotation of the 2d Brigade. Guardian Sword was followed by Operation Sanguine Thunder after the completion of final rotations in September. The operation entailed a range of goals, including training and arming Iraqi police in northern Babil Province, transferring Karbala and an-Najaf to Iraqi local control, and in general supporting Operation Liberty Ex-

Marines from the 3d Battalion, 2d Marines, and Iraqi Special Forces prepare to enter a building in Karabilah during Operation Spear in July 2005.

Photo by Cpl Neil A. Sevelius, Defense Imagery VIRIN 050618-M-2819S-131

Photo by Cpl Robert R. Attebury, Defense Imagery: VIRIN: 050629-M-3301A-007

Marines from Company A, 1st Battalion, 6th Marines, search a car for weapons during Operation Shadyville in Saqlawiyah. The operation was conducted by the 2d Marine Division and Iraqi security forces.

press, the Coalition program for safeguarding and supporting the December national elections.

Major General Richard A. Huck predicted favorable results for Operation Guardian Sword in a 30 May message to his division:

> Operation Patriot Shield comes to a close today and Operation Guardian Sword is ready to commence 6 June. I feel confident that we will be able to pick up the tempo of operations and apply more Iraqi security forces to operations in Guardian Sword. As you know, the Iraqi security forces projections for Operation Patriot Shield fell short of the mark. Our ability to train, integrate and operate with Iraqi security forces will allow us to significantly increase our forces. Put an Iraqi face on all of our operations.

As noted in the preceding chapter, the battalions of Regimental Combat Team 2, Regimental Combat Team 8, and the Army's 2d Brigade continued to execute the same types of operations as under Guardian Sword. These organizations truly had few new options for kinetic or offensive combat operations because their extensive static security responsibilities aggravated the relative paucity of units available for offensive operations. In addition, the routine logistical and administrative support for the three major units of 2d Marine Division, spread over the 335-kilometer corridor from al-Qaim to Abu Ghraib, required frequent recourse to armed convoys, road sweeps, and other force protection tasks that reduced even more the resources available for

commanders to employ against enemy targets.

In westernmost al-Anbar Province, Regimental Combat Team 2 commander Colonel Stephen W. Davis deployed 3d Battalion 25th Marines, to find arms caches and to interdict insurgent flow near Dulab, on the left bank of the Haditha Dam reservoir. The 3d Battalion, 2d Marines, continued its normal cordon and knock operations and similar cache searches in its zone, exclusive of Husaybah and Karabilah which remained highly contested, while beginning a site survey for polling stations. The 2d Light Armored Reconnaissance Battalion continued patrolling main routes, especially against bomb and mortar teams and provided direct support to the Army 224th Engineer Battalion, assigned to clear and to maintain the main supply routes for the regiments as Task Force Ironhawk. The 1st Force Reconnaissance Company continued its sniper operations, and the Azerbaijani Company, charged with internal security at the Haditha Dam, prepared for its own relief slated for early July.

The Army's 2d Brigade employed 1st Battalion, 5th Marines, with combined U.S.-Iraqi combat patrols, cache sweeps, and stay-behind ambushes in western Ramadi, partnered with the Iraqi 2d Battalion, 1st Brigade, 7th Division. On the other side of Ramadi, 1st Battalion, 503d Infantry, conducted a company movement in the Mulaab district. In Tammin, the 1st Battalion, 9th Infantry, patrolled, deployed snipers, and planned company-size attacks if targets appeared. The 1st Battalion, 506th Infantry, partnered with the Iraqi 3d Battalion, 2d Brigade, 1st Division, for patrols in Civil Camp and Abu Flies.

Colonel Charles M. Gurganis continued the Regimental Combat Team 8 program of security and counterinsurgency operations in Fallujah and the rest of Area of Operations Raleigh. His tank and assault amphibian company teams continued to operate in the "regimental security area" extending north of Fallujah to the Lake Tharthar resort. The 3d Reconnaissance Battalion covered the comparable security area to the south of Fallujah, where potential polling stations also required survey and assessment. The newly secured Karmah area also required combined operations with the Iraqi 1st Battalion, 4th Brigade, 1st Division, now based there.

Force Rotation in Mid-deployment

For the rest of July, Regimental Combat Team 2 conducted Operation Saber, an umbrella operation that assigned each battalion to conduct counterinsurgency actions in their respective zones from 23–31 July. Aimed at disrupting insurgents while unit rotations took place in the other areas of operations, it netted an average amount of cached arms and munitions but also resulted in 39 insurgents killed and 177 people detained.

The last major operation planned by Regimental Combat Team 2 before the rotation of its battalions was Operation Lightning Strike II in August. This multi-battalion attack on the south bank of the Euphrates River roughly midway between al-Qaim and Haditha targeted the city of Anah and nearby village of Qadisiyah. In addition to disrupting insurgent activities and eliminating foreign fighters in the zone, the operation aimed at demonstrating the deployment by the Iraqi government of a competent security force in the form of its 2d Battalion, 1st Infantry Division. The Army's 2d Squadron, 14th Cavalry, assisted in isolating the objective area by blocking the bridge over the river in the direction of Rawah in its sector. Regimental Combat Team 2 planned to employ elements of 2d Light Armored Reconnaissance Battalion, 3d Battalion, 2d Marines, and 3d Battalion, 25th Marines, as well as tank, assault amphibian, engineer, and Iraqi Army support to cordon the two towns, to raid specific targets, and then to clear them of insurgents.

That operation never occurred because the 3d Battalion, 25th Marines, was ambushed. The battalion had completed its transfer to Hit by mid-July but also kept units in its former garrison in Haditha. On 1 August, insurgents attacked two sniper teams of the battalion scout-sniper platoon operating together in a firing position 3.5 kilometers northwest of Haditha on the east bank of the Euphrates overlooking Barwanah. A third sniper team, Team Six, located 2 kilo-

The lack of adequate manpower to patrol Iraq's often porous western borders was a perennial challenge faced by Coalition forces in 2005. Here, Iraqi students stand in formation before their graduation ceremony at the al-Asad Iraqi Border Patrol Academy in April 2005.

Photo by Cpl Alicia M. Garcia, Defense Imagery, VIRIN: 050409-M-5607G-008

Soldiers from the 1st Battalion, 155th Brigade Combat Team, uncover the grave of a victim of an insurgent attack near al-Iskandariyah.

meters to the north heard a few seconds of small arms and machine gun fire coming from that location, then radioed the two teams without receiving a response. Team Six requested permission to move south and investigate. The battalion approved and also launched its quick reaction force from Haditha Dam. On the scene, Team Six found five Marines dead and one missing, and their weapons and weapon systems were missing.

Lieutenant Colonel Urquhart detailed the L and Weapons Companies of 3d Battalion, 25th Marines, to cordon Barwanah to search for the insurgents responsible for this attack. In the early hours of 2 August, reports from tip lines indicated that a body was located 3 kilometers south of Haditha on the west bank of the Euphrates. The body was the sixth Marine, and they recovered his remains that day from the village of Haqlaniyah. This killing of a trained and experienced team of Marine rifleman brought a rapid response from Colonel Davis' regiment. The forces slated for Operation Lightning Strike II instead were reset for Operation Quick Strike (3–6 August, extended to 11 August), a cordon and search of Haqlaniyah and Barwanah.

While 2d Light Armored Reconnaissance Battalion screened the flanks, 3d Battalion, 2d Marines, moved with Companies K and L and 2d Platoon, Company A, 1st Tank Battalion, into an assembly area on the west bank of the Euphrates after an Iraqi Special Operations Company had secured it. At the same time,

a 3d Battalion, 25th Marines, task force comprised of L and Weapons Companies, and Company A, 1st Tank Battalion, prepared to clear Barwanah on the east bank of the river, where the 3d Battalion, 25th Marines, task force had been operating for three days, fighting insurgent small arms and mortar teams with infantry and tank weapons and precision air strikes. The Marine battalions had with them the 3d and 2d Companies, respectively, of the Iraqi 2d battalion, 1st Infantry Division. These companies had reported to Regimental Combat Team 2 on 17 July. The 1st Force Reconnaissance Company provided raid and sniper support as required. Late in the first day of the operation, an assault amphibian vehicle carrying Marines of Company L, 3d Battalion, 25th Marines, was hit by an explosive device of such size that it badly damaged and overturned the vehicle, killing 15 crewmen and passengers.

On 4 August, Marine battalions attacked north and conducted cordon and searches through the villages. The 3d Battalion, 2d Marines, encountered only sporadic resistance in Haqlaniyah and established a base to support continuing actions. Resistance then stiffened for both engaged battalion task forces, and a number of air strikes were used to destroy buildings from which insurgents fired small arms and rocket launchers.

Operation Quick Strike, which began as a response to the killing of Marine snipers, uncovered a considerable nest of resistance in the three towns located only a few kilometers south of Haditha. The operation netted the destruction of nine car bombs and 23 improvised explosive devices. Marines destroyed seven buildings defended by insurgents, killing 15 and detaining another 63. Friendly casualties included 14 U.S. killed, six wounded, one Iraqi Special Forces soldier killed, three wounded and one assault amphibian vehicle a total loss. During 9–10 August, the participating units returned to their bases.

The 3d Battalion, 25th Marines, lost 19 men in three days in an Iraq deployment which cost the unit 48 killed in action. The loss sustained by this reserve forces unit proved especially devastating to the Marine Corps, the families of those lost, and the public. During 12–18 August, the units received visits from the commanders of 2d and 4th Marine Divisions, II MEF and Multi National Force–Iraq.

The next increase in insurgent activity in Area of Operations Denver took place 24–29 August at Husaybah. The outbreak in violence was possibly prodded by the departure of Company L, 3d Battalion, 2d Marines, from al-Qaim to Kubaysah, where it joined 2d Force Reconnaissance Company and Company C, 2d Light Armored Reconnaissance Battalion, in a cordon and knock clearing operation. Camp Gannon exchanged small arms and rocket fire with insurgents on 24 August. Two days later, the Regimental Combat Team 2 targeting staff identified an al-Qaeda safe house and leveled it with multiple air strikes, delivering two GBU-38 joint direct attack munition bombs, six GBU-12 laser-guided 500-pound bombs, three Maverick guided missiles, and five 5-inch unguided rockets on the target. A similar effort the next evening brought eight buildings down with a total of 5 GBU-12s, 1 GBU-38, and 7 Mavericks. The regiment now considered all the enemy's safe havens inside the Regimental Combat Team 2 area of operation destroyed. Small arms fire hit Marines of Company I, 3d Battalion, 2d Marines, the evening of 29 August, and another air strike destroyed an insurgent house with a GBU-38. As these actions continued, the relief battalion, 3d Battalion, 6th Marines, began to arrive at al-Qaim.

The force turnover in II MEF, covered in part by Operation Guardian Shield, spanned a two-month period. In addition, the Army replaced 2d Brigade, 2d Infantry Division, with the 2d Brigade, 28th Infantry Division, under the command of Colonel John Gronski, formed principally from the Pennsylvania, Utah, and Vermont National Guard. With a one-for-one replacement of battalions in operations Area of Operations Topeka, no let-up in the struggle to pacify and shape Ramadi would occur.

In addition, the 2d Marine Division exchanged artillery batteries and force reconnaissance, tank, combat engineer, and assault amphibian companies with fresh units from the U.S. During the same rotation period, ground support aviation units and the 2d Force Service Support Group remained in place, with a rotation of personnel. The Ramadi-based intelligence services of II MEF also rotated battalions, as 3d Radio Battalion relieved 2d Radio Battalion on 11 June and 2d Intelligence Battalion replaced 1st Intelligence Battalion on 24 September 2005.

The aircraft squadrons of 2d Marine Aircraft Wing mostly rotated during August–September. The wing retained two fixed-wing, four rotary-wing squadrons, and the aerial refueler detachment based at al-Asad and two rotary wing squadrons and the unmanned aerial vehicle unit at Taqaddum.

The combat power now available for II MEF to employ in Area of Operations Atlanta thus amounted to the following as of 1 September 2005 (see table 9-3).

Operation Guardian Sword ended with the relief in place of the Army brigade assigned to the 2d Marine Division. In its last weeks (through 15 August), Guardian Sword planned for the newly arrived units to assist with election preparations and economic development programs and enhance the ability of local leaders to exercise authority. The Army's 2d Brigade, 28th Infantry Division, received tactical control of the Iraqi 3d Brigade, 1st Division, and conducted its first major action, Operation Heavy, on 29 August with a counterinsurgency clearing of Jazirah. The units of Regimental Combat Team 8, carrying out rotations from late July to early October in Area of Operations Raleigh, continued actions in and about Fallujah and searched for weapon caches in Operations Vital Ground (2–14 June), Scimitar (7–14 July), and Southern Fire (24–29 August).

Securing the Border: Operation Hunter

The emphasis on Regimental Combat Team 2 operations in July and August continued after Operation Guardian Sword because of a higher headquarters order. With Operation Hunter, the commander of Multi National Force–Iraq, General George W. Casey Jr., required operations within the II MEF Area of Operations Atlanta to secure the Syrian border by establishing a presence along the frontier and capturing al-Qaeda fighters north of the Euphrates River. The operation lasted from the middle of July until late August. During this period, Operation Hunter combat operations continued within the Euphrates River valley, specifically in the cities already targeted by Regimental Combat Team 2: Hit, Haditha, Husaybah and al-Qaim. Operation Hunter included a task force from 3d Armored Cavalry Regiment operating out of Combat Outpost Rawah in the former Regimental Combat Team 2 zone of operations north of the Euphrates River, now designated Area of Operations Saber by the cavalry regiment. The timeline for the operation extended until 15 December and became part of Operation Liberty Express, the series of operations conducted to protect the Iraqi elections.

The occupation of border posts experienced continuous delays, however, and during September, the Multi National Force–Iraq commander restored Area of Operations Saber to II MEF and transferred tactical control of four U.S. Army units to 2d Marine Division and Regimental Combat Team 2 for the continuation of Operation Hunter: 4th Squadron, 14th Cavalry; 3d Battalion, 504th Parachute Infantry; Task Force 2d Battalion, 114th Field Artillery; Company F, 51st Infantry; 519th Military Intelligence Battalion; and Task Force Phantom, an intelligence, surveillance, and reconnaissance unit.

The 4th Squadron, 14th Cavalry, cleared the village of al-Ash on 16 September in Operation Mustang and repeated the effort at Qadisiyah and Anah on 28-29 September in Operation Lightning Strike. The 3d Battalion, 504th Parachute Infantry, cleared a military housing compound at Baghdadi during Op-

eration Green Light (21-22 September), and the 2d Battalion, 114th Field Artillery, road marched from the 155th Brigade Combat Team (155th BCT) in Area of Operations Biloxi to Hit, beginning on 20 September, effecting a relief of 3d Battalion, 1st Marines, there on 28 September.

The reinforcement of Regimental Combat Team 2 by Task Force 2d Battalion, 114th Field Artillery, provided a boost for the over-extended forces in western al-Anbar Province. It also demonstrated an early success for the 155th Brigade in achieving provincial and regional control in Area of Operations Biloxi, where the cities of Karbala and an-Najaf remained relatively quiet. That situation thus precipitated the reinforcement of Colonel Davis' regiment.

The border forces that General Casey sought to bolster on the Syrian frontier with Operation Hunter did not yet exist in the II MEF area of operations. In 2005, only the three border zones covering ports of entry at Ar Ar (from Saudi Arabia), Trebil (from Jordan) and Walid (from Syria) operated with battalions of three Department of Border Enforcement Brigades manning the border forts in an-Najaf and al-Anbar Provinces. Iraq operated no port of entry in an-Najaf Province. The U.S. units stationed in Camp Mudaysis and at Camp Korean Village operated to support the al-Anbar and Nukhayb Department of Border Enforcement Brigades in al-Anbar Province, and the

Marines from 2d Platoon, Company K, 3d Battalion, 8th Marines, and the 2d Combat Engineer Battalion scan the area for weapons caches near the town of Zaidon in July 2005.

Photo by LCpl Matthew Hutchison, Defense Imagery VIRIN: 050710-M-9470H-009

Table 9-3: II MEF Combat Power, September 2005

Combat Power (Air)					
AH-1W	AV-8B	CH-46E	CH-53E	EA-6B	FA-18A+
25/20	10/7	38/35	16/14	5/4	6/6
80%	70%	92%	88%	80%	100%
FA-18D	KC-130	RQ-2B	UC-35	UH-1N	
12/11	6/4	8/7	1/1	15/10	
92%	67%	88%	100%	67%	
Combat Power (Ground-USMC)					
Tank M1A1	LVA	AAV	Howitzer M198	HMMWV Hardback	UAH M114
34/31	67/63	89/84	14/14	307/288	574/537
91%	94%	94%	100%	94%	94%
Combat Power (Ground) (2-28th BCT)					
M1A1/A2	M2/M3	Mortar 120MM	Howitzer M109A6	Scout HMMWV Armored	UAH M114
43/32	49/47	15/14	8/7	176/158	226/201
74%	96%	93%	88%	90%	89%
Combat Power (Ground-155th BCT)					
M1A1/A2	M2/M3	Mortar 120MM	Howitzer M109A6	Scout HMMWV Armored	UAH M114
74%	90%	100%	83%	100%	93%
M113					
79/72					
91%					

Army's 155th BCT covered the an-Najaf Department of Border Enforcement Brigade in Area of Operations Biloxi. The Department of Border Enforcement services planned a fourth battalion of its al-Anbar Brigade at al-Qaim to occupy nine border forts covering the rest of the Syrian border in al-Anbar Province northeast of the last manned Border Fort 10 at Akashat. After it was properly secured, that sector of the frontier would reopen for commerce with Syria by reactivating the abandoned port of entry facilities at Husaybah.

The Iraqi Armed Forces and Its Problems

In mid-2005, however, the Iraqi forces were inadequate for operations along the al-Anbar Province border. The third and fourth battalion of the al-Anbar Province Department of Border Enforcement Brigade had not formed, and the building of forts had not even begun. In any case, the Marine Corps had yet to send the required 10 border transition teams for assignment to each brigade and battalion of the border forces in the II MEF area of operations. These ten-man teams, specially prepared and trained at Camp Lejeune, arrived during July and by August and evaluated the border forces based at an-Najaf, Trebil, and Waleed. Given the continuing delays in con-

struction and operations, three of the border transition teams converted to military transition teams and assisted in the stand-up of new Iraqi Army units at Ramadi. In the last two months of the year, the border posts began to take form north of Walid, and the makings of a three-brigade Department of Border Enforcement structure emerged: 1st Brigade operating from an-Najaf and covering all the posts facing Saudi Arabia; 2d Brigade at Waleed operated four battalions covering the posts facing Jordan and Syria, and a new 3d Brigade at al-Qaim operated a single battalion stationed in Area of Operations Saber. The seven Marine Corps transition teams operated with the 2d and 3d Brigades, and two units of Regimental Combat Team 2 provided the decisive military power if required: 1st Light Armored Reconnaissance Battalion (Korean Village) and 3d Battalion, 6th Marines (al-Qaim).

From the outset of its campaign, the II MEF staff planned to eventually receive control of two Iraqi Army divisions comprising six brigades and 18 battalions for operational commitment in al-Anbar Province, with another brigade and three battalions established in an-Najaf and northern Babil Province. In tandem with the political consolidation of the Iraqi government through the national elections, establishing a trained and viable Iraqi security force remained the real pillar of achieving regional control.

The Iraqi Army lacked a combat service support capability and remained dependent upon Coalition support. Contractors built a support base at Habbaniyah for a division headquarters and two brigades. Some form of base support unit was proposed for Habbaniyah as the initial Iraqi logistics hub for al-Anbar Province with the addition of another when a second division came to al-Anbar Province. A nearby "India" base was built to support the third brigade.

The units of the new Iraqi Army replaced the last of the Iraqi National Guard battalions that had proven ineffective in al-Anbar Province because of their evident tribal affiliation and vulnerability to the insurgent murder and intimidation campaign. Thus, no new Army units reconstituted from formerly Sunni-affiliated National Guard forces were acceptable in al-Anbar Province, and the Iraqi Ministry of Defense policy took recruits from al-Anbar Province to units outside the province.

Initially, the Ministry of Defense and the Coalition command assigned the 1st and 7th Iraqi Army Divisions to II MEF for employment in counterinsurgency operations. In addition, the 25th Brigade, organic to the 8th Division, drew the assignment to the an-Najaf and northern Babil Province sector (Area of Operation Biloxi). In all, the Coalition planned sending seven Iraqi brigades to Multi National Force–West in addition to the specialized military and paramilitary units designed for border and internal security tasks.

Under the same plan, the Iraqi 1st Division headquarters at Habbiniyah exercised control over all Ministry of Defense units from Ramadi to the eastern boundary of Area of Operations Raleigh. From Ramadi, the 7th Division headquarters controlled similar forces west of Ramadi to the Syrian border.

Numerous operational requirements existed throughout the Marine Corps zone of action and several Iraqi Army battalions and brigades deployed to al-Anbar Province before the 7th Division established its headquarters in the province.

The conditions demanded considerable operational flexibility by the fledgling Iraqi units to operate with their American counterparts before the rest of the Iraqi Army had in fact developed as a fully capable and manned combat force.

Timing, as usual, counted for almost everything. By October 2005, the 1st and 4th Brigades of the 8th Division, based at an-Najaf and Karbala, operated three battalions, all partnered with the U.S. 155th Brigade in Area of Operations Biloxi with military

transition teams provided by the 155th. These teams rated the battalions as becoming militarily capable in three to six months. The Iraqi 1st Division, which had a Marine Corps transition team since May, arrived in Camp Habbiniyah in October. Most of its three brigades and nine battalions preceded it, but it required another three to four months to reach a "capable" rating. That tentative status did not apply to the 1st and 2d Battalions, 1st Brigade, 1st Division, which had joined the U.S. Army's 2d Brigade at Ramadi and Regimental Combat Team 2 at Hit and Haditha during Operation Guardian Sword.

Characteristic of the initial operations of the Iraqi security forces, those two battalions had operated without their parent brigade (never assigned to al-Anbar Province) under direct control of 2d Marine Division, yet remained two to six months short of being fully fighting capable because of their chronic shortage of personnel. The Iraqi 7th Division headquarters lagged considerably in arriving in the province, first to Fallujah in January and then to the Iraqi compound in Camp Blue Diamond, Ramadi in late February 2006. Its 1st and 2d Battalions, 1st Brigade, had joined the U.S. Army 2d Brigade at Ramadi during Operation Guardian Sword. Their personnel, leadership, and equipment shortfalls placed them in an 8- to 10-month delay in reaching full fighting capability. Their transition teams came from the three Marine Corps border transition teams left unassigned because of delays in activating the Iraqi units to cover the Syrian frontier. The remaining units of 7th Division formed in July–September 2005 and after training deployed to al-Anbar Province from September 2005 to January 2006.

The manpower requirements for the military transition teams, providing liaison and training advice for elements of the Iraqi Army sent to the II MEF area of operations, proved demanding. In addition, local U.S. commanders and staffs spent considerable effort mentoring their counterparts. These demands fell upon the combat units despite efforts by Marine Corps Headquarters and the Multi National Forces–Iraq to provide them from the United States and allied nations. In all, the Marine Corps provided 366 officers and enlisted personnel to the teams in 2005, 170 of whom came from II MEF. A few of the II MEF Marines became involved with the unending police training team mission in Fallujah as did Army soldiers in Ramadi. The Iraqi security forces began to assemble under the tactical direction of 2d Marine Division in al-Anbar Province and under the Army 155th Brigade in an-Najaf, northern Babil Province.

Chapter 10

Protecting the Emerging Iraq

The U.S. and Coalition strategy for 2005 was based on two pillars. The first, building security and stability, was showing little headway due to the slow development, provisioning, and deployment of Iraqi military and paramilitary forces. The second, self-government, became the focus of operations in late 2005. Despite the lack of improvement in the security situation, plans proceeded to hold elections for a new national government. Concurrent with these plans, Coalition forces continued to conduct counterinsurgency operations.

Supporting the Election

Operation Liberty Express, lasting from 1 September to 30 December 2005, covered the military actions of II Marine Expeditionary Force and its subordinate units as they provided security and ensured conditions for a successful Iraqi national constitutional referendum on 15 October 2005 and national election on 15 December. Although the 2d Marine Division provided the major contribution to this operation, the 2d Marine Aircraft Wing and the 2d Marine Logistics Group (the new designation for the 2d Force Service Support Group) remained indispensable throughout the operation.

Major General Richard A. Huck published his operations order for Liberty Express on 30 July, setting three phases: completing unit rotation, as an extension of Operation Guardian Sword; supporting the referendum; and supporting the national election. He identified his mission as:

> 2d Marine Division continues partnership with the Iraqi security forces and conducts combined counterinsurgency operations in al-Anbar Province to neutralize anti-Iraqi forces, secure designated polling centers, and provide support to the Independent Election Commission–Iraq to maintain operational momentum, prevent anti-Iraqi force interference with unit rotations, and ensure the conduct of free, fair and legitimate constitutional referendum and national elections.

To support the referendum, the 2d Marine Division planned continuing counterinsurgency campaigns in al-Anbar Province that would provide the secure environment for polling sites managed by the Iraqi transitional government and the election commission. In particular, the subordinate commands would "execute focused disruption operations from 1–12 October, targeting extremist groups with the capability and intent of interfering with the referendum to disrupt their operational planning and execution cycle."

Using Iraqi security forces remained essential to securing and operating the polling sites and providing force protection, transportation, and sustainment. The U.S. and Iraqi forces would have to provide an election support team for each polling site within the zone for liaison with and support to the election workers.

According to the 2d Marine Division estimates, the expected threat to the elections included both Muslim extremists and the Sunni Arab resistance. Muslim extremists sought to inflict a high U.S. and Coalition casualty rate in Iraq while also waging an aggressive information operations campaign to erode public support and force a Coalition withdrawal from Iraq. They also aimed to prevent any strong central government from establishing itself in Iraq. The Sunni Arabs in Iraq had lost ground to the Shi'a and Kurdish factions in the 2004 election, and moderates in their ranks sought to regain some degree of Sunni influence through the political process.

Marine Corps intelligence estimates predicted that insurgents would focus on Ramadi because of its significance in the governmental process and Fallujah because of its symbolic importance. Their expected tactics included attacking polling sites and the areas around them using proven techniques such as indirect fire, improvised explosive devices, and sniping. Their information campaign painted the elections as a conspiracy of the Shi'a, Kurdish, U.S., and Zionist interests against the Sunni Arabs. Thus, the extremists portrayed themselves as the defenders of Sunnis in Iraq.

The Coalition hoped that the moderate Sunnis and some insurgent groups would urge their followers to vote and avoid the debacle caused by the Sunni boycott of the 2004 elections. The Coalition feared that uncontrollable sectarian violence would persuade

Photo by SSgt Michael E. Schellenbach, Defense Imagery, VIRIN 050708-M-9708S-020

MajGen Richard A. Huck, commanding general, 2d Marine Division, speaks with Marines from Regimental Combat Team 8 at Camp Fallujah in the summer of 2005.

Sunni Arabs that a favorable outcome in the elections remained impossible. Such an outcome could lead Sunnis to align with extremist elements.

General Huck and 2d Marine Division planners sought to meet these conditions by combining the types of combat operations successfully used in Operation Guardian Sword with a civil affairs campaign that focused on the local Sunni leaders and public opinion. The II MEF Campaign Plan thus continued in effect with the goals of interdiction in Regimental Combat Team 2's Area of Operations Denver, neutralizing extremists in the Army 2d Brigade, 28th Infantry Division's Area of Operations Topeka (which included ar-Ramadi), while continuing to control al-Fallujah and the remainder of Regimental Combat Team 8's Area of Operations Raleigh. Marines estimated that they could maintain operational momentum throughout al-Anbar Province and thereby disrupt insurgent operations, develop and act upon intelligence, and establish a "relatively secure environment" for the Iraqi referendum and election. In contrast to 2004, Marines could look to newly arriving Iraqi units, with up to three brigades joining to add combat power and an improved measure of in-

ternal security in the cities. The orders to civil affairs commanders and planners were equally clear. They were to continue efforts supporting the nascent provincial councils and provincial reconstruction development committees and to improve economic and infrastructure development throughout al-Anbar Province. Specific actions, however, would also support the elections. These included persuading local Iraqi leaders to encourage their followers to participate in the electoral process and to themselves educate the populace about the elections and their importance. On the other hand, the U.S. forces had to avoid a perception that they controlled or directed the election process, which had to remain an autonomous and fair Iraqi action in the eyes of all. Finally, Marine commanders ordered a surge in counterinsurgency operations immediately before the voting days that, combined with the civil-military engagement of the al-Anbar leaders at municipal and provincial level, would persuade the Iraqi public that participating in the voting was safe.

Supporting the elections required considerable planning and allocation of resources for both the 15 October and 15 December polls. Throughout the II

MEF zone of responsibility, Marines set up several dozen voting centers, encompassing 15 to 24 sites in each area of operations to handle the voter turnout, which the Iraqi Independent Election Commission estimated would be some 575,000 persons in al-Anbar Province. At each of the polls, election support teams of one or two Marines or soldiers and an interpreter would maintain order over the election commission workers and equipment provided by the Coalition. They also served to maintain liaison and communications at each site with the U.S. and Coalition forces. In the 2d Marine Division areas of responsibility, for example, more than 170 military personnel and 70 interpreters comprised this contingent. Although many of these Marines and soldiers came from the civil affairs units, the combat and support units of the division provided approximately half of these personnel.

Logistical support for the estimated 3,000 poll workers included flying them from Baghdad International Airport to al-Asad and al-Taqaddum Air Base, and driving workers to camps where they received billeting and subsistence, and instruction from the election commission. Poll workers hired within the province reported to local bases for transportation to the camps. From there, the election workers were driven to military forward operating bases near their polls three or four days before the elections. At each point of entry, the forces screened and processed the poll workers and segregated potential security risks for further scrutiny. At all assembly locations for the poll workers, Coalition forces provided emergency medical care, billeting, feeding, and hygienic facilities.

Security measures for the poll worker camps and voting sites required dedicated security forces in both close and distant protection modes and materials for segregating the inner and middle cordons and the traffic and entry checkpoints. Fortification material came from the 30th Naval Construction Regiment while 2d Force Service Support Group provided all other items. Election materials arrived in packaged containers for each site, and election commission personnel retained responsibility for the chain of custody and accountability of ballots. Route security measures included surged sweeps by both ground

LCpl Mike O'Rielly, attached to Company A, 1st Battalion, 5th Marines, checks an ID card as he searches Iraqis in Ramadi for weapons and contraband. Throughout 2005, Anbar's capital city was targeted by insurgents because of its administrative and political importance.

Photo by LCpl Kenneth Lane, Defense Imagery, VIRIN: 050518-M-0616L-016

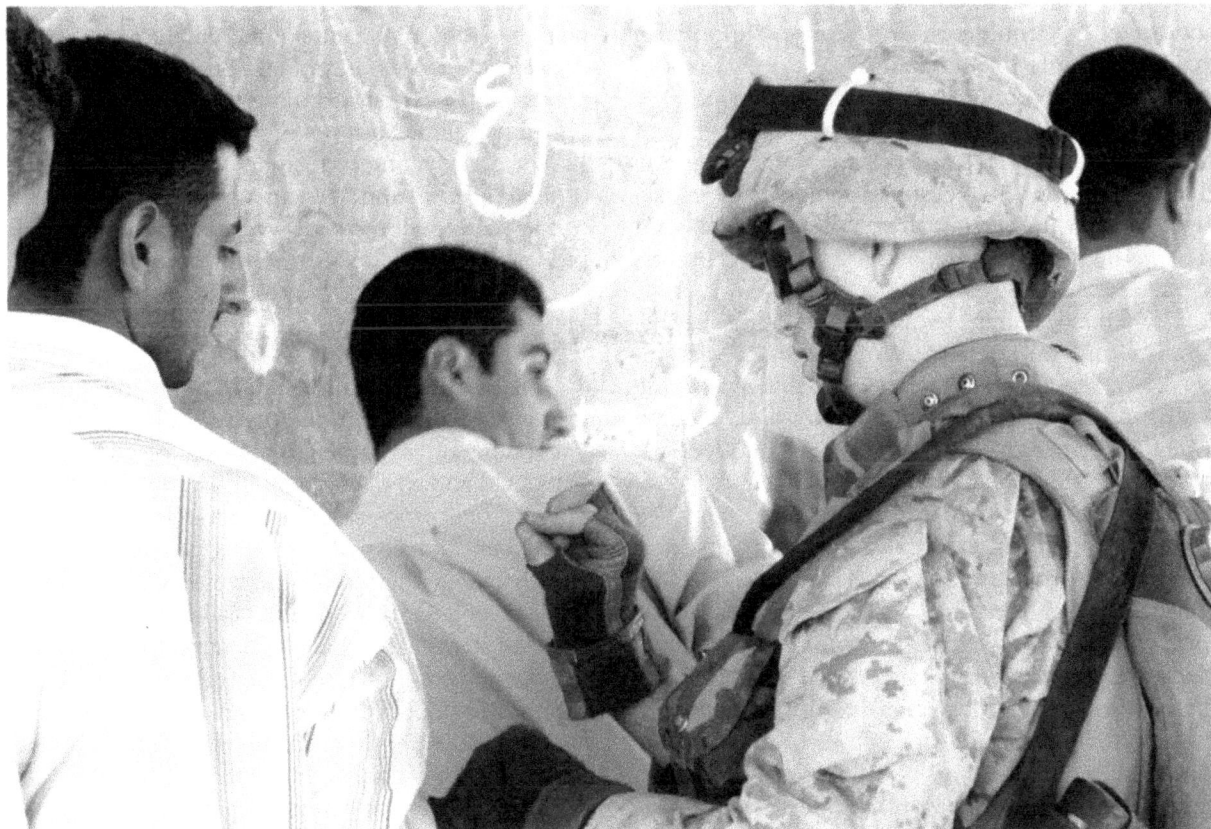

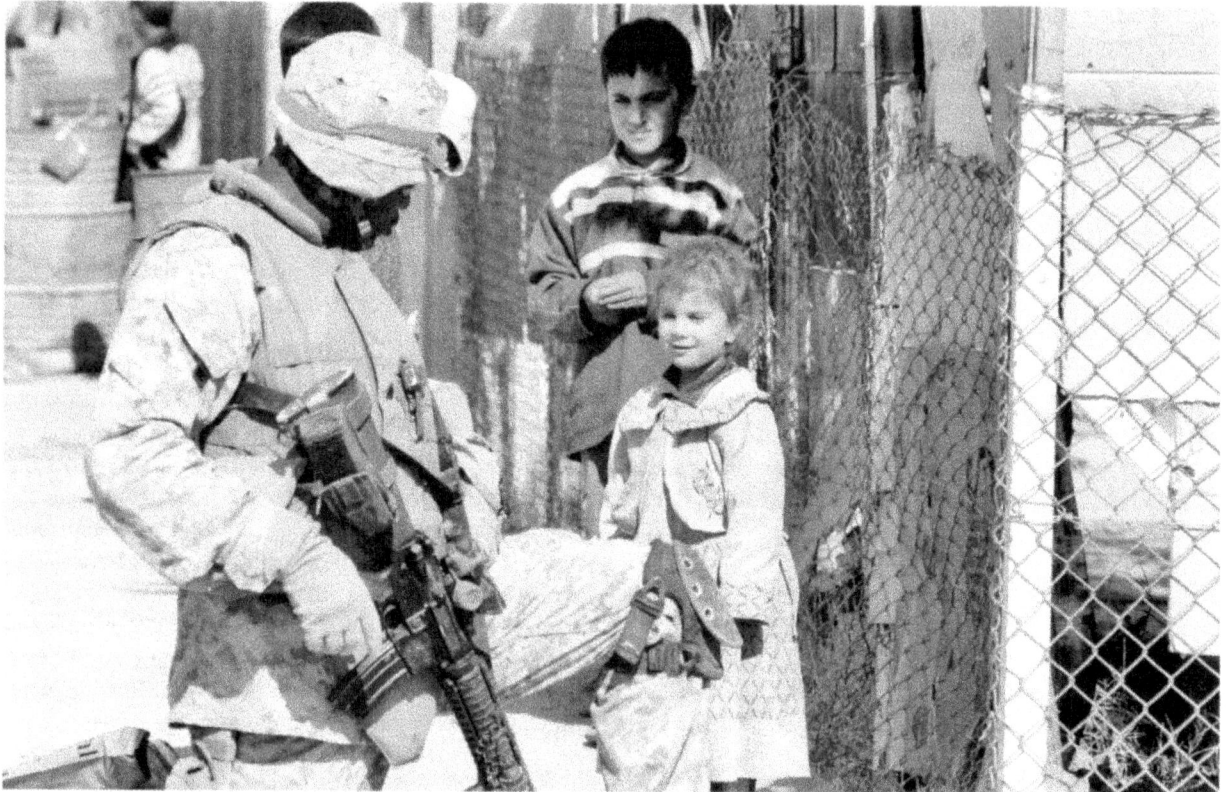

Sgt Dennis Howard of the 6th Civil Affairs Group interacts with Iraqi children at the displaced persons compound in Husaybah during Operation Steel Curtain.

and aerial electronic devices. Aviation support remained dedicated to normal military operations in September and early October, although the KC-130 transport-refueler aircraft would support movement of election commission and polling workers into the air bases. During 11–14 October, and on election day, most rotary-wing aircraft (transport and attack) increased flights to support aerial and ground movements.

The 6th Civil Affairs Group relieved the 5th Civil Affairs Group between 8 September and 22 September 2005. Much of the efforts required in working with local leaders and public affairs would come from the newly arrived group. Colonel Paul W. Brier's concept of support called for a major effort to engage the provincial and local civilian leadership. The governor, provincial council, and mayors received briefings to inform them of the importance of the constitutional referendum, to encourage them to inform their constituents, and to provide them with election materials for their constituents. Working with the governorate election official of the Independent Election Commission, Marines of the 6th Civil Affairs Group sought to help develop ideas and strategies to identify poll workers from al-Anbar Province and

help the election commission inform the public about the election processes. Colonel Brier's command also played a key role in planning the movement, billeting, and training of polling workers for al-Anbar Province, providing civil affairs Marines as members of the election support teams as well as liaison personnel during all the poll workers' movements and processing.

Counterinsurgency Operations Before the Elections

The combat operations supporting the summer turnover of units and personnel gradually evolved into a new series of operations designed to shape the battlefield and to disrupt any insurgent disruption of the electoral processes. The operational pattern remained unchanged, as noted above, in Major General Huck's orders: interdict in the west, neutralize insurgents around Ramadi, and hold Fallujah and areas further east under firm Coalition control. Largely for this reason, Operation Hunter continued as Operation Hunter II. Not only did the operations support the establishment of the Iraqi forces in al-Anbar Province and strengthen the border defenses, but they also covered the desired interdiction of the al-Qaim–Hit

Throughout 2005, many of the strategic border forts along the Syrian-Iraqi Border were incomplete and in a state of disrepair. Among them was Border Fort 4 near Husaybah, shown earlier in August 2004.

corridor of the western Euphrates River Valley.

Phase II of Operation Hunter in September continued the efforts to restore Iraqi control of its border with Syria. In addition, II MEF received orders to construct two combat outposts, north and south of the river. These would support the border defenses that the Department of Border Enforcement began to reconstruct on the Syrian border region. Coalition engineers would build the combat outpost in the south while an Iraqi contractor built the other on the northern side of the river valley. The planned presence of Coalition forces, mostly border units and Iraqi Army units, would at last cover the western Euphrates River Valley. The Iraqi Army would also establish permanent garrisons in al-Qaim, Rawah, Haditha, and Hit. By default, combat service would have to provide support for all the Iraqi and Marine Corps forces in western al-Anbar Province. In addition, Marines established random vehicle checkpoints on the routes connecting al-Qaim, Haditha, and Hit. As a new initiative, they destroyed bridges across the Euphrates at key crossing sites near the Syrian border, thus depriving infiltrators their usual line of communication. As a matter of priority, the Haditha sector was chosen

for special attention before the referendum, and al-Qaim before the national election. This prioritization clearly reflected the relative security of each sector and the limited military resources, a perennial problem in western al-Anbar Province. Destroying the bridges also indicated the weakness of the border security, and the construction of Border Forts 1 through 8 remained slow, with Forts 1 through 4 still incomplete at year's end.

After receiving approval from Central Command and Multi National Corps–Iraq headquarters to remove the bridges from the "No Strike" target list, Marine air started bombing the bridges (the Al Bu Hardan and Mish Al Bridges crossing the Euphrates northeast of Karabila and east of al-Ubayd) on 3 September. On 3 September, the aircraft dropped inert guided BDU-type 500-pound cement-filled practice bombs, reporting some damage to the bridges, but imagery showed three of the eight bombs did not strike the bridges. Accordingly, the Regimental Combat Team 2's planners requested another attack. On 6 September, aircraft dropped GBU-12 bombs directed at the bridge abutments. Again, desired effects were not achieved and required an additional strike.

Table 10-1: October 2005 Voting Patterns

Governorate	Demographics	Votes	Percentage For	Percentage Against
Karbala	Shi'a Arab majority	264,674	96.58	3.42
An Najaf	Shi'a Arab majority	299,420	95.82	4.18
Al-Anbar	Sunni Arab majority	259,919	3.04	96.9
Total		9,852,291	78.59	21.41

On 11–12 September, the attacks resumed after preparing targeting packages employing M270A1 guided multiple-launched rocket systems supporting the Army units in Area of Operations Sabre. Six rockets hit the Mish Al Bridge and destroyed it. Aircraft attacked Al Bu Hardan Bridge with GBU-38 and GBU-12 bombs following a mechanical malfunction of both M270A1 launchers. The eight 500-pound bombs used this time achieved the desired effects.

Due to the lack of available forces in western al-Anbar Province, the 2d Marine Division concurred in the destruction of the bridges without using forward controllers or the direct involvement of ground troops. Given the number of units rotating in Regimental Combat Team 2 during the month, small scale local raids and patrolling remained the norm except for the Army units operating in Area of Operations Sabre.

The 2d Light Armored Reconnaissance Battalion developed Operation Cyclone with Regimental Combat Team 2 support to clear ar-Rutbah of persistent insurgent activity. Assembling reinforcements at nearby Camp Korean Village on 9 September, the battalion commander, Lieutenant Colonel Austin E. Ren-

forth, and his staff briefed and incorporated 2d Force Reconnaissance Company; Company K, 3d Battalion, 6th Marines, and an Iraqi special forces unit into his task force. Moving out of their camp at 0100 on 11 September, the light armored reconnaissance units established a cordon of the city and launched two assault forces to clear its eastern and western parts. The force reconnaissance and Iraqi Special Forces troops cleared their sectors from north to south. Moving in the opposite direction, the Marines of Company K, reinforced by a section of amphibious assault vehicles and a platoon of Company C, 2d Light Armored Reconnaissance Battalion, cleared their zone. At 1100 the next day, the troops had detained a total of 61 people and had confiscated numerous weapons and explosive devices.

The relative lull during September permitted the planning of several larger scale operations for October, and here Operation Hunter II began to show some results. The operations of October coincided with the arrival of three battalions of the Iraqi 7th Division's 3d Brigade, deploying to Hit, Haditha, and Rawah. At the same time, the Iraqi 1st Brigade, 1st Division, established its headquarters at al-Qaim with its

SSgt Dan Jamison, crewchief of a UH-1N Huey helicopter of Marine Light Attack Squadron 369, checks his GAU-16/A machine gun while flying close air support over Ubadyi during Operation Steel Curtain in November 2005.

Photo by Cpl James P. Aguilar, VIRIN: 051115-M-6538A-154

Iraqi men and woman wait in line prior to casting their votes on the constitutional referendum at a polling station in Mosul on 15 October 2005.

1st Battalion, the beginning of a long awaited Iraqi covering force on the Syrian border in al-Anbar Province.

Lieutenant Colonel Julian D. Alford's 3d Battalion, 6th Marines, executed its first major operation since relieving 3d Battalion, 2d Marines, at al-Qaim. Beginning in the early morning hours of 1 October, the battalion began to clear the village of Sadah and the eastern half of Karabilah under Operation Iron Fist, a seven-day effort designed to eradicate insurgents, clear routes, and establish battle positions. It also provided a deception operation to distract insurgents while units assembled and prepared for Operation River Gate. Supported by a platoon each of tanks, combat engineers, and assault amphibious vehicles, Alford's task force cleared Sadah from east to west with three rifle companies on line the first day. Insurgents fought from prepared positions with small arms, rocket launchers, mortars, and explosive devices. In sporadic fighting, the Marines killed an estimated 12 enemy and encamped in positions on a wadi separating Sadah from Karabilah. A troop of the 4th Squadron, 14th Cavalry, screened the left bank of the Euphrates River, and mobile assault platoons of the Marine battalion's weapons company blocked the roads between the two towns.

The next day saw much stiffer opposition from the insurgents fighting from Karabilah. Advancing through the town over the next three days, Marines employed all their direct fire weapons and mortars, and Marine aircraft delivered rockets, Hellfire missiles, and GBU-12 and -38 guided bombs. The enemy death toll increased to 51 while the task force suffered one Marine killed and 12 wounded. The operation ended on 7 October, with two battle positions constructed for rifle platoons. Patrolling and small arms engagements continued for several weeks. The 3d Battalion, 6th Marines, now had a foothold for continued operations to the west. But that moment would await further reinforcement and Operation Steel Curtain. Until then, Marines killed an estimated 200 insurgents while operating from the new battle positions and Camp Gannon. Lieutenant Colonel Alford's double-size sniper platoon of some 38 Marines accounted for most of the enemy killed, followed in number of kills by his attached tank platoon and battalion heavy machine guns.

The Army's 2d Brigade, 28th Infantry Division, executed its own large-scale sweep at the same time on the southern outskirts of Ramadi. Operation Mountaineers sought to kill or capture insurgents and to locate arms caches on 4 October. After four Boeing CH-47E Chinook helicopters lifted A Troop, 1st Squadron, 167th Cavalry, into a blocking position southeast of the city, Company C, 1st Battalion, 172d Armor Battalion, established a cordon isolating the southeast corner of the city from the north. Two Army infantry companies, accompanied by the Iraqi 1st and 3d Battalions, 1st Brigade, 7th Division, cleared and secured their targeted districts on the southern side of the canal, while 3d Battalion, 7th Marines, cleared the northern side accompanied by the 2d Iraqi Battalion and supported by a tank platoon of Company D, 2d Battalion, 69th Armor. Marines, soldiers, and Iraqi troops searched all houses and vehicles in a major demonstration of combined U.S. and Iraqi military presence. After being attacked by explosive devices, small arms, and rocket fire, the 3d Battalion, 7th Marines, called in both fixed- and rotary-wing air support, which remained overhead until all objectives had been cleared and the ground Marines had returned to their base.

With the even larger Operation River Gate, Regimental Combat Team 2 placed more pressure on insurgent groups operating in the western Eurphrates River Valley, well-timed with Operation Iron Fist. Commencing on 3 October, elements of three U.S. and one Iraqi battalions searched the towns of Haditha, Haqlaniyah, and Barwanah, the scene of the impromptu Operation Quick Strike conducted in reaction to the killing of the Marine sniper teams of 3d Battalion, 25th Marines, in August. In addition to killing foreign fighters and insurgent groups, Colonel Davis sought to establish a U.S. and later Iraqi army presence and in general prepare these towns for elections.

Under the control of Colonel Davis and his Regimental Combat Team 2 command group, the operation opened with isolation moves blocking movement out of the target area: an Iraqi special operations company blocked movement to the north near Haditha Dam, and on the left bank of the Euphrates River, the Iraqi 7th Reconnaissance Battalion, 7th Division, covered the eastern flank while 1st Light Armored Reconnaissance Battalion screened and then occupied Barwanah. On the right bank, 3d Battalion, 504th Parachute Infantry, moved against Haqlaniyah by air assault, using 12 CH-46E helicopters supported by 3d Platoon, Company B, 1st Tank Battalion, and a company of the Iraqi 2d Battalion, 1st Brigade, 1st Division. At Haditha, 3d Battalion, 1st Marines, commanded by Lieutenant Colonel Jeffrey R. Chessani, moved into three zones supported by the tank company headquarters and 1st Platoon; another company from the Iraqi 2d Battalion, 1st Brigade; and the 2d Battalion, 3d Brigade, 7th Division.

During this operation, Iraqi troops discovered sophisticated propaganda production equipment in a house in Haditha. The items seized included numerous al-Qaeda in Iraq compact discs and audiotapes,

LCpl Christopher Ahrens of 1st Platoon, Company G, 2d Battalion, 2d Marines, uses the scope on his M4 rifle to scan the horizon during a security patrol in downtown Kharma in October 2005.

Photo by Sgt Paul S. Mancuso, Defense Imagery VIRIN: 051026-M-5213M-032

Photo by LCpl Samuel D. Corum, Defense Imagery, VIRIN: 051118-M-6412C-004

In the early morning fog outside a forward operations base in November 2005, vehicles of Company E, 2d Battalion, 2d Marines, await their drivers who are preparing for Operation Trifecta in Zaidon.

three computers, several printers, banner makers, multi-disc copiers, and thousands of blank discs and tapes. Troops later discovered a complete bomb-making facility in the same town.

When the operation terminated on 20 October, Huck reported construction of the firm bases underway and polling places secured. The damage to the enemy included 12 enemy killed and 172 suspects detained with 30 caches and 96 explosive devices discovered. The 3d Platoon, Company C, 1st Combat Engineer Battalion, built the firm bases Sparta, Raider, and Horno in the three towns (Haditha, Haqlaniyah and Barwanah). In addition to the helicopter support for the Army paratroopers, Regimental Combat Team 2 also conducted a combined air assault raid by 2d Force Reconnaissance Company and the Iraqi special operations company in the vicinity of Abu Hyat against a known, high-value target, taking several detainees in the process. Marines called for air support to deliver ordnance as large as 2,000-pound bombs, when targeting a cave complex.

Operations Iron Fist and River Gate also covered part of the continued Iraqi Army movement into al-

Anbar Province, as the three battalions of the Iraqi 3d Brigade, 7th Division, deployed to Hit, Haditha, and Rawah, while the 1st Brigade headquarters and its 1st Battalion of the 1st Division deployed to al-Qaim. On 13 October came another welcome reinforcement in the form of the 13th Marine Expeditionary Unit (13th MEU) under Colonel James K. La Vine, reporting to Huck for tactical direction after it reported to Major General Stephen T. Johnson for operations and received its own Area of Operations Tucson on 26 October, where it began counterinsurgency and route security operations.

The Constitutional Referendum, 15 October 2005

During the weekend of 1–2 October, the Independent Election Commission–Iraq, apparently on the basis of local sentiments and to demonstrate greater autonomy, changed the logistics and security arrangements for the more settled parts of al-Anbar Province. Instead of using the voting centers surveyed and secured by Coalition forces, the election commission opened approximately 87 independent centers, operated and provisioned by the local Iraqi population, with local police and unarmed guards for security. Accordingly, the centers east of Ramadi to the eastern limits of the II MEF area of operations operated with Facility Protection Service and Iraqi police security. In the western zones, the original plan prevailed for employing Iraqi Security Forces, including Iraqi Army troops, in the inner and middle cordons of the polling centers, backed up by Coalition military quick reaction forces at the outer cordon.

Despite these changes, II MEF helped to execute the referendum with few setbacks and successfully supplied, transported, and billeted the poll workers. Providing sufficient food had been more problematic. Contractors provided food to poll workers at al-Asad and Taqaddum Air Bases. Beyond these arrangements, the plan was to provide workers with halal meals and bottled water. Most remained for one to three days at the air bases before moving on to forward bases near their polling centers. In some instances poll workers staged protests due to their dissatisfaction with halal meals. Providing adequate communications for them was also an issue. At Bagh-

dad International Airport, airport security personnel confiscated the cellular telephones of election commission personnel assembled there for flights to al-Asad and Taqaddum Air Bases. Although al-Anbar Province had limited cell phone service, the commission relied on these phones for communications nationwide. Even satellite telephones failed to connect in western al-Anbar Province, and so Marines had to assist in unsnarling the communications at most polling centers.

The commission's expectations for local arrangements in the eastern part of the zone were met. Besides moving commission officials, polling center kits and ballots between air bases and local distribution points, Marines there provided little in the way of logistics support to the commission. The "local" model likely succeeded for a number of reasons such as the improved security environment, emergent Fallujah leadership, and the adaptability of Marine and Army units. The security model used by 2d Marine Division proved effective, however. On 12 October, Marine units seized polling sites and immediately moved pre-staged force protection materials to properly barricade the sites. Between 13 and 14 October, poll

EA-6B Prowler electronic warfare aircraft helped jam insurgent communications during cordon-and-knock operations. Below, a Prowler from Marine Tactical Electronic Warfare Squadron 4 taxis to a hangar at al-Asad Air Base in May 2005.

Photo by LCpl Andrew D. Pendracki, VIRIN: 050511-M-5865P-020

workers occupied the sites with U.S. units providing security escort. While insurgents conducted a few harassing attacks during the referendum, no voters or poll workers were injured at a voting site.

Imperceptible to the outside observer, several measures taken by II MEF provided for better results than in the January 2005 election. In the days leading up to the referendum, 2d Marine Division attacked locations considered likely firing positions for insurgent rocket and mortar attacks by indirect fire. During the January 2005 election, the daily average of indirect fire attacks had increased from the usual 12 to 36 the day before the election to 57 on the day of the election. Radar coverage of potential attack sites was evaluated to ensure previously used firing locations were appropriately covered. In the case of the referendum, no increase in these kinds of attacks occurred. Only five attacks by explosive devices happened during the voting period, all while the supporting electronic warfare aircraft was off-station refueling. The division requested continuous airborne fixed-wing coverage for close air support and surveillance patrols over three sectors: Ramadi-Fallujah, Hit-Haditha, and al-Qaim–Rawah. These aircraft remained on station from six hours before the polls opened until six hours after voting ended. Finally, E-8 Joint Surveillance Target Attack Radar System (J-STARS) aircraft monitored vehicle movement along routes around Ramadi during voting and curfew hours. The aircraft also remained ready to track indirect fire trajectories, although none occurred in that sector.

Due to the detailed planning and actions of Marines, soldiers, and Iraqi security troops, tens of thousands of voters in al-Anbar Province ignored the threat of attack. They cast ballots in the constitutional referendum on a remarkably calm day with isolated insurgent attacks but no major bombings or mass killings. Ramadi, however, remained a problem, and U.S. soldiers forced three of the city's main polling centers to close shortly after opening at 0700. Hospital officials said that at least seven people seeking to vote were killed by insurgents. Ammar Rawi, manager of the electoral commission in Ramadi, added that most of the "turnout came from the outskirts of the city." Muhammed Jamaili, manager of the electoral commission in Fallujah, opined that 93 percent of the city's 257,000 registered voters participated in the referendum. The population in the far west, in the area of Regimental Combat Team 2, cast a mere 7,510 votes, virtually none at Hit and Haditha.

Although Sunni Arabs rejected the terms of the constitution, they took a significant part in the voting in this referendum and therefore in the process of moving toward self-government. The soldiers, sailors and Marines under the direction of II MEF could take pride in the results posted in their areas of responsibility.

With the approval of the constitution, Operation Liberty Express remained in effect to support the required 15 December elections for a permanent government. Had the constitutional referendum failed, the National Assembly would have been dissolved, and a new transitional government would have been elected to attempt to write another permanent constitution, thus reverting to the awkward situation of the previous year.

Continued Counterinsurgency Operations Supporting 'Liberty Express'

Area of Operations Tucson furnished battle space for the newly arrived 13th MEU elements. General Huck charged it with interdicting smugglers and insurgents operating in the vast area between ar-Rutbah in the west and al-Muhammadi in the east, where Iraqi Route 10 approaches its junction with Route 12 (the main route running along the right bank of the Euphrates from Hit to al-Qaim). Because of the frequent assignments of the light armored reconnaissance battalions to operations in the western Euphrates River valley throughout the campaign, Marines had spent little time covering the valley to date. Colonel La Vine established his headquarters at al-Asad Air Base, where his Medium Helicopter Squadron 163 worked under the direction of 2d Marine Aircraft Wing. He detailed 2d Battalion, 1st Marines, to Rutbah on 26 October, where it operated out of Camp Korean Village. At the other extremity of Area of Operations Tucson, Battery C, 1st Battalion, 11th Marines, an artillery battery turned into a provisional rifle company, covered the intersection of the two highways, taking its direction directly from Colonel La Vine's command post. This security mission also served to prepare 13th MEU for its major contribution the next month in Operation Steel Curtain.

The II MEF staff also worked to support the new "Desert Protector" program, used as a form of tribal engagement to produce reliable scouts in the province. The initial cohort came from the Albu Mahal tribe of al-Qaim. They were sent to the East Fallujah Iraqi Army Camp for two weeks of training and then returned to al-Qaim to work with special operations units as scouts. Coalition and Iraqi commands released little information about special forces' missions in Iraq, but 2d Division monthly summaries indicated

Photo by LCpl Sheila M. Brooks, Defense Imagery VIRIN: 051215-M-7404B-007

Iraqi citizens in Husaybah line up to vote in parliamentary elections held on 15 December 2005.

Army, Navy, and Iraqi special forces' missions excluding Area of Operations Biloxi.

In the aftermath of the referendum, where the aim of II MEF actions focused upon the main population centers, the moment finally arrived to pacify the tumultuous border towns around al-Qaim. Operation Steel Curtain was conducted in Husaybah, Karabilah, and Ubaydi from 3 to 22 November. The operation marked the first large-scale employment of multiple battalion-sized units of Iraqi army forces in combined operations with Coalition forces since the second battle of Fallujah. The objective was to restore Iraqi sovereign control along the Iraq-Syria border and to destroy foreign fighters operating throughout the al-Qaim region. Beginning in the summer, the combat capabilities of the Iraqi forces in al-Anbar Province had grown, approaching the numerical equivalent of two full infantry divisions of Iraqi army soldiers. Iraqi soldiers now worked alongside soldiers and Marines in detailed clearing missions. In addition, Iraqi soldiers provided security and helped facilitate the care and well-being of residents displaced from their homes because of the operation. They provided perimeter security and screened displaced civilians to detect foreign fighters trying to infiltrate the shelter areas or to escape cordons. They also helped to distribute thousands of meals, blankets, and health and sanitation items to their fellow citizens. Operation Steel Curtain also saw the employment of locally recruited and specially trained scout platoons. The Desert Protectors assisted the combat units clearing the city. Because of their familiarity with the region, the local tribes and dialects, these scouts could detect suspicious individuals, including terrorists attempting to evade identification by wearing women's clothing. Twenty-one suspected insurgents were discovered hiding among the civilians in a displacement camp near Ubaydi.

Assembling more than 4,500 Marines, sailors, and soldiers, for the largest Marine Corps operation since Operation al-Fajr, Colonel Davis' Regimental Combat Team 2 began Steel Curtain with a clearing of Husaybah. His task organization for the operation included 3d Battalion, 6th Marines, Battalion Landing Team 2d Battalion, 1st Marines from 13th MEU; 1st Light Armored Reconnaissance Battalion, 2d Force Reconnaissance Company; 3d Battalion, 504th Parachute Infantry; 4th Squadron, 14th Cavalry, and the Iraqi 1st Battalion, 1st Brigade, 1st Division (later joined by 2d and 3d Battalions). Moving in the early hours of 1 November, 3d Battalion, 6th Marines, concentrated its three rifle companies at Camp Gannon facing the town with the Syrian frontier to the rear. Affecting a lodgment in the town's northwestern corner at 0400 on 5 November and then joined by a company of the Iraqi 1st Battalion, 1st Brigade, the battalion held while 2d Battalion, 1st Marines, and another Iraqi company moved into the southwest quadrant of the town and came abreast at about 1000 . Together, the two battalions then advanced to clear every structure in Husaybah, from west to east. By the end of the first day, the two battalions held a quarter of the town, inflicting several casualties on the insurgents and foreign fighters, who defended with small arms, rocket launchers, and explosive devices. In three days, the two battalions cleared the town and encamped on its eastern limits, having killed dozens of enemy and detaining more than 200 additional suspects while other elements of Regimental Combat Team 2 gathered several hundred displaced persons into holding areas where they received food, water, and medical attention, and processing.

The two battalions continued across an open triangular area between Husabayah and the next objective, western Karabalah, clearing houses and encountering explosive devices and mines the next two days, 8-9 November. Shifting to the north, the 3d Battalion, 6th Marines, cleared western Karibalah from north to south in three days, encountering mostly mines and booby traps, while 2d Battalion, 1st Marines, moved west to east in coordination. By 12 November, both of these towns had been cleared of enemy insurgents, foreign fighters, and their explosive devices.

Leaving 3d Battalion, 6th Marines, holding the two

After three months of negotiations following the 15 December 2005 national elections, Nouri al-Maliki (below) became Prime Minister of a national coalition government in Iraq.

Photo by Sgt David J. Murphy, Defense Imagery, VIRIN: 070313-M-0948M-046

cleared towns, 2d Battalion, 1st Marines, and the Army parachute infantry battalion shifted east to repeat the clearing operation, this time at Ubaydi. Beginning in the early morning of 14 November, the Army paratroopers cleared Old Ubaydi in a day, while 2d Battalion, 1st Marines, took two days to clear New Ubaydi against stiff opposition. The 2d and 3d Battalions of the Iraqi 1st Brigade also provided a company each in the clearing of this, the last targeted town of the operation. With the occupation of a battle position in Ubaydi by Weapons Company, 3d Battalion, 6th Marines, all three towns had been cleared. As Lieutenant Colonel Alford noted to a combat correspondent on 20 November, "This place has needed to be cleaned out for awhile."

The two Marine Corps assault battalions lost 10 men killed in the operation, and a total of 59 Army and Marine Corps and nine Iraqi Army wounded. The enemy lost 139 killed with one wounded prisoner. A further 388 suspected insurgents became detainees and more than 1,000 displaced persons entered Coalition humanitarian relief facilities from Husabayah and Ubaiydi. Operation Steel Curtain saw nearly continuous air support, with 67 air strikes called in by controllers. Over 100 precision-guided munitions were employed during this operation. Aviation also played a key role by providing combat re-supply of tank ammunition and water as well as multiple casualty evacuation missions.

In the aftermath of Operation Steel Curtain, the Iraqi 1st Brigade began to establish itself with headquarters at al-Qaim. As the soldiers of its 1st Battalion patrolled the streets of Husaybah, Karabilah and Ubaydi, the 3d Battalion occupied the newly built northern combat outpost on 30 November, partnering with 4th Squadron, 14th Cavalry, in backing up the reoccupied border forts to the north of the Euphrates, and the 2d Battalion occupied the southern combat outpost on 14 November, although then only 15 percent complete.

The upcoming rotation of the Army's 155th Brigade signified that a relief of its 2d Battalion, 114th Field Artillery, at Hit would become necessary. The Army declined to replace the battalion, so the II MEF and 2d Marine Division commanders alerted Colonel La Vine that 13th MEU would take responsibility for Hit and its surrounding battle space. On 23 November, Colonel La Vine assumed tactical control of the Army battalion, the Iraqi 1st Battalion, 2d Brigade, 7th Division, and a new Area of Operation Fairbanks.

This area assigned not only Hit to the 13th MEU but also maintained much of the eastern portion of former Area of Operations Tucson. After a brief period of reconstitution, 2d Battalion, 1st Marines relieved the Army unit at Hit, supported by Lieutenant Colonel Donald J. Liles' MEU Service Support Group 13, with a transfer of authority on 10 December 2005. As the national election approached, the 2d Battalion, 1st Marines, undertook a clearing action across the Euphrates from Hit in Operation Iron Hammer from 30 November to 4 December. While the 2d Battalion, 114th Field Artillery, and 1st Battalion, 2d Brigade, 7th Division, maintained security in Hit itself, the Marine battalion, the 1st Company of the Iraqi battalion, and 30 Desert Protector scouts crossed to clear the Hai Al Becker district and to establish a base for the Iraqi battalion to occupy, thereby securing the eastern side of the city. With this improvement of security, the Hit Bridge was opened to foot traffic. During this operation, troops destroyed five explosive devices and detained 19 suspected insurgents.

During the same month, Regimental Combat Team 8, now under command of Colonel David H. Berger, conducted Operation Trifecta from 10 to 20 November to disrupt insurgent activity in the Zaidon area. This operation included aviation support with a simultaneous insertion of 144 Marines into three landing zones. The 2d Battalion, 2d Marines, conducted a helicopter born cordon of Sadan Market while follow-on forces conducted the sweep. This rapid cordon prevented insurgents from escaping. The cordon and knock operation also integrated communications jamming by EA-6B Prowler electronic warfare aircraft. The 1st Reconnaissance Battalion also conducted a helicopter insertion to support its Operation Southern Hunter.

These battalion sweeps resulted in the capture of numerous arms caches and detainees, but no close combat occurred. The reconnaissance battalion also received dedicated utility helicopter support on strip alert if its sniper teams were compromised. These aircraft also performed other missions, but launched with the sniper extract locations already briefed in case they were needed. Ongoing missions included company-sized raids, cordon and knock operations, and convoy escort. For example, on 1 December, a sniper attack on civilians produced a two-company sweep by 2d Battalion, 6th Marines, aided by Iraqi Army search teams and a FAST platoon (Fleet Antiterroist Security Team) through city zones 51 and 52 to find and to kill the snipers.

The 2d Brigade, 28th Infantry Division, conducted Operation Tigers (25–26 November), a clearing operation in the Mulaab District of eastern Ramadi with both fixed- and rotary-wing aircraft in support. Colonel Gronski then sent the 3d Battalion, 7th Marines, and the 2d Battalion, 1st Brigade, 7th Division, against the same area for a cordon and search operation and targeted raids, continuing into the adjacent al-Dubaht District in his Operation Shank during 2–3 December to find weapons caches and to disrupt enemy activity. Similar operations covered most other districts of the city, along with an intensive route clearance effort and several terrain-denial artillery missions, all in late November through mid-December. In a local setback, soldiers had to raid the home of Brigadier General Shakir to recover the Iraqi Police payroll on 4 November. New Iraqi units arrived in Ramadi, including the 2d Special Police Commando Brigade on 7 December and the 1st Company, 9th

Table 10-2: Operations Sayaid 2004–05 Summary

II MEF Direct Action	Enemy Direct Action	Casualty Summary
176 Air strikes	26 Complex attacks	
2 Ground guided missile strikes	315 Indirect fire attacks	50 U.S. killed
279 Engagements of enemy actions	310 Total explosive/mine attacks	324 U.S. wounded
678 IED and mine discoveries	241 explosives attacks	57 U.S. Non-battle Injuries
20 Vehicle bomb discoveries	3 vehicle bomb attacks	4 U.S. Non-battle deaths
499 Cache discoveries	12 Suicide vehicle bomb attacks	15 Iraqi forces killed
509 Detainee events = 2308 detainees	53 Mine attacks	89 Iraqi forces wounded
633 Escalation of force incidents	1 Suicide vest bomber	1 Iraqi force non-battle deaths
11 Battalion level operations	310 Small arms/rocket attacks	5 Iraqi forces non-battle injuries
5 Recuiting events = 150 recruits		757 Enemy killed
34 Raids, targeted		64 Enemy wounded
17 Mosque enteries		
16 Cordon and search, targeted		
2,430,000 Leaflets dropped		

Tank Battalion, equipped with T-55 tanks, on 10 December, indicating the importance of taming this most dangerous Iraqi city.

Supporting the National Election (15 December 2005)

Marine Corps and Army commanders in al-Anbar Province benefited greatly from the previous experiences with election security and support. Planning for the national election in December now incorporated the contingencies of adjusting to frequent and unpredictable changes in the concept for conduct of the election by the Independent Electoral Commission of Iraq. This aspect bore fruit right away because the commission this time allowed the citizens of Ramadi to provide security for the voting sites within the provincial capitol and surrounding area. Ultimately, this concept provided an expanded voting opportunity by adding to the number of polls on election day. The Action Plan to increase Sunni participation in Ramadi from only two percent for the October 15 Referendum was based on the assumption that intimidation by al-Qaeda of Iraq and other extremist and foreign groups was the principal cause of the province's chaos. The plan's countermeasures included the assignment of the 2d Special Police Commando Brigade and the Iraqi Army tank company to Ramadi to assist in bolstering official Iraqi presence in the city.

As before, the 2d Marine Division and 155th Brigade Combat Team began securing voting sites on 12 December and transporting poll workers and material from forward bases to election sites. In eastern al-Anbar Province, U.S. and Iraqi forces provided area security and limited logistics support for the 113 Independent Election Commission voting centers. In western al-Anbar Province the Coalition forces provided both area and point security and logistics support for 30 Coalition-established sites. By noon on 14 December, troops or police had secured all polling centers throughout al-Anbar Province with their workers inside.

To facilitate the vote and aid security measures, the Iraqi government declared a national holiday during 13–15 December, a nationwide curfew for 13–17 December from 2200 to 0600, and a prohibition on carrying of weapons, even with a valid weapons card, during 13–17 December. In addition, the government closed international and provincial borders, except for fuel, food, and medical vehicles; closed international airports; placed all security forces on full standby status; and prohibited vehicular movement during 14–17 December except for security forces and vehicles with

placards issued by the Ministry of Interior.

Essentially, the U.S. forces in al-Anbar Province employed the same measures for air and electronic support, and surveillance as in the October referendum, achieving at least equal success. Approximately 800 poll workers and election support team members were flown by helicopter between the transit centers, such as al-Asad Air Base, and nine outlying sites. While complex, the air movements were executed smoothly because lift requirements and movement plans were identified and coordinated with higher headquarters early in the planning process and then synchronized daily with subordinate units. Additionally, back up ground movement plans were developed as an alternative if inclement weather precluded air operations. Providing contracted hot meals for poll workers helped maintain morale and alleviate behavior problems. In addition, commission officials billeted at the command and control locations for extended periods required sustenance. In eastern al-Anbar Province, Coalition and Iraqi army forces provided area security, while Iraqi police and local guards gave point security. In western al-Anbar Province, Coalition and Iraqi security forces served point and area needs. The troop commitments required for security in western al-Anbar Province limited the number of voting sites the division could establish.

Only two attacks by indirect fire occurred during the national election, compared to ten during the referendum. By almost every measure, the 15 December election succeeded in al-Anbar Province beyond expectations. Sunnis turned out in such large numbers that additional ballot materials had to be provided from reserves held by the regiment and brigade commanders in each area of operations.

Just over 12 million people voted, about 75 percent of the electorate. Sunnis in particular voted in much greater numbers than in January, and perhaps more than in the October election judging by the temporary ballot shortages in al-Anbar Province. Some insurgent groups apparently kept their promised election day moratorium on attacks, even going so far as to guard the voters from attack.

Six months after the election, negotiations for a "government of national unity" succeeded and a political coalition supported it under the leadership of Prime Minister Nouri al-Maliki.

Closing Out 2005: Counterinsurgency Operations and Force Realignments

With the completion of the national election, Operation Liberty Express terminated on 22 December. That day also marked the official end of Operation

Hunter. The Iraqi government had announced the restoration of control of its borders on 30 November, with a celebration conducted for the benefit of the media. The 3d Battalion, 6th Marines, participated in a flag raising ceremony at battle position Hue at Husaybah, signifying the transfer of control of the area from U.S. to Iraqi forces. General Casey attended, accompanied by the Iraqi defense and interior ministers, and the battalion provided a rifle company reinforced by tanks as security, which also included continuous air coverage. In the view of the II MEF commander, Major General Johnson, "This is a significant milestone that will highlight the initial progress to date in border defenses, training of Department of Border Enforcement personnel, and the commitment and growing capability of the Iraqi government and its security forces." Although Border Forts 4 through 6 remained incomplete at the end of the year, Iraqi Army units had already moved into border town garrisons and manned the combat outposts north and south of the Euphrates. Construction would begin before year's end in refurbishing the former port of entry at Husaybah. In December, however, the II MEF staff urged higher headquarters to first upgrade the ports of entry at Walid and Trebil before opening the port of entry in the al-Qaim zone.

Very few named counterinsurgency operations occurred in the immediate aftermath of the December election, but the ongoing operations sufficed to keep order in the province, and a certain euphoria could be noticed among the population as well as the U.S. and Coalition fighting forces. In the Haditha area, 3d Battalion, 1st Marines, ran some sweeps through suspected cache sites in Operation Red Bull (20–31 December). A similar operation, Operation Green Trident (23–31 December), saw 1st Reconnaissance Battalion sweeping around the Coalition logistics base Area of Operations Dogwood and uncovering numerous caches. Outside Ramadi, 1st Battalion, 172d Armor, cleared Tammin and Jazirah on the eastern and northern outskirts as a disruption effort in Operation Bulldog (28–31 December) but in this case fought four engagements, taking 17 detainees and had two attacks each by indirect fire and explosive devices. Clearly, Ramadi remained a dangerous area.

In total, Operation Hunter encompassed 3,840 actions during the second half of 2005. The number reflects the vastness of western al-Anbar Province as well as the absence of adequate control over the re-

gion. At the same time that II MEF's staff reported these accomplishments, it began to adjust to reductions in its forces in the aftermath of the elections and the focus of effort that Ramadi and Fallujah had attracted from the Multi National Corps–Iraq.

The pending rotation of the Army's 2d Battalion, 112th Infantry, in December left al-Taqaddum without a local security infantry unit, and the Army offered no replacement for it. The same applied to the 3d Battalion, 504th Parachute Infantry, which had served in the 2d Marine Division only as part of the Operation Hunter reinforcements received with the return of Area of Operations Saber in October. The II MEF planners began to study base consolidation as a way to continue operations with fewer units, although the Iraqi Army forces at year's end began to approach what the campaign plan had envisioned as the minimum requirement for success. In the end, the Army made available for al-Taqaddum the Illinois National Guard 2d Battalion, 130th Infantry, one of many units it began to extend to meet increasing manpower needs. The future was clear for succeeding Marine Corps deployments: more and more of these security unit assignments would come from Marine Corps commands.

One reduction in II MEF responsibilities came with the decision by the Multi National Corps commander to realign the provinces of Karabala, An-Najaf, and northern Babil under the Multi National Division–Baghdad, commencing with the relief of the 155th Brigade and the transfer of its authority to the incoming 2d Brigade, 4th Infantry Division, on 5 January 2006. Henceforth, the Marine Corps contingent took responsibility in Iraq for al-Anbar Province.

The end of the 13th MEU's deployment to Iraq drew closer. The incoming 22d MEU had been made available for employment in al-Anbar Province in time for a relief by like units in Area of Operations Fairbanks. The decision by Central Command chief General Abizaid to permit the 13th MEU to remain ashore in Hit through mid-February allowed for its relief to be incorporated into the rotation of the entire II MEF in 2006. Accordingly, Colonel Kenneth F. McKenzie reported with his 22d MEU to 2d Marine Division on 17 December and relieved 13th MEU ten days later. Only two more months remained for the II MEF campaign at this point. Since late 2003, 470 Marines had been killed in action and 4,823 wounded in Iraq.

Chapter 11

Continuous Operations

Although no large urban battle occurred during the II Marine Expeditionary Force campaign in Iraq, the myriad of tasks confronting its Marines, soldiers, and sailors differed little from the previous year's effort. The immediate military tasks included the continuous requirements for military checkpoints, patrols, police patrols, road sweeps, offensive missions, raids, cordons, and searches. The force protection requirements were equally large, and the additional penetration by 2d Marine Division units into the towns and villages surrounding the major cities and in the western Euphrates River valley multiplied greatly the number of forward operating bases and camps requiring garrisons and guards.

These continuous missions required everyone to perform typical infantry roles and tasks regardless of the type of unit or its members' specialties. Everybody had his or her duty manning guard posts and check points, mounting convoy security, and conducting all forms of surveillance. Proper force protection in populated areas, however, required more than sentry duty; it also required frequent sweeps well outside the perimeter, local counterinsurgency measures, and serving in quick reaction forces designated for responses both inside and outside the camps. Marines and soldiers of all specialties found themselves conducting offensive missions such as raids and neighborhood sweeps. Because of the shortage of women in combat units, most female Marines, sailors, and soldiers were assigned to search female civilians, suspects, and detainees.

In addition, the Marine Corps employed many units in the Iraq campaign in "provisional" roles, i.e., performing missions they were not trained or meant to perform. Combat engineer, amphibious assault, and artillery units were often used as provisional infantry units. The Iraq campaign saw the fielding of such units in an increasingly widespread fashion. The initial employment of the entire 3d Battalion, 11th Marines—an artillery unit—as a provisional military police battalion in 2004 set the mark for using other artillery units in similar roles. What followed was their widespread use as well as headquarters and line companies from 4th Tank and 4th Assault Amphibian Battalions as military police units. Provisional small boat detachments for Haditha Dam security came

from assault amphibian, reconnaissance, light armored reconnaissance units, and an infantry regiment headquarters. In the Marine aircraft wings, the 2d and 4th Light Antiaircraft Defense Battalions were employed as provisional infantry battalions defending al-Asad Air Base. Antitank platoons, not needed as such, were used as convoy escorts and mobile reaction forces. The scarcity of civil affairs units and graves registration or personnel remains platoons caused the formation of provisional units to perform these tasks as well, drawing from various organizations of the Marine Corps Reserve.

Civil Affairs

One of the most persistent challenges in the Marine Corps campaign in Iraq remained the lack of civil affairs organizations available for employment. The Marine Corps had only two civil affairs groups, both comprised of Selected Marine Corps Reservists: 3d Civil Affairs group based at Camp Pendleton, California, and 4th Civil Affairs group based at Anacostia, Washington, D.C. As the campaign in Iraq entered its third year, the tempo and duration of operations made clear that the 3d and 4th groups would deploy to Iraq every seven months. Accordingly, Marine Corps Commandant Michael W. Hagee approved establishing two provisional civil affairs groups to provide operational and personnel relief for the two existing groups, the 5th and 6th Civil Affairs groups (Provisional). On 4 January 2005, the Marine Corps activated the 5th Civil Affairs group (Provisional), using cadres drawn primarily from the 4th Combat Engineer Battalion, 4th Marine Division, and deployed it to Iraq from March to September 2005 with the initial II MEF contingent.

Planning continued to prepare and activate the 6th Civil Affairs group (Provisional) for activity beginning in September 2005. The 6th was activated on 1 June 2005, less than a month after it had been established, using cadre drawn principally from the 4th Maintenance Battalion.

In each case, the challenge remained to identify more than 190 Marines and sailors from Marine Corps Reserve Forces to comprise a complete group and to qualify most of them in the civil affairs military occupational specialties required for officers and non-

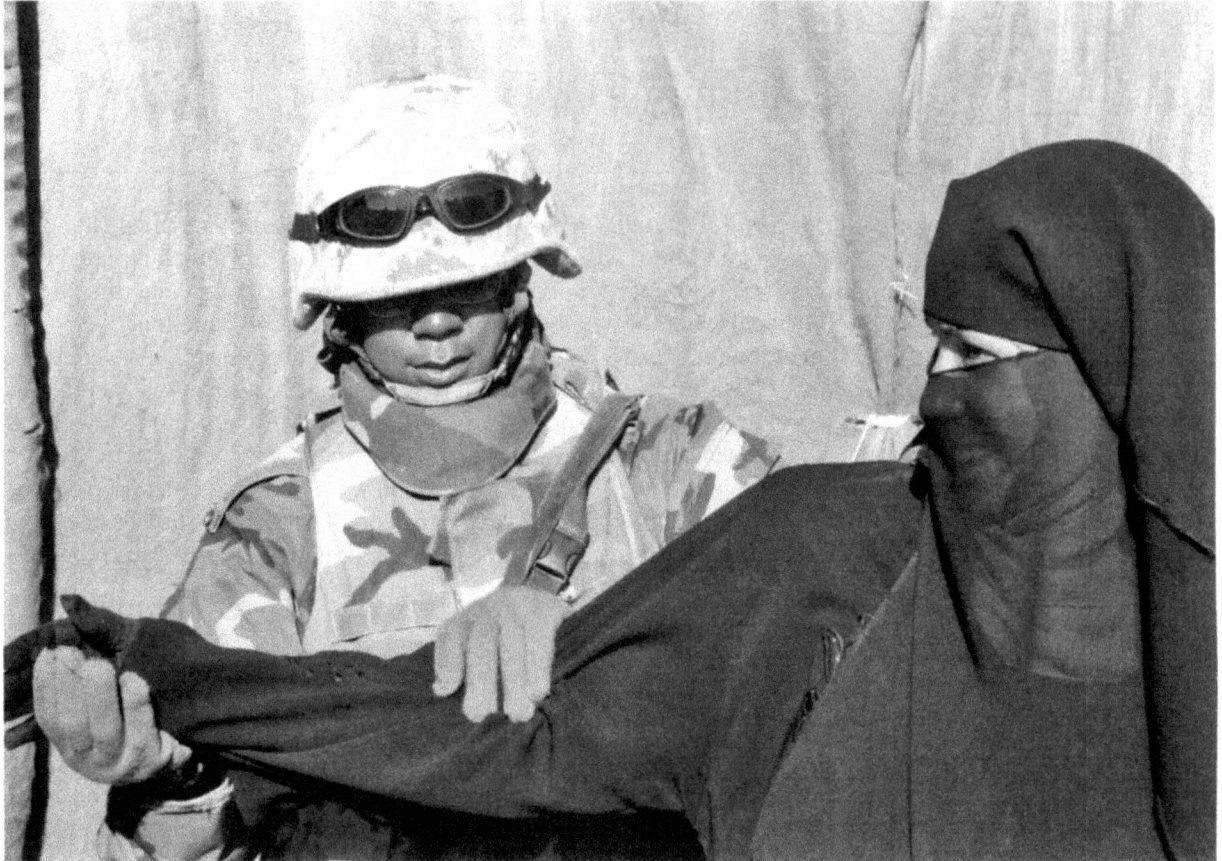

Photo by LCpl Ryan B. Busse, Defense Imagery, VIRIN: 041228-M-5585B-011.

Cpl Erica Renee Steel searches an Iraqi woman at an entry point outside Fallujah in December 2004.

commissioned officers. For instance, only the commanding officer and 14 Marines who joined the 6th Civil Affairs group had civil affairs qualifications, The need for this training greatly complicated existing requirements to complete other required combat skills training they would need for deployment to Iraq.

Civil affairs training began using mobile training teams formed by the 3d and 4th Civil Affairs groups after their return from Iraq. As a result of their experiences, the training teams brought not only "book" training to the provisional civil affairs groups, they also provided recent experience and lessons-learned from their tours of duty in Iraq. The training covered a full range of civil affairs topics: roles and missions units, civil-military operations, the Iraqi Transitional Government, and interactions with U.S. government agencies, nongovernmental organizations, and the media. Additional training focused on the law of war, information operations, psychological operations, human exploitation teams, interpreters, negotiations, and mediations. In addition to the classroom training, the Marines of the provisional groups participated in practical exercises such as how to hold town meetings and manage crowds while conducting pa-

trols. The civil affairs training conducted by the 3d and 4th Civil Affairs groups, combined with the mandatory completion of the U.S. Army correspondence course and three months on-the-job training, finished the necessary qualification of the provisional groups.

Each civil affairs group organized personnel into a headquarters detachment and four detachments. Detachment 1 comprised the government support team and the Marines who would man the civil-military operations center collocated with the II MEF operations center in al-Fallujah. Detachments 2, 3, and 4 would support the ground combat elements in the field. Each detachment comprised five civil affairs teams of six to seven Marines each.

The 5th Civil Affairs group deployed to Iraq with II MEF and relieved the 4th Civil Affairs group at Fallujah on 10 March 2005. It immediately began to work with the temporary Fallujah city council, established a civil-military operations center in al-Karmah, and began to facilitate completion of key projects, such as reopening the ar-Ramadi glass factory. In western al-Anbar Province, teams worked with Regimental Combat Team 2 to support operations. During June, the group was reassigned to the 2d Marine Division because it contained most of the key civil affairs functions. The 5th Civil Affairs group formed the Provincial Reconstruction Development Committee, and a new provincial civil-military operations center opened at Ramadi. On 21 September, the 6th Civil Affairs group took over the civil affairs functions and continued the mission, with increasing attention to the pending constitutional and national elections.

The 6th Civil Affairs group continued to maintain its Headquarters Detachment with the 2d Marine Division headquarters at Camp Blue Diamond. A civil affairs cell of ten Marines from the group served in the G-5 (Plans) staff section of II MEF at Camp Fallujah, where Detachment 1 operated the government support team and civil-military operations center at Fallujah and the second (provincial) center at Ramadi in the governor's complex. Detachment 2 supported the Army brigade in Ramadi. Detachment 3 aided Regimental Combat Team 2 operations in western al-Anbar Province. Detachment 4 remained at Camp

Fallujah to help Regimental Combat Team 8 in Area of Operations Raleigh. Between September and December 2005, three events influenced the 6th Civil Affairs group's operations and civil affairs operations: Operation Hunter; the constitutional referendum on 15 October 2005; and the election of the permanent Iraqi National Assembly on 15 December 2005.

The civil affairs groups provided military support for the provincial and local governments critical to the success of the Coalition throughout al-Anbar Province. Before 2005 the provincial government of al-Anbar Province and the city councils of most major cities there remained mostly ineffective. Insurgents continued to intimidate and infiltrate these bodies. Fallujah remained the sole major exception, where the insurgents had been removed, and the citizens were attempting to begin self-governance. During 2005 the 2d Marine Division strove to remove the insurgents from all the major cities: Ramadi, Habbaniyah, al-Qaim, and Rutbah. In the process several smaller towns became safer. Immediately after each city or town was cleared of insurgents the civil affairs

Civil affairs groups were an integral means for engaging the Iraqi population and supporting counterinsurgency efforts. In November 2006, Capt Charece D. Martin of the 4th Civil Affairs Group participated in an Iraqi Woman's Engagement to provide solutions and aid to Iraqi women and their children.

Defense Imagery, VIRIN: 061105-M-8213R-010

Photo by LCpl Daniel J. Klein, Defense Imagery VIRIN: 050128-M-8096K-026

It was not all combat for the Marines in Fallujah. They helped out the local population when they could, such as these Marines from the 4th Civil Affairs Group aiding Iraqis in loading a water tank onto a pickup truck to move it to a more accessible area.

detachments began to work with the leadership of the city. The Marines spoke continuously with local officials to address their needs and determine priorities for projects to improve the quality of life for civilian inhabitants.

Headquarters Battalion, 2d Marine Division, installed a communications network at the Provincial Civil Military Operations Center at Ramadi. This service helped facilitate a more expeditious flow of information to research and staff for provincial reconstruction projects. The civil affairs detachment supporting Regimental Combat Team 8 rehabilitated the Fallujah mayor's building, which became the center for the ongoing efforts by local officials to make Fallujah autonomous and self-sufficient in governmental matters.

A key civil affairs function in every operation in the Marine Corps campaign in Iraq aimed at building positive relationships and securing the trust of Iraqi citizens and influential local officials. This process began with the distribution of 150 billion Iraqi dinars as financial compensation for damages and loss caused by the insurgents and operations against

them. The Iraqi Provincial Reconstruction Development Committee promoted provincial government capability and legitimacy as it acted to determine the allocation of Coalition projects. Two water treatment facilities were restored in addition to constructing five new facilities for villages in al-Anbar Province to provide fresh water for more than 100,000 inhabitants. The civil affairs relationship with electrical representatives brought improvements to three substations, and the installation of additional electrical transformers increasing electrical output. Using funds from the Commander's Emergency Response Program (CERP) allowed the refurbishing of over 25 schools for use by more than 10,000 students as well as providing medical supplies, incubators, and funding for new medical clinics. Civil affairs Marines provided food, water, shelter, clothing, blankets, and medical assistance to 4,000 displaced persons in al-Ubaydi. In the Hit area they provided 1,200 hygiene kits, 2,000 water buckets, 1,600 kerosene heaters, 1,700 sweaters, 10,000 blankets, and several thousand pounds of food items. Additionally, civil affairs personnel delivered 39 primary care health care kits enabling the Iraqi Ministry of Health to provide service to 1.5 million citizens of al-Anbar Province. The overall reconstruction efforts resulted in completing 483 projects worth $18.3 million with 183 projects valued at $13.3 million in progress.

The civil affairs effort discovered the absence of a functioning plan for economic development, so one was developed to engage U.S. agencies to determine programs for economic development and what funding was available to begin pursing an economic development plan in Fallujah. The city was chosen based on its improved security situation. Execution typically began in a simple meeting with Iraqi businessmen and quickly grew to include more businessmen, key leaders, representatives from the United States Agency for International Development, the Iraq Reconstruction Management Office, and nongovernmental organizations. Civil affairs Marines developed relationships to fund a micro-financing program and develop a business center to promote economic growth, training, and better business practices. The plan injected more than $5 million in Iraq Reconstruction Management Office funds for al-Anbar Province. From this beginning in Fallujah, the same plan was used in Ramadi where 6th Civil Affairs

group began developing a business center and systematic micro-financing. Civil affairs actions also established an agriculture development plan addressing irrigation as the primary means to improve crop production. Canals were cleared of debris using funds primarily from the United States Agency for International Development Office of Transitional Initiative.

The Regional Reconstruction Operation Center supported II MEF, the Iraqi government, the U.S. Embassy, and all organizations involved in reconstructing Iraq by coordinating reconstruction efforts, information, logistics, and security between the contracting community, military, and Iraqi government. The reconstruction program included 531 projects in al-Anbar Province, valued at $440 million with 92 percent contracted and 45 percent work-in-place by February 2006. The reconstruction projects restored essential services in several infrastructure sectors including electrical, water, wastewater, health, education, security, justice, transportation, and communication.

Aviation Support

The chief aviation challenge in 2005 continued to be the excessive operation of aircraft because of the continuous need for numerous mission types. The

School supplies are distributed to Iraqi children in Fallujah by Marines of the 4th Civil Affairs Group. The pupils were returning to school in February 2005.

Photo by Cpl Thomas D. Hudzinski, Defense Imagery, VIRIN: 050205-M-7403H-027

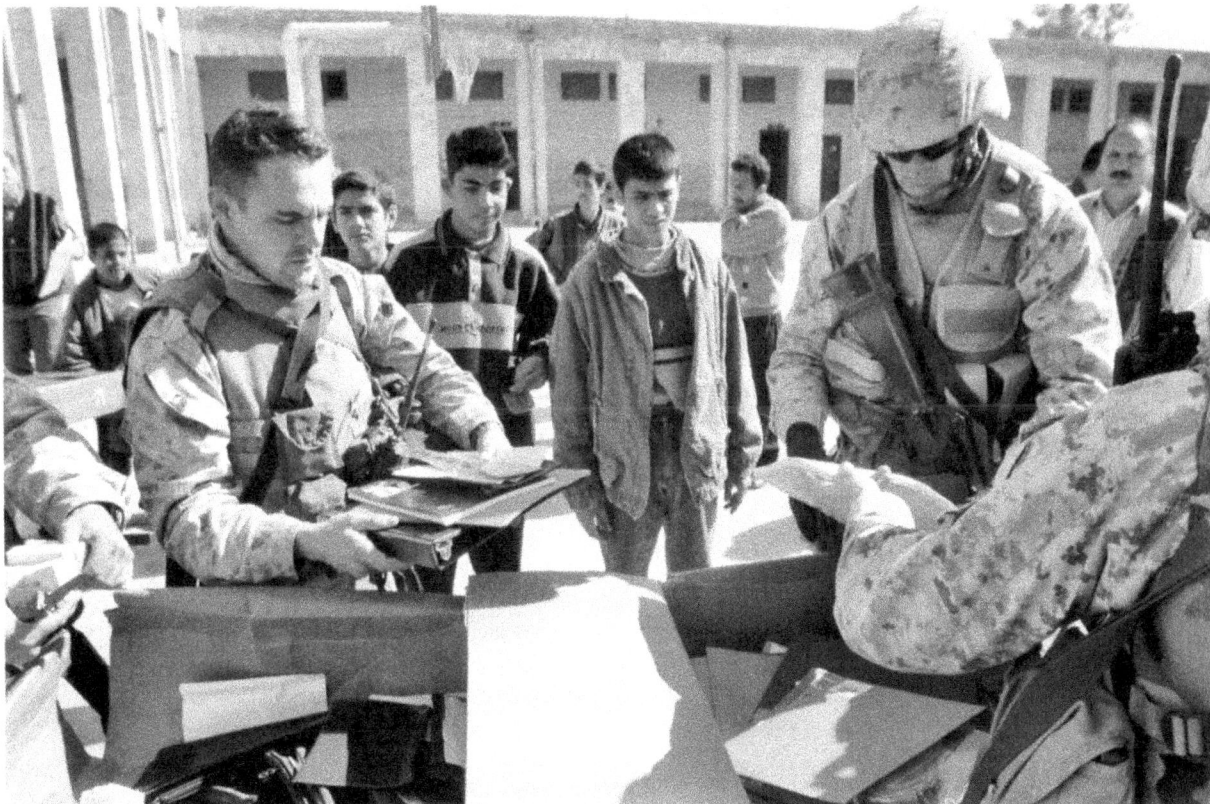

daily routine support of personnel and cargo movements directly aiding combat operations required strip alert aircraft constantly ready to provide casualty and medical evacuation, tactical recovery of aircraft and personnel, quick reaction forces, and both rotary- and fixed-wing close air support responding to "troops in contact." Other mainstay missions, usually conducted daily, included convoy escort, armed reconnaissance, intelligence surveillance, reconnaissance over-watch of critical areas and routes, fixed-wing aerial refueling, and radio relay.

Specialized requirements included electronic surveillance and jamming missions flown by Marine Corps and Navy detachments of EA-6B aircraft in frequent rotation from bases in the United States to al-Asad Air Base. While technical details and capabilities remain classified, the efforts of the detachments and aircrews frequently required 14 hours per day of coverage of priority areas such as Ramadi and important surface routes. In general, aircraft of all types under control of 2d Marine Aircraft Wing during the 2005–2006 campaign operated at 2.5 times greater than acceptable usage specified in technical documents. Few measures existed to reduce this high rate given the global commitments of Marine Corps aviation and the high priorities of almost all the missions being flown. One possible remedy remained the unmanned aerial vehicle program, the drones flown by Unmanned Aerial Vehicle Squadrons (VMU) 1 and 2. The only such squadrons—each comprising three detachments—existed in the Marine Corps, and their Pioneer and Scan Eagle drones already flew to the

A Pioneer unmanned aerial vehicle of Marine Unmanned Vehicle Squadron 2 departs on a mission in al-Taqaddum in June 2006.

Photo by Sgt Jennifer L. Jones, Defense Imagery, VIRIN: 060621-M-8484J-024

maximum extent that the craft and their operators could sustain, exceeding 1,100 hours a month. Ironically, more mission capabilities and new technical upgrades had been developed and introduced by operators since 2004, which increased the demand for the drones, now employed day and night.

Second Marine Aircraft Wing's close air support remained highly valuable on the battlefield. In an action typical of the larger, multi-battalion operations, the week-long combat of Task Force 3d Battalion, 2d Marines in Operation Matador (May 2005), numerous air strikes contributed to success in battle: strikes from one armed drone, 12 helicopters, and 16 fighter-bombers damaged enemy forces during the action.

As the 2d Marine Aircraft Wing and Marine Aircraft Group 26 prepared to relinquish operations to the 3d Marine Aircraft Wing in 2006, the tabulated statistics below show the pace of aviation operations in the first II MEF campaign in Iraq.

Table 11-1: II Marine Epeditionary Force Air Operations

Total Sorties	56,267 (102,797 flight hours)
Unmanned Aerial Vehicle Sorties	1,997 (10,847 flight hours)
Air Traffic Control Actions	297,633
Casualty and Medical Evacuations	4,417
Passengers carried	164,349
Cargo lifted	9,080 short tons
Tactical air requests completed	12,038
Air support requests completed	40,810

In executing the tactical air requests, the aircraft, both fixed- and rotary-wing, expended 209 tons of ordnance, including 3,176 rockets and 614 precision guided munitions. The aircraft flew some 3,900 convoy escort missions, and the ground support services pumped 64 million gallons of aviation fuel, while another 30 million gallons were used in aerial refueling.

Logistics Operations

Although often overlooked in combat reports and the press, logistics remained at the heart of the II MEF campaign in Iraq. The activities of Brigadier General Wissler's 2d Force Service Support Group, (renamed 2d Marine Logistics Group in 2005), at the al-Taqaddum Air Base centered on the overall coordination of non-aviation logistics activities in al-Anbar Province. This included theater responsibilities for route and convoy security, support to almost all Coalition forces in the area of operations, operations and security of Camp al-Taqaddum, and supervising tenant activities sup-

A convoy of vehicles from Combat Logistics Battalion 2 leaves Camp al-Asad for Camp Haditha on a resupply mission in March 2005.

porting II MEF. The principal subordinate units (8th Engineer Support Battalion, Combat Logistics Regiment 25, and Combat Logistics Battalions 2 and 8) all executed continuing and special tasks specific to their missions and assigned areas. These units provided the critical and continuous logistic aid to the 2d Marine Division and all its attached units and partially to the Army's 155th Brigade as well. Related tasks included convoy and route security, road sweeps, and repair and explosive ordnance disposal support, aided in the last three functions by companies of the 8th Engineer Support Battalion usually in direct help to the combat logistics battalions.

Locally at Camp Taqaddum, the Marine Armor Installation Site operated throughout the year installing kits and new protective features on the wheeled tactical vehicles of the force, principally Humvees and seven-ton trucks. Although the rate of installation increased, the continued turnover of vehicles gave an endless aspect to this work. Improvement of the cargo and personnel capacity of the airfield came with the completion of the Joint Air Cargo Operations Terminal in late June 2005. The consolidated passenger and air cargo facility improved the ability of Taqaddum to function as an air logistics hub. Because of the growing threat to ground transportation, air transport continued to grow in priority and quantity through the campaign. The group engineers also consolidated the use of Taqaddum as a primary stop in the theater ground resupply system operated by the Army support system. A convoy marshalling yard entered service the same month, a vast graveled lot suitable for handling the new convoy routes also was introduced in the theater.

The theater transportation network depended to a great extent on privately contracted flat-bed delivery systems, drivers, and commercial equipment items supplied by the principal contractor, Kellogg Brown, & Root. By December 2005, the contracted support was so inadequate that 2d Marine Logistics group had to employ organic tactical vehicles and engage in open contracting of third country national equipment and drivers. The demands in December grew partly from the national election support but also from the decision made by the commander, Multi National Corps–Iraq, to close the

An explosive ordnance disposal (EOD) technician, among Marines and soldiers attached to Combat Logistics Battalion 8, 2d Marine Logistics Group, stages unexploded ammunition at Camp Fallujah. The EOD technicians were preparing the ordnance for destruction.

Photo by LCpl Bobby J. Segovia, Defense Imagery. VIRIN: 051119-M-3717S-114

Coalition logistics base at Camp Dogwood, further ordering II MEF to effect the transfer of U.S. equipment, munitions, and supplies to Taqaddum. On 28 December the last convoy departed Dogwood for Taqaddum, completing the movement of 599 tractor-trailers in the month.

Related to all the reshuffling of storage capacity, the group completed the enlargement of Taqaddum's field ammunition storage point in December by adding seven new magazines to accommodate a new explosive weight of 35 million pounds,. An equally important task performed by the group came in the maintenance of worn equipment to the Arifjan, Kuwait, rework facility operated by Commander, Marine Forces Central Command, and to depots in the United States. A constant flow of generators, material-handling and construction equipment, and combat systems moved by air and ground transportation in and out of Iraq.

Security at Taqaddum largely centered on the assigned infantry battalion provided by the Army: first by the 2d Battalion, 112th Infantry, of the Texas National Guard, and then by the 2d Battalion, 130th Infantry, from the Illinois National Guard. These soldiers not only provided point defense of the base and related facilities but also mounted most of the essential security patrols in the surrounding areas required to stop insurgents capable of firing mortar shells and rockets into the base or firing hand-held missiles at aircraft.

In the field, Colonel Robert Destafney's Combat Logistics Regiment 25, based at Camp Fallujah, essentially provisioned the two direct support combat logistics battalions aiding Regimental Combat Teams 2 and 8 and the Army brigade at Ramadi. The primary means of resupply was by convoy in the eastern part of Area of Operations Atlanta and by air in western al-Anbar Province. The latter effort required a daily C-130 sortie dedicated to the regiment's requirements, but occasionally operations in the west required up to three daily flights as well as ground convoys sent as far as Camp Korean Village.

The situation for the two direct support battalions varied drastically with the terrain and end organizations. At Camp Fallujah, Lieutenant Colonel Patrick N. Kelleher directed his Combat Logistics Battalion 8 to aid Regimental Combat Team 8 and the Army brigade at Ramadi, especially its attached Marine Corps infantry battalion, with occasional missions to the 155th Brigade in Area of Operations Biloxi. In a typical month, the battalion dispatched up to 100 supply convoys, also termed combat logistics patrols, to needy units as well as hundreds of crane and material handling missions. The military police and explosives ordnance disposal platoons performed dozens of convoy escort, road sweep, road repair, and explosives disposal missions each week. The battalion maintenance company provided dozens of vehicle recovery missions and contact team visits each week, including several dozen "rapid requests" in the same interval. The battalion also coordinated explosive ordnance disposal for the region, handling responses called in on the telephone hotlines for that purpose. Because of its personnel composition, the battalion also provided a squad of female Marines each day for duty with Regimental Combat Team 8 entry control points and checkpoints to assist in screening and searching Iraqi women. Battalion engineers constructed several of the control and checkpoints for the combat team and provided engineer support to it as well as the II MEF headquarters group, and Iraqi security forces in Area of Operations Raleigh.

In the non-urban "wild west" of al-Anbar Province, Colonel William S. Aitkin's Combat Logistics Battalion 2 relied much more on aviation support in performing its mission as well as using three ground supply routes while assisting Regimental Combat Team 2 and its units from al-Asad Air Base. With Company A, 8th Engineer Support Battalion, in direct support, the battalion also undertook road sweeps, road repair, and explosives disposal tasks throughout Area of Operations Denver. The surface convoys, several dozen per month, drove to Korean Village, Hit, Haditha, and al-Qaim initially, expanding their routes as other towns came under control of Regimental Combat Team 2 and Iraqi forces. The initial airdrops began in April and became a regular adjunct to helicopter support to the outlying operating bases.

The frequency varied according to operations, but the routine became three helicopter missions and two airdrops to al-Qaim per week with one additional airdrop to Camp Korean Village. The engineers of the battalion and attached engineer support company worked to expand the al-Asad Air Base ammunition capacity and found considerable work constructing forward operating and permanent bases, as well as platoon battle positions in the area as more towns and villages came under presence and control of U.S. and Iraqi forces.

Because of the distances involved and relative scarcity of quick reaction forces, the convoys and road sweeps of Combat Logistics Battalion 2 and its attachments almost always relied upon reconnaissance, escort, and close air support by light and attack helicopters of the 2d Marine Aircraft Wing. The air logistics effort in al-Anbar Province supporting II MEF forces contributed in no small way to the high operating tempo of the 2d Marine Aircraft Wing. At the end, the 2d Marine Logistics group staff calculated that it had saved 3,115 outbound and 5,034 inbound tractor-trailer equivalent loads of cargo by employing air transportation. Using aircraft to move supplies undoubtedly prevented many casualties that many have been incurred in ground transportation especially given the increasing mine and improvised explosive device threat in theater.

In summarizing its activities in this first II MEF campaign in Iraq, the 2d Marine Logistics Group noted that it had completed the following (Table 11-2):

The 30th Naval Construction Regiment used its considerable capabilities to improve camps and facilities throughout the II MEF area. Typical contributions included electrical and force protection

Table 11-2: 2d Marine Logistics Group Accomplishments

Activity	Number
Combat logistics patrols	3,900
Security and transportation escorts	17,500
Miles driven	2,800,000
Explosive ordnance disposal calls	4,937
Patients treated at six trauma centers	20,380
Dental patients attended	23,390
Surgeries performed	818
Units of blood transfused	1211
Route repairs	1,126
Gallons of fuel dispensed from 16 sites	138.756,000
Short tons of ammunition distributed	1,230
Supply transactions handled	2,325,000
Short tons of mail delivered	10,847

upgrades to existing buildings, constructing roads and berms, runway repairs, and building camps for Iraqi security forces ranging from the 670-man combat outpost south in the border defense scheme to the Iraqi 1st Division's headquarters camp at Ramadi for 2,100 people.

Chapter 12

Redeployment and Relief

Although the optimism following the second battle of al-Fallujah and January 2005 elections had faded for the Marines of II Marine Expeditionary Force, indications suggested in early 2006 that the insurgency had passed its apogee and that self-government and security for Iraq would be obtained in the near future. Hope existed that the culmination of these efforts would occur in 2006 and that II MEF's relief units from I Marine Expeditionary Force (Forward) might be the last deployment of Marines as the Multi National Forces–West in Iraq.

In addition to the December 2005 national election and the noteworthy Sunni participation that took place, Marines and soldiers also took heart in the long-awaited arrival of new Iraqi military and security forces in al-Anbar Province. The Iraqi divisions and brigades even began to take over forward operating bases previously manned by U.S. forces and emboldened thoughts that they would replace American forces in their roles and tasks as well. Although fielding an effective police force remained a difficult objective, planners sought to produce a new police force in the same manner that an effective national Army seemed to be taking form.

Near Term Missions Assessed

The II Marine Expeditionary Force (Fwd) commander Major General Stephen W. Johnson and his staff presented their assessment to the incoming Multi National Corps–Iraq commander, Army Lieutenant General Peter W. Chiarelli and his V Corps staff in January. Although Marines and soldiers had registered success in 2005, al-Anbar Province remained a dangerous place with a local active Sunni insurgency. It was also frequently targeted by insurgent forces operating across the Iraqi state. A persistent and permanent presence of Coalition troops continued as a requirement for future success. Only with such a sound military presence could the development of the Iraqi Army and police forces be undertaken.

Operating in tandem, Coalition and Iraqi forces needed both experience and numbers to carry the fight to the enemy and deny it sanctuary and freedom of movement. Only when augmented by sufficient and capable Iraqi forces would the Coalition begin to effectively interact with the local civilian population. Thus, no reductions in force levels for the foreseeable future would be considered. Rather, the existing Coalition forces had to maintain their presence and to exploit the successes claimed for Operation Hunter.

The enemy situation by year's end indicated that a change in the Sunni resistance in the province might be occurring. The insurgency continued to demonstrate resiliency with the ability to re-arm and reconstitute forces and to fund itself. At this point, the insurgency included religious extremists, former regime elements, emerging elites, tribal groups, and criminals.

The oft-touted foreign fighter element in the overall insurgency posed less of an immediate problem. In all of 2005, forces under II MEF had detained 9,695 Iraqis as suspected insurrectionists, some 40 percent of those captured nationally, compared to only 141 third-country nationals detained or killed, amounting to 30 percent of those taken across Iraq.

Marines and soldiers at the forward operating bases had reported incidents of combat between competing insurgent groups during the year. Analysts determined that the second half of 2005 had seen a widening schism developing. Extremists and moderate Iraqi groups pursued divergent agendas, mainly over the alternatives of participating in the Iraq political process or in continuing to wage war. The Sunni who had previously rejected the political alternative began to see participation as a means to counter the perceived Shi'a threat and to restore Sunni power and influence in what seemed now an emerging, democratic Iraqi state.

If the Coalition forces could demonstrate the power to restore at last the damaged infrastructure and to provide local security for the population, U.S. analysts foresaw a possible weaning of the Iraqi insurgents from violence and redirecting them into supporting the political processes. The reconstruction effort in al-Anbar Province drew from a fiscal pooling of $202.5 million from the Iraq Relief and Reconstruction Relief Fund, $65.5 million of the Development Fund for Iraq and $92.3 million of the Commander's Emergency Response Program. The first two programs supported 239 projects in al-Anbar Province, all but ten under contract by 10 January

2006. These projects completed by then amounted to those shown in Table 12-1.

The Commander's Emergency Response Program added local projects reported in separate categories During the same year, the fielding of Iraqi security forces to al-Anbar Province had improved markedly The missing link at this juncture was the police forces required for the Euphrates River Valley west of Fallujah.

Table 12-1: Commander's Emergency Response Program

Amount ($million)	Project
33 (25%)	Electrical substations and distribution
39 (30%)	Potable water; wastewater systems
26 (20%)	Healthcare and education facilities
28 (20%)	Police and fire stations; army and border enforcement
8 (5%)	Roads and bridges
Local Projects	
Water and sanitation	$26.1 million
Telecommunication	$11.4 million
Education	$9.2 million
Healthcare	$5.8 million
Others	$39.8 million
Iraqi Security Forces Fielded	
Nov 04	No effective forces
Mar 05	2,829 personnel
Jan 06	19,000 personnel
Mar 06	Projected: 21,000 personnel 2 division headquarters 7 army brigades (21 battalions) 2 special police battalions 7 Border Defense Force battalions 1,700 Fallujah police

The 'Year of the Police' in Al-Anbar Province, 2006

Using a model developed in Fallujah, Marine Corps commanders and their planners saw a solution to establishing a police force. Beginning in al-Qaim and working through the Haditha-Hit corridor, assessment teams engaged the local leadership to determine their level of support, calculating numbers of former police officers, equipment, and infrastructure remaining and required for each town and village. The teams included engineers able to assess station suitability and begin drafting the renovation projects. After finishing their surveys, the teams returned to al-Qaim and began screening candidates for the police academy. Police transition teams then took over and sustained the process.

The fielding of an effective police force in al-

Anbar Province was the priority task for the Multi National Forces–West during 2006: the goal was to transition from Coalition and Iraqi security forces to civilian police. The plan for reconstruction of the police sought to establish nine districts deploying 11,330 policemen in the province, with the main concentrations at these locations (Table 12-2):

Table 12-2: Concentration of Police Officers

al-Qa'im and Hussayba	2,000
Hadithah	800
Hit	900
Ramadi	4,000
Fallujah	1,700

The "Fallujah Model" consisted of screening and vetting the candidates and training them at the Baghdad or Joint Iraqi Police Center. After their training and equipping, the police units would deploy with advisors, local military assistance, and with a system of mentoring and partnering with experienced police officers including transition teams from Coalition nations. Ongoing assessment and retraining remained the last crucial parts of the model.

The establishment of local police would signal the ability of Iraqi security forces to at last take the lead in providing local security, freeing U.S. and Coalition forces for purely military operations to support the pacification of the province.

Combat Operations Continue with the Rotation of Forces

Operations in al-Anbar Province in the first two months of 2006, leading up to the relief of II MEF by the incoming I MEF, fell under Operation Patriot Shield II (2 January–4 April). Because of the almost continuous rotation of battalions and squadrons during the period, no major operations occurred in January and February. The operational objective remained to disrupt, neutralize, and interdict insurgent operations in every area of operations while the reliefs took place.

A few examples must suffice for the many reported in the period. Operation Red Bull II teamed 3d Battalion, 1st Marines, with the Iraqi 2d Battalion, 2d Brigade, in counterinsurgency operations aimed at three towns downstream from the Haditha Dam. Beginning on 14 January, companies and sniper teams moved into assigned zones and then commenced clearing operations simultaneously in four zones. Company K cleared South Dam Village, while Companies I and L and the Mobile Assault Company cleared Senjick, Khaffayrah, and the nearby train sta-

Table 12-3: Combat Operations

Jan 2006	Operation	Unit
4–8	Morgan	4/14th Cavalry
4–14	Bullshark	3d Battalion, 1st Marines; Dam Security Unit
6–10	Hedgehog	1st Battalion, 2d Marines
9–25	Sky Train	1/506th Infantry
14–25	Red Bull II	3d Battalion, 1st Marines
15–26	Koa Canyon	1st Battalion, 2nd Marines
16–25	Cache Sweeps	2d Battalion, 2d Marines
18–25	Western Shield	1st LAR Battalion
22–29	Lakota Sunrise	1st Reconnaissance Battalion
23–24	Arabian	4/14th Cavalry

tion. The last phase, ending on 25 January, saw companies L and I clearing each side of the river up to the Area of Operations Fairbanks boundary with 22d MEU. The operation netted only one detainee but uncovered 31 caches and two explosive devices.

At nearly the same time, Colonel McKenzie's 22d MEU launched 1st Battalion, 2d Marines, in Operation

In January 2006, LtGen Peter W. Chiarelli, USA (below), relieved LtGen Thomas F. Metz, USA, as the head of Multi National Corps–Iraq and as second in command of Coalition forces.

Photo by LCpl Gabriela Garcia, Defense Imagery, VIRIN: 061118-M-4937G-010

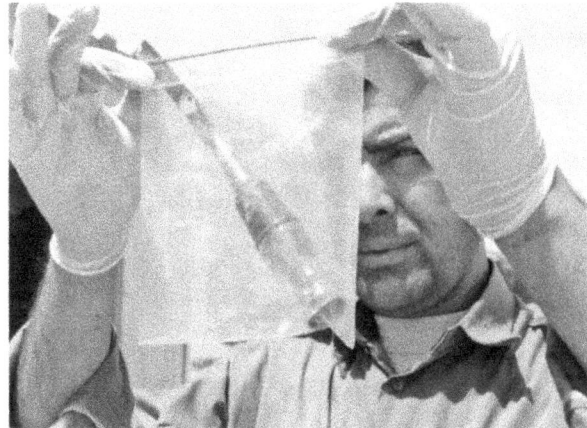

Photo by Cpl Seth Maggard, Defense Imagery, VIRIN: 080425-M-1391M-005

An Iraqi policemen bags a piece of evidence during a crime investigation course in al-Asad.

Koa Canyon (15–26 January), a combined sweep on both sides of the Euphrates with the Iraqi 1st Battalion, 2d Brigade, moving north to south from Jubbah to the Hit operating base. The operation resulted in 20 detainees and the discovery of three explosive devices while uncovering 44 caches of weapons and ordnance.

Far to the west, the 1st Light Armored Reconnaissance Battalion conducted a novel isolation action on ar-Rutbah in Operation Western Shield (18–25 January). After establishing three traffic control points and battle positions, Lieutenant Colonel Robert R. Kosid's Marines brought in three teams of four bulldozers each and progressively excavated a berm surrounding the town, thus preventing any traffic from entering or departing except through the control points. This effort considerably reduced the city's value as a logistical haven for insurgents.

North of Fallujah, 1st Reconnaissance Battalion inserted teams by helicopter to scout suspected insurgent locations and disrupt activities during the changeover of an infantry battalion in the city. Dubbed Operation Lakota Sunrise (22-29 January), the effort sent teams ranging widely in a cordon and search southward from the shore of Lake Tharthar and also in interdiction operations along an east-west corridor some 20 kilometers north of the city.

The relief of II MEF by I MEF in early 2006 demonstrated once again the value of replacing like organizations as well as indicating some new aspects of the deployment effort in the continuing campaign for al-Anbar Province. Although relieved of its operational responsibility for an-Najaf and Karbala Provinces upon the departure of the 155th Brigade, Major General Johnson negotiated with the Army commands for specific replacements for the 22d MEU, 1st Battalion,

MajGen Richard C. Zilmer (left) meets with BGen Tarq Abd-Al Whab-Jassem of the 1st Iraqi Army Division before a transfer of authority ceremony in August 2006. Zilmer served as both commander of I MEF (Fwd) and of I MEF's ground combat element in Iraq from 2006 to 2007.

506th Parachute Infantry, at ar-Ramadi, and Task Force Phantom. Although not successful in replacing the last, a highly specialized unit, he did receive assurance by 20 January that the 1st Battalion, 36th Infantry, would replace the 22d MEU in Area Of Operations Fairbanks and that the airborne battalion would not depart its current Ramadi assignment.

The combat power fielded by II MEF, with the departure of the 155th Brigade, became the following for 2006, intermittently swelled by the addition of a Marine expeditionary unit:

The relief of the 2d Battalion, 69th Armor, by the 1st Battalion, 506th Parachute Infantry, 2d Brigade, 28th Infantry Division, at Ramadi officially began the 2006 transfer of authority effort, and the first Marine Corps organizations to participate in the process executed their transfers on 23 January, when the 2d Battalion, 7th Marines, turned over its sector in Fallujah to the 3d Battalion, 5th Marines, newly arrived on its third rotation to Iraq.

In contrast to previous turnovers of Marine Corps forces in Iraq, the transfer of authority between II MEF and I MEF lasted over three months instead of two. The last unit of the 2d Marine Division, Company A, 2d Assault Amphibian Battalion, departed Iraq in mid-April. In particular, the aircraft squadrons arrived and departed with little or no overlap, and the gaps in the Marine Corps air order of battle perhaps reflected the global demands on the aviation arm. When Colonel Jonathan G. Miclot relieved Brigadier General Robert E. Milstead as Multi National Forces–West's aviation component commander on 8 February at al-Asad Air Base, his 3d Marine Aircraft Wing (Forward) only had ground support units, and both his wing staff and that of Marine Aircraft Group 16, which had relieved Marine Aircraft Group 26 on 7 February, operated at half-strength until more personnel arrived from the United States. Effectively, this measure guarded against a perceived personnel manning trend of major rotations occurring increasingly early in the calendar year. All of Colonel Miclot's aircraft squadrons, however, continued en route to the theater of operations, and squadrons of the 2d Aircraft Wing's order of battle maintained the required functions. Such flexibility remained characteristic of Marine Corps aviation, but there was more variation: two of the usual three medium helicopter squadrons in the Marine aviation order of battle were replaced in this period by a heavy helicopter squadron of CH-53D helicopters and a Virginia Air National Guard helicopter battalion that

Table 12-4: II MEF Combat Power, January 2006

Combat Power (Air)					
AH-1W	AV-8B	CH-46E	CH-53E	EA-6B	FA-18A+
25/19	10/6	35/33	16/14	5/4	11/10
76%	60%	94%	88%	80%	91%
KC-130	RQ-2B	UC-35B	UH-1N		
6/5	8/7	1/1	11/9		
83%	88%	100%	82%		
Combat Power (Air) (22d MEU)					
AH-1W	UN-1H	CH-46E	CH-53E	AV-8B	
4/2	2/2	12/11	4/4	6/5	
50%	100%	92%	100%	83%	
Combat Power (Ground) (USMC)					
Tank M1A1	LAV FOV	AAV FOV	Howitzer M198	HMMWV Hardback	UAH M1114
33/27	75/73	94/92	12/12	313/293	709/661
82%	97%	98%	100%	94%	93%
Combat Power (Ground) (2d Brigade)					
M1A1/A2	M2/M3	TRK Mortar	Howitzer M109A6	Scout HMMWV Armored	UAH M114
43/43	50/45	16/16	8/8	177/170	279/270
100%	90%	100%	100%	100%	100%
Combat Power (Ground) (22d MEU)					
Tank M1A1	LAV FOV	AAV FOV	Howitzer M109A6	HMMWV Hardback	
4/3	5/4	15/14	6/4	18/16	
75%	80%	93%	67%	89%	

operated the UH-60–series Blackhawk helicopters.

This turnover also maintained an element of continuing Army ground reinforcement in the province, but it could only be temporary until the Army spring rotations were completed. The Army, as strained as the Marine Corps, could not leave all its units in Iraq—most would have to rotate to the United States

BGen Robert B. Neller (left) served as I MEF (Fwd) Deputy Commanding General for Operations.

following their normal rotation schedule. In some instances, their return dates were extended, but in the end I MEF would be reinforced by one Army brigade, as it had been during its al-Anbar Province campaign in 2004.

The last turnover of major subordinate commands under the two Marine expeditionary forces came on 14 February when the forward deployed headquarters of the 1st Marine Logistics Group, led by Colonel David M. Richtsmeier, relieved Brigadier General Wissler and his 2d Marine Logistics Group at Taqaddum. The 2d Marine Division headquarters departed Iraq during February.

In contrast to earlier deployments, the 1st Marine Division headquarters did not deploy with I MEF. This unusual departure from standard Marine Corps organization and doctrine began with the consolidation of the 2d Marine Division and II MEF staffs and operations centers at Camp Fallujah on 31 January. The measure had its origins in 2004, when Major General James N. Mattis assumed responsibility from the 82d Airborne Division and noted how that division handled the ground command and control requirements—specifically, the Army's method of detailing a commanding general and two deputy commanders for maneuver and support. He also sensed that the

BGen David G. Reist (second from right), the 1st Marine Logistics Group commander, served as MajGen Zilmer's second deputy—the Deputy Commanding General for Supply.

physical division of Marine Corps headquarters staffs between Camp Fallujah and Camp Blue Diamond might not be efficient. "This was a ground intensive campaign, with no deep battle and only limited aviation play, apart from the persistent interest of USAF commands in the use of USMC aviation. On the other hand, the support function remained as intensive as any corps level operation. It made little sense to have layers of command and we could make economies." General Mattis approached the Commandant, General Hagee, with his ideas. The concept lay fallow until the following year. During his visit of April 2005, the Commandant asked II MEF (Fwd) commander, Major General Johnson, to study cutting manpower needs between the two staffs. After planning discussions with Major General Huck and staff lasting two months, Johnson assured General Hagee that they could consolidate the staffs early enough so that I MEF would be able to duplicate the structure upon arrival. The restructuring of the II MEF command element provided a single staff capable of functioning both in the MEF role of Multi National Forces–West and in directing the ground war, as had the staff of the Marine division in 2004 and 2005.

The resulting organization essentially charged the II MEF current operations staff section with perform-

ing the daily ground operations coordination among the remaining ground combat elements, two regiments and an Army brigade combat team. The commanding general of the Marine expeditionary force received two deputy commanders, one for operations and the other for logistics. These actions reorganized the expeditionary force command structure so that the force now resembled an Army ground corps headquarters. The resulting economies in manpower and materiel could be realized in this instance only because of the much less demanding air-ground coordination and the fixed set of military requirements in the current counterinsurgency campaign. In the end, the incoming I MEF command headquarters exercised control over three regimental-sized ground combat elements, an aircraft wing, and a logistics group.

1st Marine Expeditionary Brigade commander Major General Richard C. Zilmer headed I MEF's forward command element. He was assisted by a deputy commanding general for operations, Brigadier General Robert B. Neller, and a deputy commanding general for support, Brigadier General David G. Reist, who was also commanding general of 1st Marine Logistics Group. On 28 February, Major General Huck relinquished his responsibilities to Major General

Table 12-5: Ground Combat Turnover January–April 2006

Initial Deployment	Replacement Unit	Base	Transfer of Authority
2-69th Armor	1-506th Inf	Ramadi	4 Jan
2d Bn, 7th Mar	3d Bn, 5th Mar	Fallujah	23 Jan
2d Bn, 2d Mar	1st Bn, 1st Mar	Fallujah	5 Feb
22d MEU	1-36th Inf	Fairbanks	14 Feb
RCT-2	RCT-7	Denver	16 Feb
RCT-8	RCT-5	Topeka	21 Feb
3d Bn, 6th Mar	1st Bn, 7th Mar	Denver	16 Mar
1st LAR (-)	3d LAR (-)	Denver	21 Mar
3d Bn, 7th Mar	3d Bn, 8th Mar	Topeka	25 Mar
3d Bn, 1st Mar	3d Bn, 3d Mar	Denver	26 Mar
2nd Bn, 6th Mar	1st Bn, 25th Mar*	Fallujah	7 Apr
1st Recon Bn	2d Recon Bn	Fallujah	11 Apr

*Of the Marine Corps Reserve infrantry battalions, the 1st Bn, 25th Mar became the first to deploy for a second tour in Iraq, March 2006.

Zilmer as Commanding General, Multi National Forces–West. The first campaign of II MEF in Iraq had come to its conclusion.

As the first units of II MEF began to redeploy to their home bases at the end of January, the final tally of operations showed that its Marines sailors and soldiers had conducted 9,476 direct actions consisting of the following: discovering and destroying 2,141 improvised explosive devices, destroying 1,950 arms caches, taking 4,607 offensive actions of various types, firing 638 counter-battery fire missions, and conducting 140 formal operations. These actions killed 1,702 and wounded 405 insurgents, and detained 10,578 suspected insurgents.

The human cost to friendly forces was heavy. During this initial campaign in Iraq II MEF units sustained some 2,942 casualties. At the time of the transfer of authority between Major Generals Huck and Zilmer on 28 February, the combat losses to I MEF and II MEF in Iraq since the first departure of forces in September 2003 totaled 5,541 (500 killed and 5,041 wounded in action).

Major General Johnson Reflects on Marine Corps Operations in Iraq in 2005

I believe 2006 is going to be another decisive year for Iraq and for her people. They'll begin to see the benefits of the recent election and the increased capability and strength of their developing security forces. Since I last briefed you, the Iraqis of al-Anbar have stepped forward and exercised their right to vote in unprecedented numbers. Al-Anbar saw more than 250,000 Sunnis vote in the October referendum and approximately 370,000 in the December election. The people have shown their resolve by participating in a new and unfamiliar process, but one that offers hope for the citizens of Iraq.

If you look back over the past year at al-Anbar Province, the growth of the Iraqi Army in size, capability and professionalism has been quite remarkable. Last April, there were two Iraqi Army brigades in al-Anbar Province. Today, partnered with Multi National Force–West units, we have two divisions of the Iraqi Army that comprise nearly 20,000 soldiers. Currently three brigades have the lead in counterinsurgency operations in their own area, and across the region, Iraqi Army battalions are bearing an increasingly larger share of the counterinsurgency fight. Along the entire border with Saudi Arabia, Jordan, and Syria, construction is complete on all but a few of the forts, and the soldiers of the Iraqi border forces are patrolling and providing security.

In the coming year in al-Anbar Province, I think you're going to see continued progress in four key areas. First, that of presence. After the recent and successful operations along the western Euphrates River Valley, a persistent presence has been established at key points with Coalition forces and increasingly capable Iraqi Army forces. This presence is providing the conditions under which Iraqi police will be introduced and assist the local governments in assuming a greater role in providing services to their people.

Secondly, Coalition force partnering with the Iraqi security forces will be key. Coalition partnership with Iraqi security forces for training of operations is key to their continued growth. Through this partnership, Iraqi security forces and readiness will grow, security conditions will improve, and opportunities for good governance, reconstruction and economic development will appear.

Third, police. The reestablishment of Iraqi police in Fallujah has been a success story. With 1,200 trained police on the streets supported by limited numbers of Iraqi Army and Coalition forces, Fallujans were able to vote safely and in large numbers in the recent election and the referendum. With 350 locally recruited police in training and 160 more in training, the force will soon reach its authorized strength of 1,700.

In other parts of the province, an assessment of conditions conducive to the introduction of police in towns and cities is under way. Police stations are being identified for repair. The local police chief has been nominated in the al-Qaim region, and Iraqis are screening and recruiting potential policemen. The reintroduction of a professional police force in al-Anbar will provide local leaders with security and stability that they need to take care of their own. These police will start to be introduced over the coming months in conjunction with the completion of their training. And finally, the political process. As a result of the recent elections and increased persistence conditions are favorable for change and for providing Iraqis with an opportunity to take advantage of the choices that are before them.

We are hearing an increasingly larger number of moderate voices. We want to give the political opportunities, political process a chance. The people want an inclusive government that provides an alternative to the violence like we saw yesterday in Ramadi and to sectarian divisiveness. They want to focus on the needs of their community: schools, hospitals, jobs and their families. We're continuing to see a Sunni insurgency in al-Anbar Province, and I think we will continue to see it manifested until the political process has time to develop. The people have gone to the polls and voted. They've elected officials. Those officials will be seated and that process will allow people to see that they have the opportunity for success, that they have the opportunity to be heard, and that there are alternatives to violence.

The detainees that we take in this province are primarily local. They are people who live in the towns in the Euphrates River Valley. When we fight them, we fight them locally. That's where they live, and that's where they come from. The vast majority is local. And while there is an element of foreign fighters who influence or who try to influence the local insurgency, it's a very, very small part of the insurgency.

Ramadi is not in flames. There are key places where there are more insurgents than are others, and we, along with our Iraqi security force partners, are going after them. But I do not see that Ramadi has become a place where they are focusing a lot more effort. I think, again, it is local people, local insurgents, primarily, who are causing the difficulties in key places, not the entire town of Ramadi.

As far as turning it over [to Iraqi forces], our forces are still partnered with those Iraqi security forces. We still provide support—logistics support, communication support and so forth, and we still work very closely with them. But they're taking the lead in planning in a number of areas. Also, where and when those forces take over is a function of how long they have been together, how long their training is—or how long have they been functioning together. Some have only come out of training since September, those in the western Euphrates primarily, and those to the east are a little more mature. One size doesn't fit all with the Iraqi security forces. Some will mature more quickly, and others will take longer. I suspect within the next—probably in the next four to six months you're going to see a number of forces who will be able to take an increasing role in the lead or increasing lead here in this area, down here in the Fallujah-Ramadi area, and it'll take a little longer for those that are newer out in the Euphrates River Valley to assume a greater role in their area. But I think in 2006 you will see a continuation and a continuing to mature of these forces throughout the battlespace.

Epilogue

New and Old

The 2004–05 security and stability campaign by Marine Corps forces in Iraq began with the objective of reversing the nascent Iraqi insurgency and beginning the process of rebuilding a shattered society. The emerging resistance against the allied Coalition that had defeated Iraq in 2003 took U.S. forces and civilian authorities by surprise. Higher authorities calculated that the extended presence of occupation forces, the persistent application of counterinsurgency and security techniques, and the fielding of Iraqi security forces would pacify the country. In parallel with the establishment of security, the U.S.-directed Coalition Provisional Authority projected the creation of a provisional Iraqi government and the facilitation of democratic elections at national and regional levels such that "governance" would be established within a year of the scheduled mid-2004 "reversion of sovereignty" to the Interim Iraqi Government.

In almost every aspect, the expectations of these higher civil and military authorities proved overly ambitious and, in effect, repeated their earlier underestimation of resistance and insurgency in Iraq. The U.S. military forces deployed in Iraq remained undermanned and thus incapable of maintaining the security presence in numerous Iraqi towns that could and did shelter dissident elements that plotted and executed violent attacks upon security forces and civilians alike. Predictably, hopes that an Iraqi constabulary could be formed failed when a large contingent of the Iraqi Civil Defense Corps refused to participate in face of the Sunni revolt in al-Anbar Province and the al-Sadr uprising of April–August 2004 or otherwise failed to report for duty in assisting U.S. and coalition forces in smaller scale security operations throughout Iraq.

The Iraqi Civil Defense Corps received too little basic training, no more than three to four weeks in duration, intended for the more benign environment expected in mid-2003. Instead, these newly formed and untested units faced insurgents and extremists that had gained combat experience fighting against well-armed and seasoned troops, mostly fielded by the United States. Nevertheless, when the first annual rotation of U.S. forces began in the spring of 2004, preparations continued to move the Iraqi security

units into the towns and to shift the U.S. forces outside the urban areas in permanent base camps already under construction to replace the forward operating bases improvised from Iraqi military and government compounds.

Into this tenuous situation of early 2004 came I Marine Expeditionary Force, returning after the brief and successful 2003 operation in which the Iraqi defenses had been overcome with such quick, decisive and violent action that vast areas and major cities fell with relative ease to U.S. and coalition control. The summer and fall occupation duty experienced by approximately 8,000 Marines of the 1st Marine Division in the largely Shi'ite populated areas between Baghdad and Basrah bore little resemblance to the challenges that the new campaign in al-Anbar Province would bring.

The Marines, sailors, and soldiers comprising the Multi National Force–West comprised by I MEF and its reinforcements came prepared for the challenges in the spring of 2004 and harbored no illusions that the "Sunni Triangle" would prove easy as a security and stabilization operation. The extent to which the various Sunni insurgencies and small foreign terrorist elements thrived in both urban and rural areas exceeded all predictions. Although leaders such as I MEF commander Lieutenant Generals James T. Conway and 1st Marine Division Major General James N. Mattis sensed that the larger numbers of infantry they introduced in the area of operations would significantly effect the security situation, the number of Marines remained woefully insufficient to cover an area of approximately 32 percent of Iraq's total surface area. To that end, the Marine Corps commanders saw only the possibility of applying the patience, persistence, and presence of their troops, and attacking the insurgent leadership when detected and raiding the sanctuaries of the insurgents to destabilize their activities.

These realities came to fruition very quickly in the spring of 2004. After a few sporadic encounters with insurgents in each of the regimental zones of operations, the murder of civilian contractors in al-Fallujah and the mutilation and display of their corpses brought orders to I MEF and 1st Marine Division to clear the city of insurgents. The subsequent effort that exposed the scope and depth of the insurgencies in the province at large. The two battles for al-Fallujah remained pivotal in the I MEF campaign of 2004–2005, although the successful measures for subduing that urban center could not be repeated because of the cost and destruction wrought in its execution. Even as the scheduled election of January 2005 took place, the situation faced by I MEF and the incoming II MEF remained all too clear. Until some form of reliable Iraqi security forces could be established in sufficient numbers and competence, the U.S. Marine Corps forces in al-Anbar and neighboring provinces would have to wage an aggressive campaign. The enemy had to be dug out of their enclaves and brought to battle, but in selected cases and in situations in which the rest of the province would not suffer without sufficient security. At the same time, what few Iraqi security forces could be established had to be nurtured and mentored to the point that they could at least operate with U.S. forces such that the coalition could begin to overcome the cultural barriers that separated the public from the coalition forces that sought to protect it.

The firepower and military technology wielded by Marine Corps forces with all their training and expertise remained decisive, vital weapons when combat occurred: armored vehicles, artillery, and various forms of air support could and did dominate portions of the battlefield, but in the end the Marines soldiers and sailors used rifles, grenades, and explosives to confront insurgents at close quarters to eliminate their hold over the population. Such work did not always fall to the lot of the infantrymen, who remained sorely under strength for the distances and scope of the assignments. Many military personnel, regardless of specialty, found themselves engaged in routine scouting, patrolling, convoying, and screening tasks in which ambushes or other forms of combat led to counterattacks, pursuit, or search and clearing operations that many men and women of I MEF and II MEF and other services experienced for the first time.

The progress in fielding an Iraqi security force proved slow. What the Marines of I MEF initially found in al-Anbar Province largely comprised only seven Iraqi Civil Defense Corps battalions, renamed Iraqi National Guard after the assumption of sovereignty by the Interim Iraqi Government. These units mostly comprised local Sunnis recruited and trained by the U.S. Army. Only one such unit could be moved from its recruiting locale. When added to what local police remained on duty, this force amounted to approximately 2,000 Iraqis. A reasonable formula for counterinsurgency would have required over thirty battalions of combat troops for al-Anbar Province. The I MEF was comprised of only eleven U.S. battalions, not counting provisional units employed for base defense. II MEF arrived in early 2005 with even fewer battalions.

The Iraqi security units displayed key vulnerabilities: they were subject to local infiltration, intimidation, and threats by local Sunnis. Regardless of the degree of assistance provided by local Marine and Army units, even including the vaunted Combined Action Platoon doctrine used successfully by the Marine Corps in Vietnam, the Iraqi battalions failed to the point of wholesale breakdown. A few units manned by Shi'a or Kurdish soldiers proved much less vulnerable to the Sunni insurgents' intimidation tactics. In general, however, the Iraqi units fielded in 2004–05 lacked strength, experience, and resilience to fight the insurgents or to continue operating for sustained periods of time. The Iraqi defense establishment also failed consistently to replace losses of Iraqi soldiers and to provide adequate equipment for their forces in al-Anbar Province. With the eventual arrival of over two divisions of the Iraqi Army in the province by early 2006 along with a marked improvement in the military competence of the Iraqi soldiers, the continuing problems of violence and insecurity in the Marine Corps' areas of responsibility began to dissipate. These units drew their soldiers largely from the Shi'a population but added somewhat to the existing discontent of the Sunni population of al-Anbar Province.

Improvements in security, realized by the end of the two-year pacification campaign, meant that a certain part of the Sunni population could be persuaded to cooperate with governmental authorities and to participate in the basic restoration of Iraqi governance, rebuilding damaged towns and cities, and opposing the further use of violence. Results remained uneven, and already in early 2006, the realization that ar-Ramadi was one of—if not the most—dangerous cities in Iraq suggested that it, not the infamous al-Fallujah, functioned as the true center of the Sunni resistance and insurgency in the surrounding lands. The continuing campaign to gain control over ar-Ramadi, without resorting to the devastation wrought against al-Fallujah, remained a slow and often unrewarding process of vigilance, combat, and persistence. Aerial and artillery bombardment in many ways threatened to become counterproductive. The Sunni population continued to resent its lost status in the former regime, and local leaders were skeptical that U.S. forces would continue to fight insurgents and terrorists with vigor. The Sunni population also believed that the Iraqi national government would never earn Sunni support and participation in moderate forms of political action.

For the men and women serving in the two Marine expeditionary forces and numerous Marine expeditionary units deployed to Iraq, the tasks at hand remained all too obvious and challenging. Marines could not engage in self-doubt or self-pity. All the day-to-day violence, aggravated by devastating explosions of improvised devices, mines, and suicide bombers, had to be endured with patience, resolve, and tactical savvy. They continued to treat the population as a peaceful entity, requiring the Marines' protection and vigilance. The dissident and insurgent elements required the use of violent force, but still preserving the essential humanity of the situation such that Marines soldiers and sailors could discern the boundaries between the violence of combat and the limitations posed by a nearby civilian populace that in the end had to be "won over" to the cause of the western occupier and the awkwardly functioning native government. For the Marines, soldiers, and sailors of the Marine expeditionary forces in Iraq, service there was their "finest hour," especially since it was under great military and political pressures. These included at times being outnumbered, being watched from near and far for any signs of weakness, being second-guessed by military and civilian officials and the mass media; operating under restrictive rules of engagement preventing them from using their full array of combat power and weaponry; and fighting an enemy, often at close quarters, who did not wear a uniform and who blended in the population of noncombatant civilians. In such an environment, the thought of failure or letting down one's fellow Marines remained unthinkable. The attitude and accomplishments of the Marines inspired new legendary feats of courage in the long history of the Marine Corps.

The Marine Corps forces in Iraq, with the reinforcing organizations that joined them in Multi National Force–West operated with initial handicaps that could be overcome only by gaining experience and applying it at a rapid pace. The myriad tasks facing Marines in both urban and wide open rural terrain almost defy description. A series of broken cities and communities literally lay at their feet, occupied by inhabitants thoroughly demoralized by the shock of war and occupation, lacking any level of experience in self-government and self-sufficiency to make a concerted effort at rebuilding. The Marines, however, did not, as other armies have done, celebrate victory with triumphant parades and speeches. Their actions and attitudes were low key and those of professionals who had accomplished their missions to the best of their abilities. They did not treat the Iraqis as the enemy or a conquered people. They did not hoist American flags atop buildings in triumph.

In a remarkable series of events, the Marines and their comrades reached into themselves and drew upon their training, discipline, pride, dedication to duty, physical readiness, and fighting spirit to adapt to the novel conditions and dangers of counterinsurgency missions and executed them with steady resolve, overcoming setbacks and generally remaining benign in victory.

Those mission successes and achievements did not come without cost. During the campaign of 2004–05, some 500 Marines of Multi National Force–West were killed while serving in Iraq with thousands more wounded—many grievously—in combat. Since 20 March 2004, elements of I MEF and II MEF, augmented by the rest of the active and reserve establishments, provided continuous presence in Iraq.

The new battle streamers on the two Marine Expeditionary Forces' colors symbolize much. They represent more than a year of the lives and the service of the individual Marines and sailors. They recall the 500 fellow Marines and sailors who lost their lives for the mission and who made the journey home ahead of their comrades. They represent great courage in battle. They represent remarkable stamina over months and even years. They represent unshakable honor tested in a war against a treacherous, often invisible enemy in the worst of conditions. They represent immeasurable personal sacrifice by the Marine expeditionary forces' Marines and sailors and their families.

Notes

Chapter 1

The principal sources for this and subsequent chapters are the official records and working papers held by the Marine Corps Archives, Gray Research Center, Marine Corps University, located at Marine Corps Base, Quantico, Virginia. In addition, certain reference materials located at the Marine Corps History Division, Marine Corps University, have been used. Relevant classified records held by the archives of the Gray Research Center were examined and catalogued by the author during 2006-07. Because no formal inventory or finding aids have to date been produced by the archives, the classified records used herein are identified by use of their classified material control center (CMCC) registry number assigned by the CMCC, Marine Corps Combat Development Command, Quantico, the cognizant security management authority. These registry numbers take the form of S-1234-06, in which the letter designates a classification of secret, the four numbers the sequential assignment of the item or document by the CMCC in its registry, and the last numbers the year of accession into the control system, i.e. not the date of the document concerned. Although less satisfactory than a true inventory, the use of the CMCC registry numbers permits the researcher to locate the requisite items.

Unless otherwise noted, the material in this chapter is derived from the following material:

For the situation in Iraq following the overthrow of Saddam Hussein, see Donald P. Wright and Colonel Timothy R. Reese with Contemporary Operations Study Team, *On Point II: Transition to the New Campaign: The United States Army in Operation Iraqi Freedom, May 2003–January 2005* (Fort Leavenworth, KS, 2008); Michael R. Gordon and General Bernard E. Trainor, *Cobra II: The Inside Story of the Invasion and Occupation of Iraq* (New York: Pantheon Books, 2006); Kenneth W. Estes, "1st Armored Division: Operation Iraqi Freedom, May 2004–July 2004" (Wiesbaden: HQ 1st Armored Division, 2005); Charles E. Kirkpatrick, "V Corps Becomes CJTF-7: The Month of Plans and Decisions" (Heidelberg: HQ V Corps, draft November 2004).

For the Iraqi insurgency, see Carter Malkasian, "Counterinsurgency in Iraq," in *Counterinsurgency in Modern Warfare*, edited by Daniel Marston and Carter Malkasian (New York: Osprey Publishing, 2008) and Ahmed S. Hashim, *Insurgency and Counter-Insurgency in Iraq* (Ithaca: Cornell University Press, 2006).

For General Hagee's plans for the Marine Corps' second deployment to Iraq, see General James T. Conway Interview, in *Al-Anbar Awakening, Volume I American Perspectives: U.S. Marines and Counterinsurgency in Iraq, 2004–2009*, edited by Chief Warrant Officer–4 Timothy S. McWilliams and Lieutenant Colonel Kurtis P. Wheeler (Quantico: Marine Corps University Press, 2009); General Michael W. Hagee oral history, part I, 14 July 2005. Unedited and unreleased version provided by Dr. Fred Allison, Marine Corps Historical Center.

For the challenges and problems faced by the new deployment, see Headquarters Marine Corps, EOS Update Briefing, 15Oct03; S-3991-06; Marine Corps Chronology 2003, Reference Section, Marine Corps Historical Center; Headquarters Marine Corps Operations Center (POC) "Current Operations Briefs" for 01Dec03, 17Dec03, 23Feb04, S-1764 to 1816-06.

For the makeup of the I Marine Expeditionary Force deployment, see 1st Marine Division *Operation Iraqi Freedom II* draft manuscript, (unpublished, undated); Headquarters Marine Corps Operations Center (POC) "Current Operations Brief" 21Nov03; 1st Force Service Support Group Command Chronology (ComdC), July-Dec03; "I MEF OIF II RFP MSG FINAL," S-3937-06\ Archived OIF-II-1 Files; "Matrix_New_Baseline_09_JAN_2004_1100," S-3937-06\Archived OIFII-1 Files; Regimental Combat Team 7 ComdC Feb-Mar04 shows E/2/11 arriving Kuwait 28Feb04, S-0306-06\1MarDivClassified \Disk2\Regimental Combat Team 1 Mar04PartV\CC A/1/11 Feb–Mar04.

For the situation in al-Anbar Province and I MEF planning for operations there, see Bing West *No True Glory: A Frontline Account of the Battle for Fallujah* (New York: Bantam, Books, 2005); Commanding General Talking Points-OIF II Update, Ground Dinner-18Jan04, S-3937-06; Headquarters Marine Corps Operations Center (POC) "Current

Operations Briefs" for 5Jan04, 12Jan04, 28Jan04, "Force Flow Update" 28Jan04, S-3937-06.

Chapter 2

For information on the deployment of forces, see 1MarDiv ComdC Jan-Jun04; "Draft I MEF OM and RIP Frag 18Feb04," S-3937-06\Archived OIF-II-1 files; "First 60," S-3937-06; "I MEF input DRAFT 2 MARCENT to CJTF-7 confirmation of dates" 23Jan04 in S-3937-06\RIP&TOA; 1MarDiv ComdC Jun-Jun04 (unclassified); "Sequential Listing of Significant Events (U)" S-3801-06\1MarDiv June-Jul04; 1FSSG ComdC Jan-June04; 3MAW (fwd) ComdC 10Feb-31Mar04; Operation Iraqi Freedom–II ASE Completion Schedule, System description, Headquarters Marine Corps Operations Center (POC) "Current Operations Brief" 29Jan04; Lieutenant General Michael A. Hough, "State of Marine Aviation," *Marine Corps Gazette* 88 (May04), 5: pp. 11-27; PPO 040129; USCENTCOM msg was his 040803ZJan04; CJTF-7 reported a shortfall of 2,780 up-armored HMMWVs in Iraq; Brigadier General William D. Cato, "Rapid Acquisition in Support of Operation Iraqi Freedom II" *Marine Corps Gazette* 88 (May04), 5: pp. 48-50.

Chapter 3

For information on the geography and population of the al-Anbar province see Department of Defense, *Iraq Transitional Handbook*, Dec 2003, DOD-2630-IRQ-005-04; *Iraq Tribal Study: Al-Anbar Governorate*, Global Resources Group, June 18, 2006; Gretchen A. Sparkman "COLISEUM Requirement K506-04-0029-S," a contracted précis, S-4522-06\HistoricFiles\al-Anbar Historical; Lewis Owen, "Tigris-Euphrates river system." Encyclopedia Britannica (2007); "2004 World Data," Encyclopedia Britannica (2006).

For the deployments of I MEF's component units see Regimental Combat Team 7 ComdC Feb-Mar04; 1MarDiv ComdC Jan-Jun04, 3d MAW ComdC Jan-Jun04, 1st FSSG Comdc Jan-Jun04, 1st Marines 7th Marines ComdC Jan-Jun04, 1st BSSG ComdC Jan-Jun04; pilot controller handbook 15Jun05, S-0265-06\FECC Encl\Air Web Page Files.

For I MEF's relief of the 82d Airborne Division and initial I MEF engagements in al-Anbar see Regimental Combat Team 7 Intentions messages, 19-29Mar04, S-3933-06\Intentions Mssg\Mar04\Regimental Combat Team 7; Regimental Combat Team 7 ComdC Feb-Mar04; 1MarDiv Sequential Listing of Events, S-3801-06; 1BCT Intention messages, 21Mar04-30Mar04, S-3933-06\Intentions Mssg\Mar04\1BCT; 1MarDiv ComdC Jan-Jun04; 1MarDiv Sequential Listing of Events, S-3801-06; Michael S. Groen, "The Tactical Fu-

sion Center," *Marine Corps Gazette* 89 (April, 2005) 4: pp. 59-63; Headquarters Marine Corps Operations Center (POC) "Current Operations Brief" 18April04; Combat Power 15Apr04; S-3937-06\I MEF Sitreps\SitrepOfficer\AsstSitrepOfficer\Combat Power.

Chapter 4

For Operation Vigilant Resolve, including background of the battle and operation, see 1MarDiv ComdC Jun-Jan04; 1st Marine Division *Operation Iraqi Freedom II* draft manuscript, (unpublished, undated), Ch4; 1MarDiv Intentions 01April04, S-393306\Intentions Mssg\Apr04; 1MarDiv Intentions 03April04; Regimental Combat Team 1 ComdC Apr04; "1/5 Frag Order 005-04" 11Apr04, Ref Sect, 1-5 Historical Docs OIF1-2; 1st Bn, 2d Mar, 1st Bn, 5th Mar, A Battery, 1st Bn, 11th Mar, and Regimental Combat Team 1 ComdCApr04; U.S. Army National Ground Intelligence Center, "Complex Environments: Battle of Fallujah, 1 April 2004," S-4504-06.

For Company B, 1st Bn, 5th Mar action during the first battle of Fallujah, see J. Smith Silver Star Citation, RefSect; Robert D. Kaplan "Five Days in Fallujah," The *Atlantic Monthly* 294 (July/August 2004), 1:pp. 116-26.

For the indecisive conclusion to the first battle of Fallujah, see 1MarDiv ComdC Jan-Jun04; U.S. Army National Ground Intelligence Center, "Complex Environments: Battle of Fallujah 1," April04, S-4504-06.

For the Sadr Uprising and the Mahdi Army, see CJTF-76 April FragO 581; Estes, "1st Armored Division: Operation Iraqi Freedom, May 2004 -July 2004" (Wiesbaden: HQ 1st Arm Div, 2005); 1MarDiv 8Apr04 Intentions; 1MarDiv 11Apr04 Intentions.

For fighting in Ramadi during the spring of 2004, see 2d Bn, 4th Mar Intsum 06-07April04-7, S-0306-06\DiskFour\2-4JanApr(Sec)TabKS2\T\KS2\INTSUMS\APR; Morel and Copeland Navy Cross, Baptista, Bronzi and E. M. Smith silver star citations, RefSect.

For the redeployment of Regimental Combat Team 7 and Operation Ripper Sweep, see 1MarDiv Intentions 13Apr07; 1MarDiv Intentions 14Apr07; 1MarDiv 17Apr04 Intentions; 1MarDiv Intentions Apr-May04; 1Mar-Div ComdC June-July04; Regimental Combat Team 7 ComdC Apr-May04.

For the reorganization of the Combined Joint Task Force 7 into Multi National Force–Iraq and Multi National Corps–Iraq see Donald P. Wright and Colonel Timothy R. Reese with Contemporary Operations Study Team, *On Point II: Transition to the New Campaign: The United States Army in Operation Iraqi Freedom, May 2003–January 2005* (Fort Leavenworth, KS, 2008), pp. 173-176.

For I MEF operations during the spring and early summer of 2004, see 1MarDiv Intentions May-June04; 1Mar-Div ComdC Jan-Jun04; Regimental Combat Team 1 ComdC May04 and Jun04; Regimental Combat Team 7, ComdC May and Jun04; Silver Star citation Matthew A. Lopez, RefSect; 1MarDiv Intentions 26April04.

For the deployments of the 11th, 24th, and 31st Marine Expeditionary Units, see USMC Chronology, RefSect; Headquarters Marine Corps Operations Center (POC) "Current Operations Brief" 040518, 040621, 041004; 24 July report to 1stMarDiv by 24th MEU based upon 1MarDiv Intentions message that date; S-3937-06\IMEF sitreps\Jul04\11th MEU sitrep 31Jul04; Headquarters Marine Corps Operations Center (POC) "Current Operations Brief," 06June04; 040604; US-CENTCOM RFF serial 325 (020847Zjun04; Headquarters Marine Corps Operations Center (POC) "Current Operations Brief" 21Jun2004; COMMARFORPAC DEPORD 151900ZJun04.

For the Battle of an-Najaf see, Francis X. Kozlowski, *U.S. Marines in Battle: an-Najaf, August 2004* (Quantico, VA: Marine Corps History Division, 2009); Jackson, 89; G-3 I MEF "Information Memorandum on Operations in An-Najaf.

For the status of forces in July 2004, see Headquarters Marine Corps Operations Center (POC) "Current Operations Brief," 20July2004.

Chapter 5

For the situation in Fallujah during the summer of 2004, including security operations, the Fallujah Brigade, and attacks against I MEF forces, see I MEF Cdr Update 11May04, S-3709-06\CdrsUpdate Highlighted\May04; MajGen Amos in IMEF Cdr Updates 5May04, 20 May04, S-3709-06\CdrsUpdate Highlighted\May04; "Talking points for Fallujah Brigade Situation," S-3811-06\MEF Briefs; IMEF Cdr Updates 1May-1Sept04, S-3709-06\CdrsUpdate Highlighted \May04; "OIF II Aircraft Loss Report (as of 14Sep04)" in Headquarters Marine Corps Operations Center (POC) "Current Operations Brief" 041001; Sitrep 092200Sep04, S-3709-06\IMEF Sitrep\Sep04.

For preparations for the second battle of Fallujah, see Clifton Distinguished Flying Cross citation, RefSect; Slide, "Laptop Standalone" (7Sep04) and briefing, "Shaping Fallujah" (9Sept04), S-3811-06\MEF Briefs for Historical Purposes\VIP briefs; "TF 6-26 Fallujah Shaping Operations" (27Sept04), S-3811-06\MEF Briefs for Historical Purposes\VIP briefs\Prospective Slides; 1MarDiv Frag Orders 0295, 0300 and 0314-04, S-3925-06\1DivChron\DivClasChron IV items; 1MarDiv ComdC, July-Dec04; Headquarters Marine Corps Operations Center (POC) "Current Operations Brief"

01Oct04; Regimental Combat Team 1 and Regimental Combat Team 7 ComdC, July-Dec04; 31st MEU, "Operation Phantom Fury, Mission Analysis Briefing 28Oct04," S-3925-06\1stDivChronology\Ops History\ChronFileS3.

For the rocket attack on RCT-1's headquarters, see 1st Marines ComdC, 1Sept-31Sept04 (Gray Research Center, Quantico, VA), pp. 15-16.

For the plans for Operation Phantom Fury/al-Fajr see App 11–Intell Est, RCT7 FragO 0220-04 31Oct04, S-3813-06\Regimental Combat Team 7 docs\Operation Phantom Fury CD; "Regimental Combat Team 7 Mission Analysis and COA Development Fallujah 24Sep04," S-3815-06\Chessani\planning docs; cf. "Falluja II OPT" (1Oct04) Regimental Combat Team 1, S-3815-06\Chessani\planning docs; 1 Div Chronology July-Dec04; Regimental Combat Team 1 Intentions Messages, S-3925-06\1st MarDiv ComdC Dec04\RCT1 Part III TAB C\November Intentions; Regimental Combat Team 7 Intentions messages, S-3925-06\1st Div Chronology Dec04\Regimental Combat Team 7 July-Dec04\Regimental Combat Team 7 Command Chrono\Regimental Combat Team 7\November Supporting docs; Lee Silver Star citation, RefSect.

For the events of the second battle of Fallujah see Regimental Combat Team 1 "Air in Fallujah," S-4501-06.

For details and illustrations, see "Aviation FiresCon-Ops," S-3925-06\1stDivChronology Dec04\RCT1 Part IV\H Tab\"Phantom Fury Air Brief v.3.ppt" (11/2/2004). "I MEF OIF2.2 11 Sept for BG Mcabee," S-3811-06\MEF briefs historical\VIP briefs\VIP briefs for WEB. Fred Allison, "Urban CAS Marine Corps Style Fallujah 2004" unpublished essay, Marine Corps Historical Division (December, 2007); 1MarDiv ComdC July-Dec04; MNF-I "Fallujah Strategic Mission Analysis Briefing (3Oct 04)," S-4501-06; I MEF Sitrep of 9 Nov2004; Regimental Combat Team 1 Intentions, S-3925-06\1st Div Chronology Dec04\RCT1 Part III TAB C\November Intentions; Regimental Combat Team 7 Intentions, S-3925-133 06\1st Div Chronology Dec04\Regimental Combat Team 7 July-Dec04\Regimental Combat Team 7 ComdC\Regimental Combat Team 7\ November Supporting docs; 2-7 Cavalry, "Optimized Fallujah Storyboard, S-3925-06\1st Div Chronology Dec04\2-7 Cav; Adelsperger Navy Cross (posthumous) and Kirk Silver Star citations, RefSect; Regimental Combat Team 1 Intentions 12 Nov04, S-3925-06\1st Div Chronology Dec04\RCT1 Part III TAB C\November Intentions; 1MarDiv Jan-July04 Sign-Events, S-3801-06; Fallujah Capt Winslow\S-3515 to 3519-06; Department of Defense "Fallujah Update 05 Nov 04" S-4503-06; "Optimized Train Station Reconnaissance Results," Regimental Combat Team 1, S-3815-06\Chessani \planning docs for photos of Regimental Combat Team 1 assembly areas, routes; "Iraqi Order" Regimental Combat Team 1, S-3815-06\Chessani\planning docs for details of Regimental Combat Team 1 assault, plus detailing of Iraqi FOF for pacification, Phase IV.

For aviation operations during Operation al-Fajr see Major A. R. Milburn "Lessons Learned; Operation Phantom Fury" 5 Jan 05, S-4501-06; Regimental Combat Team 1 CommandBriefDec04, S-3925-06\1stDivChonologyDec04\RCT1 Jul Dec04 PartIV\I Tab; Regimental Combat Team 1 "Air in Fallujah", S-4501-06; Artillery table from S-4501-06, unknown provenance.

For the stabilization operations during Operation al-Fajr see Regimental Combat Team 1 Intentions (various), S-3925-06\1st Div Chronology Dec04\RCT1 Part III TAB C\November Intentions; Regimental Combat Team 7 Intentions (various), S-3925-06\1st Div Chronology Dec04\Regimental Combat Team 7 July-Dec04\Regimental Combat Team 7 Command Chrono\Regimental Combat Team 7\ November Supporting docs; Regimental Combat Team 1 intentions, 12Nov04; Kasal and Mitchell Navy Cross citations, Refsect; I MEF sitreps, Nov-Dec 04; The Regimental Combat Team 1 ComdC Dec04 also notes 23 December as the beginning of Phase IV operation; Krafft and Workman Navy Cross citations, RefSect. Colonel John Ballard comments on draft manuscript, 11Jun08; "Phantom Fury Phase IV" S-3815-06\Chessani\ planning docs; also in Regimental Combat Team 1 Frag order 001(Phase IV) to OpOrd 003-04 (Phantom Fury), S-3815\Regimental Combat Team 1 FragOsl.

For assessments of the second battle of al-Fajr, see 1MarDiv, "Phase IV ConOps" (11Oct04), S-4501-06; "Phantom Fury Phase IV" Regimental Combat Team 1, S-3815-06\Chessani\planning docs; LtGen John F. Sattler and LtCol Daniel H. Wilson, "Operation Al Fajr: The Battle of Fallujah–Part II," *Marine Corps Gazette* 89 (July, 2005) 7:12-24; "Intercept from Phantom Fury;" S-4501-06–redacted for declassification purposes. As of 27 Dec 04, cited in Headquarters Marine Corps Operations Center (POC) "Current Operations Brief" 041227 "Source: HQMC CRC manpower officer;" Headquarters Marine Corps Operations Center (POC) "Current Operations Brief" 041227.

Chapter 6

For information on the transfers of authority in al-Anbar during the winter of 2004-2005, see Headquarters Marine Corps Operations Center (POC) "Current Operations Brief" 24Nov04 and 09Dec04; 1MarDiv

ComdC July-Dec04.

For actions supporting the January 2005 elections see Headquarters Marine Corps Operations Center (POC) "Current Operations Briefs" for 09Dec04, 22Dec04, 02Feb05, 07Feb05, 11Feb05, 18Feb05, 11Jan05, 20Jan05, 24Jan05, 24Oct05; "Election draft FragO" (MNF-I), S-4522-06\HistoricFiles\Elections; I MEF sitreps26-31Jan04; I MEF sitrep, 30Jan04.

For the repopulation of Fallujah, see 1MarDiv ComdC Jan-June05.

For I MEF operations in early 2005, see I MEF, "Operation Iraqi Freedom II. 2 August, 2004-March, 2005," author files; 1MarDiv ComdC Jan-Jun05; 31st MEU ComdC Jan-Jun05; 7th Marines ComdC Jan-Jun05; Headquarters Marine Corps Operations Center (POC) "Current Operations Brief" 09Dec04 Headquarters Marine Corps Operations Center (POC) "Current Operations Brief" 24Jan05; Headquarters Marine Corps Operations Center (POC) "Current Operations Brief" 11Feb05; Headquarters Marine Corps Operations Center (POC) "Current Operations Brief" 29Mar05; Headquarters Marine Corps Operations Center (POC) "Current Operations Brief" 18Feb05050218.

Chapter 7

For Multi National Force–Iraq's operational goals and plans for 2005, see "Thoughts on the Current Situation in Raleigh and Fallujah," S-3815-06\Chessani\Planning Docs; "CASB-12Jun04, with attached OPlan Sovereign Iraq (May04 draft)," S-4521-06\TOA and After.

For the Commandant's planning guidance and deployment plans of II MEF, see 24Jun04 draft Command Marine Corps (CMC) planning guidance for Operation Iraqi Freedom III, CMC 081328ZJul04, and LOI for II MEF Operation Iraqi Freedom III OPT 2-20Aug04; S-4521-06\Operation Iraqi FreedomIII; "AO Atlanta Assessment" in 2d Intel Battalion,"Operation Iraqi Freedom III OPB 134 040902" briefing, S-4521-06\Operation Iraqi Freedom III OPT; II MEF ComdC Feb-Apr05; 2d AA Battalion ComdC JJ05; Regimental Combat Team 8 ComdC JJ05; Headquarters Marine Corps Operations Center (POC) Daily Briefs Jan-Apr05; 3d Bn, 25th Mar ComdC Jan-Jun05; Headquarters Marine Corps Operations Center (POC) "Current Operations Brief" 17Mar05.

For supply issues faced by II MEF, see Marine Corps Logistics Cmd, ComdC2004; Headquarters Marine Corps Operations Center (POC) "Current Operations Brief" 22Feb05.

For II MEF operations during the first months of deployment in 2005, see Headquarters Marine Corps Operations Center (POC) "Current Operations Brief"

17Mar05; II MEF ComdC Feb-Apr05; Regimental Combat Team 2 ComdC Jan-Jun05; Bn, 8th Mar ComdC Jan05; 3d Bn, 4th Mar ComdC Jan-Mar05; A/2d LAR Bn ComdC Jan-Apr05; Regimental Combat Team 8 ComdC Jan-Jun05; Headquarters Marine Corps Operations Center (POC) "Current Operations Brief" 050211-15; 155th BCT Sitrep 132000Feb05, S-4489-06\155BCT\05 Feb; Headquarters Marine Corps Operations Center (POC) "Current Operations Brief" 25Jan05, 08Jan05, 17Mar05, 04April05, 07April05; 1st Bn, 1st Mar ComdC Jan-Jun05; MAG-26 ComdC, Mar05 and Apr05.

Chapter 8

For Operation River Blitz and River Bridge, see 2MarDiv Sitrep 050317, S-4489-06\2MarDiv Intentions Messages\05 Mar ; Headquarters Marine Corps Operations Center (POC) "Current Operations Brief" 31Mar05; II MEF ComdC Feb-Apr05.

For the insurgent attack on Camp Gannon and other operations on the Syrian-Iraqi border, see 1stMarDiv Intentions 050221, S-4489-06\2dMarDiv\2dMarDiv Intentions, see Regimental Combat Team 2 ComdC Jan-Jun05; Steve Fainaru, "The Grim Reaper, Riding a Firetruck in Iraq: Marines Recount Dramatic Assault At Base Near Syria" *Washington Post*, (10Apr05), A1.

For II MEF counterinsurgency operations throughout Area of Operations Atlanta, see Regimental Combat Team 2 ComdC JJ05, 3d Bn, 25th ComdC Mar JJ05; for op order and maps, photos see S-4491-06\Operation Matador\S3; RCT2 ComdC Jan-Jun05 and Jul-Sep05, 3d Battalion, 2d Mar ComdC July05, 3d Battalion, 25th Mar ComdC Jan-Jun05, July-Dec05; Stann and Wimberg (posthumous) Silver Star citations, RefSect; 1st Bn, 5th Mar ComdC Jan-Jun05; Russell Silver Star citation, RefSect.

Chapter 9

For the Sunni insurgency, see Regimental Combat Team 8 ComdC Jan-Jun05; 1st Bn, 6th Mar ComdC Jan-Jun05 also featuring excellent maps; Waldron Silver Star citation, RefSect.

For II MEF's campaign plan for 2005, see MEF Campaign Plan 28Jan05,S-0259-06\MNF-WSitreps\OpOrd-Annexes.

For II MEF's combat power in al-Anbar, see Headquarters Marine Corps Operations Center (POC) "Current Operations Brief" 04Aug05; RCT2 ComdC Jul-Sep05; 3d Bn 2d Mar ComdC Aug05; 3d Bn, 25th Mar ComdC July-Dec05; A/1st Tk Bn ComdC Aug05.

For II MEF counterinsurgency operations in al-Anbar during the summer of 2005, see "Multi-National

Force West (MNF-W) Operations Order 1-05 (Title: Operation Iraqi Freedom 04-06 Campaign Plan)", S-0259-06\Opord-Annexes; 2MarDv Intentions 30May05, S-4489-06\2dMarDiv\2dMarDiv Intentions Messages\05May; 2MarDiv Intentions 06Jun05, S-4489-06\2dMarDiv\2dMarDiv Intentions Messages\05Jun; Regimental Combat Team 2 ComdC Jul-30Sep05; Headquarters Marine Corps Operations Center (POC) "Current Operations Brief" 01Aug05.

For the situation on the Iraq-Syrian border and II MEF efforts to address the weak defenses there, see II MEF Sitrep 050901; S-0259-06\MNFW Sitreps\Sep05; "Task Force Phantom Tacon To 2d MarDiv (revised)"; S-0627-06\publishedfragorders; "FECC Classified Command Chronology May 05 to Dec 05; S-4523-06\G-3\FECC; Regimental Combat Team 2 ComdC Jul-Sep05.

For information on training Iraqi military forces see "BTT Location" "POE Brief v7.1" and "Al Qaim COA Brief," S-0266-06\ISF\DBE; Headquarters Marine Corps Operations Center (POC) "Current Operations Brief" 05May05, 01Jun05, 31Aug05; "BTT Location 25 Dec," S-0266-06\ISF enclosures.

Chapter 10

For information on Iraqi Security Forces, see "Strategic Basing & ISF Laydown Narrative" (16Apr05), S-4489-06\ISF; "MNF-W ISF Monthly Status," Headquarters Marine Corps Operations Center (POC) "Current Operations Brief" 31Aug05; 7th IA Div movement in Headquarters Marine Corps Operations Center (POC) "Current Operations Brief" 15Feb06; MTT data from Headquarters Marine Corps Operations Center (POC) "Current Operations Brief" 31Oct05; 2MarDiv G-3 ComdC Nov05 and Dec05; 13th MEU ComdC July-Dec05; "021600CDec05. Cg.Loo.Briefing.Graphics," S-0261-06\Dec05.

For II MEF efforts to encourage voting in al-Anbar, see 2MarDiv Frago 0158-05 of 30Jul05: Operation Liberty Express; S-4509-06\Elections Turnover.

For counterinsurgency operations during the latter half of 2005 see "Div Liberty Express OPT Outbrief (08 Aug 05) V.2 (Optimized)" [with excellent illustrations], S-4509-06\Elections Turnover\Liberty Express Documents; II MEF Future Ops [staff section] ComdC JD05, S-4523-06\G3\FOPS; "Border FortCode Words 5-18" (15Jan06), S-0266-06\ISF enclosures\DBE; FECC Classified Command Chronology May 05 to Dec 05; S-4523-06\G3\FECC; Headquarters Marine Corps Operations Center (POC) "Current Operations Brief" 03Oct05; 3d Bn, 6th Mar ComdC Oct-Dec05; 1st Tk Bn ComdC July-Dec05; Foncon au with Lieutenant Colonel Alford, 03Jun08; Headquarters Marine Corps Operations Center

(POC) "Current Operations Brief" 03Oct05; 2MarDiv Hq Bn G-3 ComdC Oct05; 2MarDiv Hq Bn G-3 ComdC Oct05; Headquarters Marine Corps Operations Center (POC) "Current Operations Brief" 051019; I MEF Future Ops ComdC July-Dec05, S-4523-06\G3\FOPS; "270001.Cdec05.Firm Bases.Hadithah.Haqliniyah.Barwana"; S-0621-06\Dec05; 2Mardiv 061212COct05 Mod 2 To FragO 0158-05, S-4509-06\Elections Turnover\Liberty Express Documents\Div Liberty Express FragO; After action reports of 2d Marine Division, 8th Marines and 2d Brigade: S-4509-06\Elections Turnover\Liberty Express Documents\After action reports; Headquarters Marine Corps Operations Center (POC) "Current Operations Brief" 28Oct065; 13th MEU ComdC July-Dec05; 2MarDiv G-3 ComdC Sept05 and Oct, Nov05; 2MarDiv G-3 ComdC Nov05; "010001CDec05.Op.Hard.Knock;" S-0261-06\Dec05; 2MarDiv G-3 ComdC Dec05; "Div Liberty Express Transition Brief (11 Dec 05)"; S-0237-06\1-LibertyExpress Documents; 2MarDiv G-3 ComdC Dec05; "312400CDec05.3.1.Op.Red.Bull" "Green Trident" and "Bulldog," S-0261-06\Dec05; II MEF FOPS ComdC July-Dec05; 2MarDiv G-3 ComdC Dec 05; casualties from Headquarters Marine Corps Operations Center (POC) "Current Operations Brief" 03Jan06.

For information on the Constitutional Referendum Elections, see John Ward Anderson and Jonathan Finer, "Pollings Close in Iraq: Large Numbers Turn Out Despite Sporadic Violence" *Washington Post* (October 15, 2005).

For a summary of Operation Hunter see 13th MEU ComdC Oct-Dec05; ComdC 3d Bn, 6th Mar Oct-Dec05; "012400CDec05. Op.Hunter.Effects.Complete", S-0261-06\Dec05; 2MarDiv G-3 ComdC Nov05; II MEF, "012400CDec05.Op.Hunter. Effects.Complete," "012000CDec05.ISF.Laydown," S-0261-06\Dec05; 2MarDiv G-3 ComdC Nov05; MNF-W Sitrep 051110, S-0259-06. 3d Bn, 6th Mar Oct-Dec05; "012400CDec05. Op.Hunter.Effects.Complete", S-0261-06\Dec05; 2MarDiv G-3 ComdC Nov05.

Chapter 11

For the operations of Marine Corps civil affairs groups as well as reconstruction projects, see 5th CAG ComdC Sept-Dec05; 4th CAG ComdC Jul-Dec05; 5th CAG ComdC Jul-Dec05; 6th CAG, "Finding Guide for the Records of the 6th Civil Affairs group (Provi-

sional)," in a 362Mb disc filed with the ComdC Jul-Dec05 and Jan-May06. Operational archives of 5th CAG are in S-4488-06, for 6th CAG in S 0237, 0238, 0243-06; II MEF Presidential Unit Citation Award Recommendation 2005–2006, RefSect.

For aviation operations during 2005, see MAG-26 ComdC Mar05; VMU-1 and VMU-2, ComdC 2005; II MEF Aviation Universal Needs Statements on UAV, common data/ground links and pods are contained in S-0265-06; 2d MAW, "Operation Matador 8-14 May Rollup;" S-0265-06\Aviation Strike Reports; "MNF-W Combat Operations in Review (28Jan06), S-0262-06\Jan06.

For logistics operations, see 2d MLG, CLR-25, CLB-2, CLB-8 ComdC Mar-Dec05; "MNF-W Combat Operations in Review (28Jan06), S-0262-06\Jan06.

Chapter 12

For the need for police forces and plans for training them, see II MEF, "Al Anbar: Near Term Way Ahead (13Jan06)," S-4557-06\G3 1of7\V Corp Brief on Al Anbar (13 Jan) (ver5.2).

For II MEF operations during the first months of 2006, as well as the relief of II MEF by I MEF in early 2006, see MNF-W Combat Operations in Review (28Jan06)," S-0262-06\Jan06; 22d MEU ComdC JJ06; Headquarters Marine Corps Operations Center (POC) "Current Operations Briefs" 03Jan06-28Feb06; II MEF Sitrep 051231, S-0259-06\MNFW Sitreps\Dec05

For General Mattis' recommendations for new command structures for Marine Expeditionary Force deployments to Iraq, see Mattis interview 12Oct07; I MEF ComdC Jan-Jun06.

For Marine Corps casualties sustained in Iraq since 2003, see Headquarters Marine Corps Operations Center (POC) "Current Operations Brief" 01Mar06.

Major General Johnson's thoughts on the accomplishments of II MEF in Iraq can be accessed at http://www.defense.gov/transcripts/transcript.aspx?transcriptid=879.

Epilogue

For analysis of whether or not the coalition deployed enough troops to Iraq, see Carter Malkasian, "Did the Coalition Need More Forces in Iraq? Evidence from Al Anbar," (Alexandria: Center for Naval Analyses, 18 November 2006).

Appendix A

Command and Staff List[1]

I Marine Expeditionary Force (Forward)/Multi National Force-West
March 2004-February 2005

Commanding General: LtGen James T. Conway (until September 2004)
LtGen John F. Sattler
Deputy: MajGen Keith J. Stalder (until May 2004)
BGen Dennis J. Hejlik
Chief of Staff: Col John C. Coleman
G-1: Col William J. Hartig (until May 2004)
Col Eric D. Bartch
G-2: Col James R. Howcroft (until June 2004)
Col Ronald S. Makuta
G-3: Col Larry K. Brown (until June 2004)
Col Michael R. Regner
G-4: Col Bruce E. Bissett (until June 2004)
Col Andrew Reynosa III
G-5: Col Anthony L. Jackson (until June 2004)
Col Richard O. Bartch
G-6: Col Marshall I. Considine III (until June 2004)
LtCol Martin E. Lapierre Jr.

I MEF Headquarters Group
Commanding Officer: Col John C. Cunnings (until June 2004)
Col Joseph A. Bruder IV

11th Marine Expeditionary Unit (SOC)
Commanding Officer: Col Anthony M. Haslam

24th Marine Expeditionary Unit (SOC)
Commanding Officer: Col Robert J. Johnson

31st Marine Expeditionary Unit (-) (Reinforced)
Commanding Officer: Col Walter L. Miller Jr.

3d Civil Affairs Group
Commanding Officer: Col Michael M. Walker

4th Civil Affairs Group
Commanding Officer: Col John R. Ballard

Marine Ground Combat Element

1st Marine Division (-) (Reinforced)
Commanding General: MajGen James N. Mattis (until August 2004)
MajGen Richard F. Natonski
Assistant Division Commander: BGen John F. Kelly (until July 2004)
BGen Joseph F. Dunford Jr.

Chief of Staff: Col Joseph F. Dunford Jr. (until July 2004)
        Col Robert J. Knapp

1st Marine Regiment (-) (Reinforced) (Regimental Combat Team 1)
Commanding Officer: Col John A. Toolan (until September 2004)
        Col Lawrence D. Nicholson (14 September, 2004)
        Col Michael A. Shupp

7th Marine Regiment (-) (Reinforced) (Regimental Combat Team 7)
Commanding Officer: Col Craig A. Tucker

1st Brigade, 1st Infantry Division (U.S. Army)
Commanding Officer: Col Arthur W. Connor Jr., USA

2d Brigade, (-) (Reinforced), 1st Cavalry Division "Black Jack" (U.S. Army)
Commanding Officer: Col Michael D. Formica, USA

2d Brigade (-) (Reinforced), 2d Infantry Division, "Strike Force Brigade" (U.S. Army)
Commanding Officer: Col Gary S. Patton, USA

Marine Aviation Combat Element

3d Marine Aircraft Wing (-) (Reinforced)
Commanding Officer: MajGen James F. Amos (until May 2004)
        MajGen Keith J. Stalder

Assistant Wing Commander: Col Roy A. Arnold

Chief of Staff: Col Gerald A. Yingling Jr. (until July 2004)
        Col Rex C. McMillian (until October 2004)
        Col Rick W. Schmidt

Marine Aircraft Group 16 (-) (Reinforced)
Commanding Officer: Col Stuart L. Knoll (until April 2004)
        Col Guy M. Close

Marine Air Control Group 38 (-) (Reinforced)
Commanding Officer: Col Ronnell R. McFarland (until June 2004)
        Col Jonathan G. Miclot

Marine Wing Support Group 37 (-) (Reinforced)
Commanding Officer: Col Juan G. Ayala

Marine Combat Service Support Element

1st Force Service Support Group (-) (Reinforced)
Commanding Officer: BGen Richard S. Kramlich

Deputy Commander: Col John L. Sweeney Jr.
Chief of Staff: Col Tracy L. Mork

Combat Service Support Group 11 (-)
Commanding Officer: Col David B. Reist

Combat Service Support Group 15 (-) (Reinforced)
Commanding Officer: Col Michael E. Kampsen

I Marine Expeditionary Force Engineer Group

Commanding Officer: RAdm Charles R. Kubic
RAdm Raymond K. Alexander

II Marine Expeditionary Force (Forward)/Multi National Force-West
March 2005-February 2006

Commanding General: MajGen Stephen T. Johnson (until January 2006)
MajGen Richard A. Huck
Deputy: BGen Charles S. Patton
Chief of Staff: Col John L. Ledoux
G-1: LtCol John R. Armour (until September 2005)
Maj Blair S. Miles
G-2: Col John T. Cunnings
G-3: Col Glenn T. Starnes (until October 2005)
Col Thomas L. Cariker
G-4: Col John J. Fitzgerald Jr. (until July 2005)
Col. Donald C. Hales
G-5: Col Kenneth D. Bonner
G-6: Col Sean T. Mulcahy

II MEF Headquarters Group: (-) (Reinforced)
Commanding Officer: Col Daniel D. Leshchyshyn

13th Marine Expeditionary Unit (-)
Commanding Officer: Col James K. LaVine

15th Marine Expeditionary Unit (SOC)
Commanding Officer: Col Thomas C. Greenwood

22d Marine Expeditionary Unit
Commanding Officer: Col Kenneth F. McKenzie

5th Civil Affairs Group (Reinforced)
Commanding Officer: Col Steven E. McKinley

6th Civil Affairs Group
Commanding Officer: Col Paul W. Brier

155th Brigade Combat Team (Reinforced) (Army National Guard)
Commanding Officer: Col Augustus L. Collins, USA (until April 2005)

Marine Ground Combat Element

2d Marine Division (-) (Reinforced)
Commanding General: MajGen Richard A. Huck (until January 2006)
Assistant Division Commander: BGen Joseph J. McMenamin
Chief of Staff: Col Robert G. Sokoloski

2d Marine Regiment (-) (Reinforced) (Regimental Combat Team 2)
Commanding Officer: Col Stephen W. Davis

8th Marine Regiment (-) (Reinforced) (Regimental Combat Team 8)
Commanding Officer: Col Charles M. Gurganus (until August 2005)
Col David H. Berger

2d Brigade, 2d Infantry Division (Reinforced) (U.S. Army)
Commanding Officer: Col Gary S. Patton, USA

2d Brigade, 28th Infantry Division (Reinforced) (Army National Guard)
Commanding Officer: Col John L. Gronski, USA

Marine Aviation Combat Element

2d Marine Aircraft Wing (Forward)
Commanding General: BGen Robert E. Milstead
Chief of Staff Col John T. Rahm (until August 2005)
            Col Thomas M. Murray

Marine Aircraft Group 26 (-) (Reinforced)
Commanding Officer: Col Thomas M. Murray (until February 2006)
            Col David J. Mollahan

Marine Air Control Group 38
Commanding Officer: Col Jonathan G. Miclot

Marine Air Control Group 28 (-) (Reinforced)
Commanding Officer: Col Mark R. Cyr

Marine Wing Support Group 27 (Reinforced)
Commanding Officer: Col Scott M. Anderson

Marine Combat Service Support Element

2d Force Service Support Group (Forward)
Commanding General: BGen Ronald S. Coleman (until June 2005)
            BGen John E. Wissler

Chief of Staff: Col James E. McCown III

Combat Logistics Regiment 25
Commanding Officer: Col Robert W. Destafney (until September 2005)
            Col Dennis W. Ray

I Marine Expeditionary Force (Forward)/Multi National Force–West
March 2006–February 2007

Commanding General: MajGen Richard C. Zilmer
Deputy Commanding General for Operations: BGen Robert B. Neller
Deputy Commanding General for Support: BGen David G. Reist
Chief of Staff: Col George F. Milburn
G-1: Col Eric D. Bartch
G-2: Col Peter H. Devlin
G-3: Col Michael P. Marletto
G-4: Col Scott A. Dalke
G-5: Col Chad W. Hocking
G-6: Col Kirk E. Bruno

I MEF Headquarters Group
Commanding Officer: LtCol Thomas Ward

15th Marine Expeditionary Unit
Commanding Officer: Col Thomas C. Greenwood (Until August 2006)
            Col Brian D. Beaudreault

Marine Ground Combat Element

1st Marine Division (Forward)
Commanding General: MajGen Richard F. Natonski (until August 2006)
    MajGen John M. Paxton
Assistant Division Commander: Col Kevin A. Vietti
Chief of Staff: Col Kevin A. Vietti

5th Marine Regiment (-) (Reinforced) (Regimental Combat Team 5)
Commanding Officer: Col Lawrence D. Nicholson

7th Marine Regiment (-) (Reinforced) (Regimental Combat Team 7)
Commanding Officer: Col William B. Crowe

1st Brigade Combat Team, 1st Armored Division (U.S. Army)
Commanding Officer: Col Sean B. MacFarland, USA

Marine Aviation Combat Element

3d Marine Aircraft Wing
Commanding General: MajGen Samuel T. Helland
Assistant Wing Commander: Col Jonathan G. Miclot (until June 2006)
    Col Howard F. Baker
Chief of Staff: Col Rick W. Schmidt (until September 2006)
    Col Guy M. Close

Marine Aircraft Group 16
Commanding Officer: Col Guy M. Close (until May 2006)
    Col John C. Kennedy

Marine Aircraft Group 31
Commanding Officer: Col Robert Walsh (until May 2006)

Marine Air Control Group 38 (-) (Reinforced)
Commanding Officer: Col Jonathan G. Miclot (until June 2006)
    Col Mark G. Cianciolo

Marine Combat Service Support Element

1st Marine Logistics Group (-) (Reinforced)
Commanding General: BGen David G. Reist[2]
    Col David M. Richtsmeier (CO Fwd)[3]
Deputy Commander: Col Elvis E. Blumenstock[4]
Chief of Staff: Col Michael D. Malone (until January 2007)
    Col Juan G. Ayala

Combat Logistics Regiment 17
Commanding Officer: LtCol Todd A. Holmquist (until July 2006)
    LtCol James C. Caley (July-August 2006)
    LtCol Kirk C. Wille

Combat Logistics Regiment 15 (-) (Reinforced)
Commanding Officer: Col Charles L. Hudson (until June 2006)
    Col Brian J. Vincent III

Notes

1. To present a comprehensive order of battle for the entire period covered by this anthology (2004-08) would require a volume unto itself. The goal of this appendix is to give as comprehensive a list as possible within the space provided. Consequently, not all Marine Corps units deployed to Iraq between 2004 and 2008 are listed.

The majority of Marines deployed to Iraq during this time period were under the command of Multi National Force–West (MNF-West), which was coterminious with either I MEF (2004-05), II MEF (2005-06) or I MEF (2006-07). The appendix is divided by MEF deployment, and lists commanders down to the regimental level and units down to the battalion level that were at one time under the command of MNF-West during each MEF deployment.

The information is drawn from the following sources: I Marine Expeditionary Force Presidential Unit Citation Recommendation (2005), II Marine Expeditionary Force Presidential Unit Citation Recommendation (2006), I Marine Expeditionary Force Presidential Unit Citation Recommendation (2007), LtCol Kenneth W. Estes, "U.S. Marine Corps Operations in Iraq, 2003-2006" (Quantico, VA: History Division: United States Marine Corps, 2009), USMC History Division Reference Branch, "Chronology of U.S. Marines and Global War on Terror," at http://www.tecom .usmc.mil/HD/Chronologies/Campaign/GWOT_2001-2005.htm (accessed 3 June, 2009), and Institute for the Study of War, "Order of Battle, Coalition Combat Forces" at http://www.understandingwar.org /IraqOrderofBattle (accessed 3 June, 2009).

2. BGen Reist served as 1st MLG commanding general and as Deputy Commanding General for Supply. See 1st Marine Logistics Group (MLG), Command Chronology (CC), July-December 2006, p.2.

3. Col David M. Richtsmeier was Commanding Officer, 1st MLG (Fwd). See Cpl Daniel J. Redding, "Combat zone ingenuity protects Marines," Operation Iraqi Freedom—Official Website of Multi National Force–Iraq, 10 August, 2006, at http://dr15.ahp.dr1.us.army.mil/index.php?option=com_content&task=view&id=2005&Itemid=225. accessed 25 August, 2009.

4. Col Blumenstock served as Acting Commander, 1st MLG, while BGen Reist was deployed to Iraq as Deputy Commanding General for Supply, I MEF (FWD). See 1st MLG Command Chronology, July-January, 2006, p.3.

Appendix B

Unit List

U.S. Marines in Operation Iraqi Freedom
March 2004-February 2007

I Marine Expeditionary Force (Forward) [I MEF]/Multi National Force-West [MNF-W]
March 2004-February 2005

Command Element

11th Marine Expeditionary Unit (Special Operations Capable) [11th MEU (SOC)]

Battalion Landing Team 1st Battalion, 4th Marines [BLT 1/4]
Marine Medium Helicopter Squadron 166 (Reinforced) [HMM-166]
Marine Expeditionary Unit Service Support Group 11 [MSSG-11]
Task Force, 1st Battalion, 5th Cavalry (U.S. Army) [TF 1st Bn, 5th CavReg]
1st Battalion, 227th Aviation (U.S. Army) [1st Bn, 227th AvReg]
153d Engineer Battalion (U.S. Army) [153d EngrBn]
1st Battalion, 5th Special Forces Group (Airborne) (U.S. Army) [1st Bn 5th SFG]

24th Marine Expeditionary Unit (Special Operations Capable) [24th MEU (SOC)]

Battalion Landing Team 1st Battalion, 2d Marines [BLT 1/2]
Marine Medium Helicopter Squadron 263 (Reinforced) [HMM-263]
Marine Expeditionary Unit Service Support Group 24 [MSSG-24]
Task Force 2d Battalion, 24th Marines [TF 2d Bn 24th Mar]
Task Force "Blackwatch" (United Kingdom) [TF "Blackwatch"]

31st Marine Expeditionary Unit (-) (Reinforced) [31st MEU]

1st Battalion, 23d Marines (Reinforced) [1st Bn 23d Mar]
Task Force Naha [TF Naha]
Marine Medium Helicopter Squadron 265 (Reinforced) [HMM-265]
1st Battalion, 7th Marines (Reinforced) [1st Bn 7th Mar]
Battalion Landing Team 1st Battalion, 3d Marines [BLT 1/3]
3d Battalion, 5th Marines [3d Bn 5th Mar]
Marine Expeditionary Unit Service Support Group 31 [MSSG-31]
2d Force Reconnaissance Company (-) [2d ForReconCo]
2d Battalion, 11th Marines (-) (Reinforced) (Provisional MP Battalion) [2d Bn 11th Mar]

I Marine Expeditionary Force Headquarters Group [I MEF HqGru]

2d Intelligence Battalion (-) (Reinforced) [2d IntelBn]
2d Radio Battalion (-) [2d RadBn]
9th Communications Battalion (-) (Reinforced) [9th CommBn]
Battery C, 1st Battalion, 10th Marines [Btry C, 1st Bn, 10th Mar]
Battery E, 2d Battalion, 10th Marines [Btry E, 2d Bn, 10th Mar]
Detachment, 1st Air Naval Gunfire Liaison Company [Det, 1st ANGLICO]
       3d Civil Affairs Group [3d CAG]
       4th Civil Affairs Group [4th CAG]

Marine Ground Combat Element

1st Marine Division (-) (Reinforced) [1st MarDiv]

Headquarters Battalion (Reinforced) [HqBn]
Small Craft Co (-) [Small Crft Co]
2d Battalion (-) 11th Marines (Reinforced) [2d Bn, 11th Mar]
3d Battalion, 24th Marines [3d Bn, 24th Mar]
3d Battalion (-) 11th Marines (Reinforced) [3d Bn, 11th Mar]
2d Battalion, 4th Marines [2d Bn, 4th Mar]

1st Marines (-) (Reinforced)/Regimental Combat Team 1 [1st Mar/RCT-1]

2d Platoon (-), 1st Force Reconnaissance Company [2d Plt, 1st ForReconCo]
Fire Control Team, 1st Air Naval Gunfire Liaison Company [FCT, 1st ANGLICO]
2d Battalion, 1st Marines [2d Bn, 1st Mar]
3d Battalion, 1st Marines [3d Bn, 1st Mar]
2d Battalion, 2d Marines [2d Bn, 2d Mar]
3d Battalion 4th Marines (Reinforced) [3d Bn, 4th Mar]
1st Battalion, 5th Marines [1st Bn, 5th Mar]
3d Battalion, 5th Marines [3d Bn, 5th Mar]
3d Battalion, 8th Marines (Reinforced) [3d Bn, 8th Mar]
Task Force 2d Battalion 7th Cavalry (U.S. Army) [TF 2d Bn, 7th Cav]
Task Force Light Armored Reconnaissance [TF LAR]
1st Reconnaissance Battalion [1st ReconBn]
2d Reconnaissance Battalion [2d ReconBn]
Company B, 1st Battalion 4th Marines (-) (Reinforced), [Co B, 1st Bn, 4th Mar]
Company D, 2d Assault Amphibian Battalion (Reinforced) [Co D, 2d AABn]
Company C, 2d Tank Battalion (Reinforced) [Co C, 2d CmbtEngBn]
Company B, 2d Combat Engineer Battalion, (-) (Reinforced) [Co B, 2d CEB]
Battery M, 4th Battalion, 14th Marines (Reinforced) [Btry M, 4th Bn, 14th Mar]

7th Marines (-) (Reinforced)/Regimental Combat Team 7 [7th Mar/RCT-7]

1st Battalion, 7th Marines [1st Bn, 7th Mar]
2d Battalion, 7th Marines [2d Bn, 7th Mar]
3d Battalion, 7th Marines [3d Bn, 7th Mar]
1st Battalion, 8th Marines (Reinforced) [1st Bn, 8th Mar]
1st Battalion, 23d Marines [1st Bn, 23d Mar]
Battalion Landing Team 1st Battalion, 3d Marines (Reinforced) [BLT 1/3]
1st Force Reconnaissance Company [1st ForReconCo]
2d Force Reconnaissance Company [2d ForReconCo]
3d Light Armored Reconnaissance Battalion [3d LAR Bn]
Task Force 2d Battalion, 2d Infantry (-),(U.S. Army) [TF 2d Bn, 2d Inf]
Company C, 3d Battalion, 82d Field Artillery (U.S. Army) [Co C, 3d Bn, 82d FldArty]
Company A, 2d Tank Battalion (-) (Reinforced) [Co A, 2d Tank Bn]
Detachment, Company C (-), 2d Combat Engineer Battalion [Det, Co C, 2d
        CmbtEngrBn]
Detachment, Company A (-), 3d Light Armored Reconnaissance Battalion
        [Det, Co A, 3d LAR]
Marine Expeditionary Force Service Support Group 31 [MSSG-31]

2d Brigade (-) (Reinforced), 1st Cavalry Division "Black Jack" (U.S. Army) [2d Bde, 1st CavDiv]

15th Forward Support Battalion (U.S. Army) [15 FwdSptBn]

Task Force 1st Battalion, 5th Infantry "Stryker" (U.S. Army) [TF "Stryker"]
Task Force 1st Battalion, 5th Cavalry (U.S. Army) [TF 1st Bn, 5th Cav]
Battery A, 3d Battalion, 82d Field Artillery (U.S. Army) [A Btry, 82d FldArty]
Attack Helicopter (U.S. Army) [Atk Helo]
Company B, 312th Military Intelligence Battalion (U.S. Army) [B Co, 312th MilIntelBn]
Company B (-), 13th Signal Battalion (U.S. Army) [B Co, 13th SigBn]
759th Composite MP Battalion (U.S. Army) [759th Comp MPBn]
2d Reconnaissance Battalion (-) (Reinforced) [2d ReconBn]
Company A (Reinforced), 2d Light Armored Reconnaissance Battalion,
    [Co A, 2d LAR Bn]
Detachment, Explosive Ordinance Disposal Platoon (-), 63d Ordnance Battalion
    [Det, EOD Plt, 63d OrdBn]

1st Brigade, 1st Infantry Division (U.S. Army) [1st Bde, 1st InfDiv]

2d Battalion, 4th Marines [2d Bn, 4th Mar]

2d Brigade (-) (Reinforced), 2d Infantry Division "Strike Force Brigade" (U.S. Army)
    [2d Bde, 2d Inf]

2d Battalion, 2d Force Support Battalion (Reinforced) (U.S. Army),
    [2d Bn, 2dForSuppBn]
Task Force 1st Battalion, 503d Infantry (-), (U.S. Army) [TF 1st Bn, 503d Inf]
Task Force 1st Battalion, 506th Infantry (-) (U.S. Army) [TF 1st Bn, 506th Inf]
Task Force 1st Battalion, 9th Infantry (U.S. Army) [TF 1st Bn, 9th Inf]
Task Force 2d Battalion, 17th Field Artillery (U.S. Army) [TF 2d Bn, 17th FldArty]
44th Engineering Battalion (-) (U.S. Army) [44th EngrBn]
Company A, 102d Military Intelligence Battalion (U.S. Army) [Co A, 102d MilIntel Bn]
Company B(-), 122d Signal Battalion (U.S. Army) [Co B, 122d SigBn]
Company B, 5th Battalion, 5th Air Defense Artillery (U.S. Army) [Co B, 5th Bn,
    5th AirDefArty]
2d Battalion 5th Marines (Reinforced) [2d Bn, 5th Mar]

Marine Aviation Combat Element

3d Marine Aircraft Wing (-) (Reinforced) [3d MAW]

Marine Wing Headquarters Squadron 3 (-) (Reinforced) [MWHS-3]

Marine Aircraft Group 16 (-) (Reinforced) [MAG-16]

Marine Light Attack Helicopter Squadron 367, MAG-39 [HMLA-367]
Marine Light Attack Helicopter Squadron 169 (-), MAG-39 [HMLA-169]
Marine Medium Helicopter Squadron 268, MAG-39 [HMM-268]
Marine Medium Helicopter Squadron 365, MAG-29, 2d MAW [HMM-365]
Marine Medium Helicopter Squadron 774, MAG-42, 4th MAW [HMM-774]
Marine Heavy Helicopter Squadron 361 [HMH-361]
Marine Fighter Attack Squadron (All-Weather) 242, MAG-11 [VMFA(AW)-242]
Marine Attack Squadron 542 [VMA-542]
Marine Attack Squadron 311 [VMA-311]
Marine Aviation Logistics Squadron 16 (-) (Reinforced) [MALS-16]

Marine Air Control Group 38(-) (Reinforced) [MACG-38]

Marine Tactical Air Command Squadron (-) (Reinforced) [MTACS-38]
Marine Air Support Squadron 3 (-) (Reinforced) [MASS-3]

Marine Wing Communications Squadron 38 (-) (Reinforced) [MWCS-38]
Marine Air Control Squadron 1 (-) (Reinforced) [MACS-1]
Marine Unmanned Aerial Vehicle Squadron 1 [VMU-1]
Marine Unmanned Aerial Vehicle Squadron 2 [VMU-2]

Marine Wing Support Group 37 (-) (Reinforced) [MWSG-37]

Marine Wing Support Squadron 373 [MWSS-373]
4th Low Altitude Air Defense Battalion (Reinforced), 4th MAW (Prov Sec
    Battalion, Al Asad) [4th LAAD Bn]
Battery F, 2d Battalion, 10th Marines (Tactical Control from 1st FSSG) [Btry F,
    2d Bn, 10th Mar]
Battery K, 4th Battalion, 14th Marines [Btry K, 4th Bn, 14th Mar]
Battery P, 5th Battalion, 14th Marines [Btry P, 5th Bn, 14th Mar]
Detachment, Marine Air Control Squadron 1 [Det, MACS-1]

Marine Wing Support Squadron 472 [MWSS-472]
Detachment, 9th Communication Battalion [Det, 9th CommBn]
326th Area Support Group (U.S. Army) [326th AreaSptGru]
1439th Engineer Team (U.S. Army) [1439th EngrTm]
767th Engineer Team (U.S. Army) [767th EngrTm]

Marine Combat Service Support Element

1st Force Service Support Group (-) (Reinforced) [1st FSSG]

Headquarters and Service Battalion [HqSBn]
2d Battalion, 10th Marines (-) (Reinforced) [2d Bn, 10th Mar]

Combat Service Support Group 11 (-) [CSSG-11]

Combat Service Support Battalion 1 [CSSB-1]
Combat Service Support Battalion 7 [CSSB-7]

Combat Service Support Group 15 (-) (Reinforced) [CSSG-15]

I Marine Expeditionary Force Engineer Group [I MEFEngrGru]

Task Force Charlie [TF Charlie]
Task Force Echo [TF Echo]
Task Force Sierra [TF Sierra]
Task Force Tango [TF Tango]

With Participating Members From:

1st Naval Construction Battalion [1st NCB]
7th Naval Construction Regiment [7th NCR]
22d Naval Construction Regiment [22 NCR]
20th Seabee Readiness Group [20th CRG]
31st Seabee Readiness Group [31st CRG]
Naval Mobile Construction Battalion 3 [NMCB 3]
Naval Mobile Construction Battalion 4 [NMCB 4]
Naval Mobile Construction Battalion 7 [NMCB 7]
Naval Mobile Construction Battalion 14 [NMCB 14]
Naval Mobile Construction Battalion 15 [NMCB 15]
Naval Mobile Construction Battalion 17 [NMCB 17]
Naval Mobile Construction Battalion 23 [NMCB 23]

Naval Mobile Construction Battalion 74 [NMCB 74]
Naval Mobile Construction Battalion 133 [NMCB 133]
120th Engineer Battalion (Combat Heavy) (U.S. Army) [120th EngrBn]

II Marine Expeditionary Force (Forward)/Multi National Force–West [II MEF (FWD)/MNF-W] March 2005-February 2006

Command Element

13th Marine Expeditionary Unit (-) [13th MEU]

Command Element
Battalion Landing Team 2d Battalion, 1st Marines [BLT 2/1]
Marine Medium Helicopter Squadron 163 [HMM-163]
Marine Expeditionary Unit Service Support Group 13 [MSSG-13]

22d Marine Expeditionary Unit (-) [22d MEU]

Command Element
Battalion Landing Team 1st Battalion, 2d Marines [BLT 1/2]
Marine Medium Helicopter Squadron 261 [HMM-261]
Marine Expeditionary Unit Service Support Group 22 [MSSG-22]

II MEF Headquarters Group (-) (Reinforced) [II MEF HqGru]

Headquarters and Service Company [HqSCo]
Headquarters and Service Company, 4th Tank Battalion, 4th Marine Division
(Provisional MP) (Reinforced) [HqSCo 4th Tank Bn, 4th MarDiv]
Company A, 4th Tank Battalion [A Co, 4th Tank Bn]
Company B, 4th Tank Battalion [B Co, 4th Tank Bn]
Battery C, 1st Battalion, 14th Marines [Btry C, 1st Bn, 14th Mar]
Battery D, 2d Battalion, 14th Marines [Btry D, 2d Bn, 14th Mar]
Headquarters Battery, 5th Battalion, 14th Marines [HqBtry, 5th Bn, 14th Mar]
Battery N, 5th Battalion, 14th Marines [Btry N, 5th Bn, 14th Mar]
Battery O, 5th Battalion, 14th Marines [Btry O, 5th Bn, 14th Mar]
Company E, 2d Battalion, 25th Marines [Co E, 2d Bn, 25th Mar]
Battery D, 2d Battalion, 14th Marines [Btry D, 2d Bn, 14th Mar]
Battery C, 1st Battalion, 14th Marines [Btry C, 1st Bn, 14th Mar]
Weapons Company, 1st Battalion, 23d Marines [Wpns Co, 1st Bn, 23d Mar]
1st Platoon, 2d Fleet Antiterrorism Security Team Company [1st Plt, 2d FAST]
Antiterrorism Battalion, Combined Antiarmor Team [AT Bn, CAAT 3]
1st Intelligence Battalion (-) (Reinforced), I MEF [1st IntelBn]
2d Radio Battalion (-) [2d RadBn]
8th Communications Battalion (-) (Reinforced) [8th CommBn]
5th Civil Affairs Group
6th Civil Affairs Group

155th Brigade Combat Team, Army National Guard (Reinforced) [155th MissANG]

Task Force 2d Battalion, 11th Armored Cavalry Regiment (U.S. Army) [TF 2d Bn, 11th
    ArmCavReg]
Marine Air Support Squadron 1 [MASS-1]
Marine Aircraft Group 14 [MAG-14]
Marine Air Control Squadron 2 [MACS-2]
Marine Wing Support Squadron 271 [MWSS-271]
Marine Wing Communications Squadron 38 [MWCS-38]

30th Naval Construction Brigade (U.S. Navy) [30th NCBde]
Task Force 2d Battalion, 198th Armor Regiment [TF 2d Bn, 198th AR]
Task Force 1st Battalion, 198th Armor Regiment [TF 1st Bn, 198th AR]
Task Force 1st Battalion, 155th Infantry Regiment [TF 1st Reg, 155th BCT]
106th Service Battalion [106th ServBn]
150th Engineer Battalion (-) [150th EngrBn]
Task Force, 2d Battalion, 114th Field Artillery Regiment [TF 2Bn, 114th FldArtyReg]
5th Battalion, 14th Marines [5th Bn, 14th Mar]

Marine Ground Combat Element

2d Marine Division (-) (Reinforced) [2d MarDiv]

Headquarters Battalion (-) (Reinforced) [HqBn]
2d Air Naval Gunfire Liaison Company (-) (Reinforced) [2d ANGLICO]
1st Air Naval Gunfire Liaison Company (-) (Reinforced) [1st ANGLICO]
Detachment, 3d Air Naval Gunfire Liaison Company (-) [Det, 3d ANGLICO]
1st Force Reconnaissance Company (-) (Reinforced), I MEF [1st ForReconCo]
2d Force Reconnaissance Company (-) (Reinforced) [2d ForReconCo]
74th Multi-Role Bridge Company, 130th Engineering Brigade (U.S. Army) [74th
     MRB Co, 130th EngrBde]
1st Battalion, 5th Marines [1st Bn, 5th Mar]
3d Battalion, 7th Marines [3d Bn, 7th Mar]

2d Marines/Regimental Combat Team 2 (-) (Reinforced) [2d Mar, RCT-2]

3d Battalion, 1st Marines (Reinforced) [3d Bn, 1st Mar]
3d Battalion, 2d Marines (-) (Reinforced) [3d Bn, 2d Mar]
3d Battalion, 6th Marines (Reinforced) [3d Bn, 6th Mar]
3d Battalion, 25th Marines [3d Bn, 25th Mar]
3d Battalion, 504th Infantry [3d Bn, 504th Inf]
1st Light Armored Reconnaissance Battalion (-) (Reinforced) [1st LAR Bn]
2d Light Armored Reconnaissance Battalion (-) (Reinforced) [2d LAR Bn]
Detachment, 2d Air Naval Gunfire Liaison Company [Det 2d ANGLICO]
4th Battalion, 14th Cavalry Regiment, (U.S. Army) [4th Bn, 14th CavReg]
Fleet Antit-Terrorism Security Team, 172d Brigade Support Battalion [FAST,
     172d BSB]
Battery A, 2d Battalion, 20th Field Artillery Regiment (U.S. Army) [A Btry, 2d
Bn, 20th FldArtyReg]
Battery A, 1st Battalion, 11th Marines [A Btry, 1st Bn, 11th Mar]
Battery K (Reinforced), 3d Battalion, 10th Marines [Btry K, 3d Bn, 10th Mar]
Company A (Reinforced), 1st Tank Battalion [Co A, 1st TkBn]
Company A (Reinforced), 4th Assault Amphibian Battalion [Co A, 4th
     AABn]
Information Company, Azerbaijani [InfCo, Azj]

8th Marines (-) (Reinforced)/Regimental Combat Team 8 [8th Mar, RCT-8]

Company B (Reinforced), 2d Tank Battalion [Co B, 2d TBn]
Company B (Reinforced), 2d Assault Amphibian Battalion [Co B, 2d AABn]
Battery A (Reinforced), 1st Battalion, 10th Marines [Btry A, 1st Bn, 10th Mar]
3d Reconnaissance Battalion (-) (Reinforced), 3d Marine Division [3d ReconBn]
3d Battalion 1st Marines (Reinforced) [3d Bn, 1st Mar]
2d Battalion, 2d Marines (Reinforced) [2d Bn, 2d Mar]
1st Battalion, 4th Marines (Reinforced) [1st Bn, 4th Mar]

3d Battalion, 4th Marines (Reinforced) [3d Bn, 4th Mar]
1st Battalion, 6th Marines [1st Bn, 6th Mar]
2d Battalion, 6th Marines (Reinforced) [2d Bn, 6th Mar]
3d Battalion, 6th Marines [3d Bn, 6th Mar]
2d Battalion, 7th Marines (Reinforced) [2d Bn, 7th Mar]
3d Battalion, 8th Marines [3d Bn, 8th Mar]
1st Reconnaissance Battalion (Reinforced) [1st ReconBn]
Company D (Reinforced), 2d Tank Battalion [Co D, 2d TkBn]
Company A (Reinforced), 2d Assault Amphibian Battalion [Co A, 2d AABn]

2d Brigade (Reinforced), 2d Infantry Division (U.S. Army) [2d BCT 2d Inf]

1st Battalion, 503d Infantry (U.S. Army) [1st Bn, 503d Inf]
1st Battalion, 506th Infantry (U.S. Army) [1st Bn, 506th Inf]
Air Defense Artillery, Battery B, 5th Battalion, 5th Field Artillery (-) [ADA, Btry B, 5th Bn, 5th FldArty]
1st Battalion, 9th Infantry Regiment (U.S. Army) [1st Bn, 9th InfReg]
2d Battalion, 17th Field Artillery Regiment (U.S. Army) [2d Bn, 17th FldArty]
44th Engineer Battalion (U.S. Army) [44th EngrBn]
3d Battalion, 82d CSE (U.S. Army)
Battery B, 1st Battalion, 4th Artillery, 2d Forward Support Battalion (U.S. Army) [Btry B, 1st Bn, 4th Arty, 2d ForSptBn]
1st Battalion (Reinforced), 5th Marines [1st Bn, 5th Mar]

2d Brigade, 28th Infantry Division (Reinforced) (Army National Guard) [2d Bde, 28th InfDiv]

228th Forward Support Battalion (U.S. Army) [228th FwdSptBn]
1st Battalion, 506th Infantry (U.S. Army) [1st Bn, 506th Inf]
1st Battalion, 110th Infantry (U.S. Army) [1st Bn, 110th Inf]
1st Battalion, 172d Artillery (U.S. Army) [1st Bn, 172d Arty]
2d Battalion, 222d Field Artillery (U.S. Army) [2d Bn, 222d FldArty]
2d Battalion, 116th Field Artillery Regiment (U.S. Army) [2d Bn, 116th FldArty]
3d Battalion, 7th Marines (Reinforced) [3d Bn, 7th Mar]

224th Engineer Battalion (C) (M) (Reinforced) [224th EngrBn]

Company C, 4th Tank Battalion [Co C, 4th TkBn]

54th Engineer Battalion (U.S. Army) [54th EngrBn]

Battery E, 2d Battalion, 11th Marines (Provisional MP) [Btry E, 2d Bn, 11th Mar]

Marine Aviation Combat Element

2d Marine Aircraft Wing (Fwd) [2d MAW]

Marine Wing Headquarters Squadron 2 (-) [MWHS-2]

Marine Aircraft Group 26 (-) [MAG-26]

Marine Headquarters and Headquarters Squadron 26 [MHHS-26]
Marine Fighter Attack Squadron 224 [VMFA-224]
Marine Fighter Attack Squadron 332 [VMFA-332]
Marine All Weather Fighter Attack Squadron 142 [VMFA(AW)-142]
Marine All Weather Fighter Attack Squadron 242 [VMFA(AW)-242]
Marine All Weather Fighter Attack Squadron 224, MAG-31 [VMFA(AW)-224]
Marine Fighter Attack Squadron 142, MAG 42, 4th MAW [VMFA-142]

Marine Attack Squadron 223 [VMA-223]
Marine Attack Squadron 311 (-) MAG- 13, 3d MAW [VMA-311]
Marine Tactical Electronic Warfare Squadron 1 [VMAQ-1]
Marine Tactical Electronic Warfare Squadron 2 [VMAQ-2]
Marine Tactical Electronic Warfare Squadron 4 [VMAQ-4]
Marine Light Attack Helicopter Squadron 167 [HMLA-167]
Marine Light Attack Helicopter Squadron 269 (-), MAG-26 [HMLA-269]
Marine Light Attack Helicopter Squadron 369 [HMLA-369]
Marine Light Attack Helicopter Squadron 775, MAG-46, 4th MAW [HMLA-775]
Marine Medium Helicopter Squadron 161 [HMM-161]
Marine Medium Helicopter Squadron 264, MAG-26 [HMM-264]
Marine Medium Helicopter Squadron 266 [HMM-266]
Marine Medium Helicopter Squadron 364, MAG-16, 3d MAW [HMM-364]
Marine Medium Helicopter Squadron 764, MAG-46, 4th MAW [HMM-764]
Marine Medium Helicopter Squadron 774 [HMM-774]
Marine Heavy Helicopter Squadron 465 (-) (Reinforced), MAG-16, 3d MAW [HMH-465]
Marine Medium Helicopter Squadron 466 [HMM-466]
Marine Transport Squadron 1 [VMR-1]
Marine Aviation Logistics Squadron 26 [MALS-26]

Marine Air Control Group 28 (-) (Reinforced) [MACG-28]

Marine Tactical Air Command Squadron 28 (-) (Reinforced) [MTACS-28]
Marine Air Control Group Headquarters [MACG-28 Hq]
Marine Air Control Squadron 2 (-) (Reinforced), MACG-28 [MACS-2]
Marine Wing Communications Squadron 28 (-) (Reinforced) [MWCS-28]
Marine Air Support Squadron 1 (-) (Reinforced), MACG-28, [MASS-1]

Marine Air Control Group 38 Headquarters [MACG-38 Hq]

Marine Unmanned Aerial Vehicle Squadron 1 [VMU-1]
Marine Unmanned Aerial Vehicle Squadron 2 [VMU-2]
Marine Air Control Squadron 1 [MACS-1]

Marine Wing Support Group 27 (-) (Reinforced) [MWSG-27]

Marine Wing Support Squadron 271 [MWSS-271]
Marine Wing Support Squadron 371 [MWSS-371]
2d Low Altitude Air Defense Battalion [2d LAAD Bn]
Marine Wing Support Squadron 272 [MWSS-272]
Marine Wing Support Squadron 372 [MWSS-372]

Marine Combat Service Support Element

2d Force Service Support Group/2d Marine Logistics Group (Forward) [2d FSSG]

Headquarters Service Battalion (-) (Reinforced) [HqSBn]
Communications Company (Reinforced) [CommCo]
8th Engineer Support Battalion (-) (Reinforced) [8th EngrSBn]
Combat Logistics Battalion 2 [ComLogBn 2]
Combat Logistics Battalion 8 [ComLogBn 8]

Combat Logistics Regiment 25 [ComLogReg 25]

Headquarter Service Company (-), 2d Transportation Support Battalion [HqSCo, 2d TransSptBn]

30th Naval Construction Regiment (-) (Reinforced), 1st Naval Construction Division (U.S. Navy) [30th NCR, 1st NCD]

Naval Mobile Construction Battalion (-) 24 [NMCB-24]
Naval Mobile Construction Battalion (-) 1 [NMCB-1]
Naval Mobile Construction Battalion (-) 3 [NMCB-3]
Naval Mobile Construction Battalion (-) 5 [NMCB-5]
Naval Mobile Construction Battalion (-) 22 [NMCB-22]
Naval Mobile Construction Battalion (-) 23 [(NMCB-23]
Naval Mobile Construction Battalion (-) 24 [NMCB-24]
Naval Mobile Construction Battalion (-) 133 [NMCB-133]
983d Engineer Combat Battalion (Heavy), (U.S. Army) [983d EngrCbtBn]
46th Engineer Combat Battalion (Heavy), (U.S. Army) [46th EngrCbtBn]

I Marine Expeditionary Force (Forward)/Multi National Force–West [I MEF (FWD)/MNF-W]
March 2006–February 2007

Command Element
15th Marine Expeditionary Unit [15th MEU]

Battalion Landing Team 2/4 [BLT 2/4]
Marine Medium Helicopter Squadron 165 [HMM-165]
Combat Logistics Battalion 15 [CLB-15]

I Marine Expeditionary Force Headquarters Group (-)(Reinforced) [I MEF Hq Gru]

1st Intelligence Battalion (-) (Reinforced) [1st IntelBn]
2d Intelligence Battalion (-) (Reinforced) [2d IntelBn]
1st Radio Battalion (-) (Reinforced) [1st RadBn]
2d Radio Battalion (-) (Reinforced) [2d RadBn]
9th Communication Battalion (-) (Reinforced) [9th CommBn]
1st Air Naval Gunfire Liaison Company (-) (Reinforced) [1st ANGLICO]
1st Force Reconnaissance Co (-) (Reinforced) [1st ForRecon Co]
3d Civil Affairs Group [3d CAG]
4th Civil Affairs Group [4th CAG]
6th Civil Affairs Group [6th CAG]

Marine Ground Combat Element

1st Marine Division (Forward) [1st MarDiv]

Headquarters Battalion [HqBn]
1st Battalion, 14th Marines [1st Bn, 14th Mar]
3d Battalion, 14th Marines [3d Bn, 14th Mar]
5th Battalion, 14th Marines [5th Bn, 14th Mar]

5th Marines/Regimental Combat Team 5 (-) (Reinforced) [5th Mar/RCT-5]

1st Battalion, 1st Marines [1st Bn, 1st Mar]
2d Battalion, 2d Marines [2d Bn, 2d Mar]
3d Battalion, 2d Marines [3d Bn, 2d Mar]
3d Battalion, 5th Marines [3d Bn, 5th Mar]
2d Battalion, 6th Marines [2d Bn, 6th Mar]
2d Battalion, 8th Marines [2d Bn, 8th Mar]
1st Battalion, 24th Marines [1st Bn, 24th Mar]
1st Battalion, 25th Marines [1st Bn, 25th Mar]

1st Reconnaissance Battalion [1st ReconBn]
2d Reconnaissance Battalion [2d ReconBn]
3d Reconnaissance Battalion [3d ReconBn]

7th Marines/Regimental Combat Team 7 (-) (Reinforced) [7th Mar/RCT-7]

1st Force Reconnaissance Company (-) (Reinforced) [1st ForReconCo]
4th Force Reconnaissance Company (-) (Reinforced) [4th ForReconCo]
4th Reconnaissance Battalion [4th ReconBn]
2d Battalion, 37th Armor Regiment (U.S. Army) [2d Bn, 37th AR]
1st Light Armored Reconnaissance Battalion (-) [1st LAR Bn]
2d Light Armored Reconnaissance Battalion (-) [2d LAR Bn]
3d Light Armored Reconnaissance Battalion (-) [3d LAR Bn]
1st Battalion, 7th Marines [1st Bn, 7th Mar]
3d Battalion, 1st Marines [3d Bn, 1st Mar]
3d Battalion, 3d Marines [3d Bn, 3d Mar]
3d Battalion, 6th Marines [3d Bn, 6th Mar]
3d Battalion, 4th Marines [3d Bn, 4th Mar]
3d Battalion, 7th Marines [3d Bn, 7th Mar]
3d Battalion, 8th Marines [3d Bn, 8th Mar]
1st Battalion, 6th Marines [1st Bn, 6th Mar]
1st Battalion, 36th Infantry Regiment (Mechanized) (U.S. Army) [1st Bn, 36th Inf]
4th Battalion, 14th Stryker Cavalry Regiment (U.S. Army) [4th Bn, 14th Stryker CavReg]

1st Brigade Combat Team, 1st Armored Division "Ready First" (U.S. Army)
[1st BCT, 1st ArmDiv]

1st Battalion, 6th Marines [1st Bn, 6th Mar]
3d Battalion, 8th Marines [3d Bn, 8th Mar]
1st Battalion, 506th Infantry Regiment (U.S. Army) [1st Bn, 506th InfReg]
1st Battalion, 9th Infantry Regiment (U.S. Army) [1st Bn, 9th InfReg]
1st Battalion, 37th Armor Regiment (U.S. Army) [1st Bn, 37th ArmReg]
2d Battalion, 37th Armor Regiment (U.S. Army) [2d Bn, 37th ArmReg]
1st Battalion, 77th Armor Regiment (U.S. Army) [1st Bn, 77th ArmReg]
1st Battalion, 35th Armor Regiment (U.S. Army) [1st Bn, 35th ArmReg]

Marine Aviation Combat Element

3d Marine Aircraft Wing (Forward) (Reinforced) [3d MAW]

Marine Wing Headquarters Squadron 1 (-) [MWHS 1]

Marine Aircraft Group 16 [MAG-16]

Marine Aircraft Logistics Squadron 16 (-)(Reinforced) [MALS-16]
Marine All Weather Fighter Attack Squadron 533 [VMFA(AW)-533]
Marine All Weather Fighter Attack Squadron 242 [VMFA(AW)-242]
Marine Attack Squadron 223 (-) [VMA-223]
Marine Attack Squadron 513 (-) [VMA-513]
Marine Attack Squadron 211 (-) [VMA-211]
Marine Light Attack Helicopter Squadron 369 [HMLA-369]
Marine Light Attack Helicopter Squadron 169 [HMLA-169]
Marine Light Attack Helicopter Squadron 269 [HMLA-269]
Marine Light Attack Helicopter Squadron 367 [HMLA-367]
Marine Light Attack Helicopter Squadron 167 (-) [HMLA-167]
Marine Medium Helicopter Squadron 268 [HMM-268]

Marine Medium Helicopter Squadron 364 [HMM-364]
Marine Medium Helicopter Squadron 774 [HMM-774]
Marine Medium Helicopter Squadron 266 [HMM-266]
Marine Heavy Helicopter Squadron 463 [HMH-463]
Marine Heavy Helicopter Squadron 363 [HMH-363]
Marine Heavy Helicopter Squadron 466 [HMH-466]
Marine Heavy Helicopter Squadron 361 [HMH-361]
Marine Heavy Helicopter Squadron 465 [HMH-465]
Det, Marine Aerial Refueler Transport Squadron 252 [VMGR-252]
Det, Marine Aerial Refueler Transport Squadron 352 [VMGR-352]

Marine Aircraft Group 31 [MAG-31]

Marine Air Control Group 38 (-) (Reinforced) [MACG 38]

Marine Unmanned Aerial Vehicle Squadron 1 [VMU-1]
Marine Unmanned Aerial Vehicle Squadron 2 [VMU-2]
Marine Tactical Air Command Squadron 38 [MTACS-38]
Marine Air Support Squadron 3 [MASS-3]
Marine Wing Communications Squadron 38 [MWCS-38]
Marine Air Control Squadron 1 [MACS-1]
Marine Wing Support Squadron 37 (-) (Reinforced) [MWSG-37]
Marine Wing Support Squadron 273 [MWSS-273]
Marine Wing Support Squadron 373 [MWSS-373]
Marine Wing Support Squadron 274 [MWSS-274]
Marine Wing Support Squadron 374 [MWSS-374]
3d Low Altitude Air Defense Battalion [3d LAADBn]

Marine Combat Service Support Element

1st Marine Logistics Group (Forward) (-) (Reinforced) [1st MLG]

Combat Logistics Regiment 17 [CLR-17]

Headquarters Company (-) (Reinforced), 7th Engineer Support Battalion
        [HqCo, 7th ESB]
Combat Logistics Battalion 5 [CLB-5]
Headquarters and Service Co, Combat Logistics Battalion 7 [H&SCo, CLB-7]
Combat Logistics Battalion 1 [CLB-1]

Combat Logistics Regiment 15 (-) (Reinforced) [CLR-15]

9th Engineer Support Battalion [9th EngrSptBn]

30th Naval Construction Regiment (-) (Reinforced) [30th NCR]

46th Engineer Battalion (U.S. Army) [46th EngrBn]
Naval Mobile Construction Battalion 133 [NMCB-133]
84th Engineer Construction Battalion (U.S. Army) [84th EngrConBn]
Naval Mobile Construction Battalion 22 [NMCB-22]

3d Naval Construction Regiment (-) (Reinforced) [3d NCR]

Naval Mobile Construction Battalion 18 [NMCB-18]
Naval Mobile Construction Battalion 74 [NMCB-74]

Appendix C

Selected Glossary of Terms and Abbreviations

AIF–Anti-Iraqi Forces

ACR–Armored Reconnaissance Regiment

AFDD–Air Force Doctrine Document

AQI/AQIZ–al-Qaeda in Iraq/al-Qaeda in Mesopotamia

AOR–Area of Responsibility

ASC–Anbar Salvation Council

BATS–Biometric Automated Tool Set

BBC–British Broadcasting Company

BCT–Brigade Combat Team

BIAP–Baghdad International Airport

BLT–Battalion Landing Team

BPC–Building Partnership Capacity

CAP–Combined Action Program

CAV–Cavalry

CEB–Combat Engineering Battalion

CERP–Commander's Emergency Reconstruction Program

CENTCOM–U.S. Central Command

CF–Coalition Forces

CG–Commanding General

CGS–Common Ground Station

CIA–Central Intelligence Agency

CJTF–Combined Joint Task Force

CLB–Combat Logistics Battalion

CLR–Combat Logistics Regiment

CMO–Civil-Military Operations

CMOC–Civil-Military Operations Center

CP–Command Post

CPA/CPA–Coalition Provisional Authority

CSS–Combat Service Support

CSSB–Combat Service Support Battalion

DIA–Defense Intelligence Agency

DOD–Department of Defense

ECP–Entry Control Points

EFDC–Expeditionary Force Development Center

EFIC–East Fallujah Iraqi Camp

EKMS–Electronic Key Management System

EOD–Explosive Ordnance Disposal

FLT–Fallujah Liaison Team

FOB–Forward Operating Base

FSS–Fast Sealift Ships

FSSG–Force Service Support Group

GIC–Gulf Investment Company

GCE–Ground Combat Element

HIDACZ–High Density Airspace Control Zone

HQMC–Headquarters Marine Corps

IA–Iraqi Army

IDF–Israeli Defense Force

IECI–Independent Electoral Commission of Iraq

IED–Improvised Explosive Device

IED WG–Improvised Explosive Device Working Group

IIF–Iraqi Intervention Force

IIG–Interim Iraqi Government

IMO–Information Management Officer

ING–Iraqi National Guard

IO–Information Operations

IPT–Integrated Process Team

IPSA–Intermediate Pumping Stations

IRMO–Iraq Reconstruction Management Office

ISF–Iraqi Security Forces

ISR–Intelligence, Surveillance, Reconnaissance

IW–Irregular Warfare

JCC–Joint Coordination Center

JDAM–Joint Direct Attack Munition

JIDI–Joint IED Defeat IPT

KIA–Killed in Action

LAR–Light Armored Reconnaissance

MA–Mortuary Affairs

MACCS–Marine Air Command and Control Squadron

MAG–Marine Air Group

MAGTF–Marine Air-Ground Task Force

MARCORSYSCOM–Marine Corps Systems Command

MarDiv–Marine Division

MAW–Marine Aircraft Wing

MCCDC–Marine Corps Combat Development Command

MCIA–Marine Corps Intelligence Activity

MCWL–Marine Corps Warfighting Laboratory

MCWP–Marine Corps Warfighting Publication

MEB–Marine Expeditionary Brigade

MEF–Marine Expeditionary Force

MEG–MEF (Marine Expeditionary Force) Engineer Group

MEU–Marine Expeditionary Unit

MHG–Marine Expeditionary Force (MEF) Headquarters Group

MLG–Marine Logistics Group

MNC-I–Multi National Corps–Iraq

MNF-I–Multi National Force–Iraq

MNF-W–Multi National Force–West

MNSTC-I–Multi National Security Transition Command–Iraq

MNSTC-I–Multi National Support and Training Command–Iraq

MOD–Ministry of Defense (Iraq)

MOI–Ministry of the Interior (Iraq)

MSR–Main Supply Route

MWSG–Marine Wing Support Group

MWSS–Marine Wing Support Squadron

NCO–Noncommissioned Officer

NCR–Naval Construction Regiment

NGO–Nongovernment Organization

OEF–Operation Enduring Freedom

OIF–Operation Iraqi Freedom

OIF II–Operation Iraqi Freedom II

PA–Public Affairs

PL–Phase Line

POE–Points of Entry

POW–Prisoner of War

PRDC–Provincial Reconstruction Development Committee

PRT–Provincial Reconstruction Teams

PSYOP–Psychological Operations

RCT–Regimental Combat Team

RLT–Reconstruction Liaison Team

RPG–Rocket-Propelled Grenade

RROC–Regional Reconstruction Operations Center

SAM–Surface-to-Air Missile

SVBIED–Suicide Vehicle-Borne Improvised Explosive Device

SERT–Seabee Engineer Reconnaissance Teams

SOF–Special Operations Forces

TACON–Tactical Control

TAL–Transition Administrative Law

TF–Task Force

TOC–Tactical Operations Center

TTP–Tactics, Techniques, and Procedures

UAV–Unmanned Aerial Vehicle

USAF–United States Air Force

USA–United States Army

USMC–United States Marine Corps

USN–United States Navy

VBID/VIED–Vehicle-Borne Improvised Explosive Device

VCP–Vehicle Checkpoints

WIA–Wounded in Action

Appendix D

Chronology of Events

2004

March 20	The 82d Airborne Division transfers command of Multi National Force–West to I Marine Expeditionary Force who takes responsibility for al-Anbar Province.
March 31	Four civilian Blackwater USA contractors are ambushed and their bodies mutilated by insurgents in Fallujah.
April 5	Units from I Marine Expeditionary Force launch Operation Vigilant Resolve in Fallujah.
April 9	Gen John P. Abizaid, USA, Commanding General of U.S. Forces Central Command, orders Marines to suspend offensive operations against the insurgency in Fallujah.
April 9–30	Units from I Marine Expeditionary Force engage in skirmishes and firefights throughout Fallujah.
May 1	I Marine Expeditionary Force withdraws from Fallujah and hands authority over to the Fallujah Brigade.
June 28	The official transfer of sovereignty to Iraq, dissolution of the Coalition Provisional Authority, and transfer of power to the Iraqi Interim Government. Two days later, Marines raise the American flag over the new U.S. Embassy in Baghdad.
July 16	First units of the 11th Marine Expeditionary Unit arrive in an-Najaf.
July 23	Six Marines from 1st Reconnaissance Battalion, 1st Marine Division, complete the first combat, high-altitude parachute drop in the history of the Marine Corps.
July 31	11th Marine Expeditionary Unit assumes operational control of an-Najaf and al-Qadisiyah Provinces.
August 2	Marines from the 11th Marine Expeditionary Force begin battling units of the Mahdi Militia insurgency in Najaf and Kufa.
August 9	Multi-National Force–West assumes tactical control of 11th Marine Expeditionary Force with the arrival of I Marine Expeditionary Force (Forward) Command Element.
August 11	11th Marine Expeditionary Force forces engage insurgents southwest, northwest, and northeast of Najaf.

August 21	1st Battalion, 4th Marines raid Kufa.
August 26	In Najaf, 1st Battalion, 4th Marines, surround the Imam Ali Mosque Shrine. Multi National Corps–Iraq orders Marines to cease offensive activities and allow Iraqi officials to peaceably resolve the removal of Mahdi Militia forces.
August 27	Grand Ayatollah al-Sistani negotiates a truce in Najaf. Iraq government declares that hostilities will officially end at 1000.
September 10	The Fallujah Brigade disbands, having failed in its efforts to secure the city.
September 12	LtGen John F. Sattler becomes commanding general, I Marine Expeditionary Force, relieving LtGen James T. Conway.
September 26	Two suicide car bombers try to drive into a base used by U.S. Marines and Iraqi National Guardsmen in Karma, near Fallujah. When challenged, they detonate the cars. No injuries are reported.
October 5	More than 3,000 U.S. and Iraqi troops, including the 24th Marine Expeditionary Force, launch an offensive operation in the southern approaches to Baghdad and take control of a bridge across the Euphrates River.
October 14	Marines launch air and ground attacks against an insurgent stronghold in Fallujah after peace talks are suspended. The peace talks fizzle over the demand that the insurgent mastermind Abu Musab al-Zarqawi and other foreign fighters be handed over to the authorities.
November 7	Marines from I Marine Expeditionary Force conduct operations in preparation for a second battle to clear Fallujah of insurgents. These include securing key bridges, surgical air strikes, and seizing insurgent nodes outside the city.
November 2	George W. Bush re-elected as U.S. President.
November 8	I Marine Expeditionary Force launches Operation Phantom Fury (Operation al-Fajr) against insurgents in Fallujah. The second battle of Fallujah begins.
November 11	Northern area of Fallujah falls to U.S. Marine forces.
November 13	The initial attack on Fallujah is completed. Search and attack operations commence.
November 14	3d Battalion, 5th Marines, takes the Jolan district in Fallujah. Marines successfully occupy the city.
November 23–27	Elements of the 24th Marine Expeditionary Force, along with U.S. Army soldiers and Iraqi forces, launch Operation Plymouth Rock against insurgents in North Babil Province.
December 21	The 11th Marine Expeditionary Force assumes operational control of Karbala Province from the Polish-led Multi National Division Central–South.
December 23	Operation Phantom Fury concludes. Fallujah secured and cleared of insurgents. Repopulation of the city commences.

2005

January 14	All districts of Fallujah are opened for resettlement.
January 26	CH-53 helicopter crashes in western Iraq, claiming the lives of 30 Marines and one sailor. Currently the single deadliest event for U.S. forces during the war.
January 30	Iraqi national elections held for a Transitional National Assembly. Sunnis largely boycott the vote.
February 20–March 5	Marines and Iraqi security forces launch Operation River Blitz throughout al-Anbar Province. The operation targets insurgents in cities along the Euphrates River including Hit, Ramadi, and Baghdadi.
March 10–25	Regimental Combat Team 7 and its relieving unit, Regimental Combat Team 2, conduct Operation River Bridge.
March 27	II Marine Expeditionary Force (Forward) relieves I Marine Expeditionary Force as Multi National Force–West.
March	II Marine Expeditionary Force (Forward) builds 1,700-man police department in the city of Fallujah.
April 1–May 4	Marines from the 2d Marine Division conduct Operation Outer Banks and Operation Patriot Shield to clear the Haditha-Hit corridor of insurgent operations.
April 11	Insurgents attack Camp Gannon at Husaybah. Three Marines are wounded.
March–June	II Marine Expeditionary Force (Forward) disbands the 60th Iraqi National Guard and integrates 2,000 former ING soldiers into the regular Iraqi Army.
May 2	Two F/A-18 Hornet fighters from Marine Fighter Attack Squadron 323 collide over Iraq, killing both pilots.
May 7–14	Regimental Combat Team 2 conducts Operation Matador against insurgents operating along the Syrian border.
May 25–29	Marines conduct Operation New Market in Haditha to battle entrenched insurgents.
June 6–July 31	Operation Guardian Sword: 2d Marine Division conducts operations against insurgents to support Iraqi Constitutional Referendum.
June 17–22	Operation Spear: Marines focus on the rebel stronghold of Karabilah near the Syrian border.
June 18	Regimental Combat Team 8 launches Operation Dagger against insurgent networks in al-Anbar Province.
June 23	Iraqi insurgents carry out the deadliest attack involving U.S. female service members to date when a suicide car bomber rams a convoy in Fallujah. Five

	Marines and one female sailor—three males and three females—are killed in the attack and 13 others are wounded, 11 female.
June 28–July 6	Regimental Combat Team 2 conducts Operation Sword in Hit and Haditha.
July	Marine, Army, and Iraqi Army units conduct Operation Sayaid (Hunter) to continue efforts to secure Anbar Province.
July 7	Operation Scimitar begins with raids in the village of Zaidan, approximately 20 miles southeast of Fallujah, and at least 22 suspected insurgents are detained.
August 3	Fourteen Marine reservists and a civilian interpreter are killed in Haditha when the amphibious assault vehicle they are traveling in is struck by a roadside bomb. Two days earlier, six other Marines are killed near the same city by enemy gunfire.
August 3–10	Marines participate in Operation Quick Strike, an offensive operation aimed at disrupting insurgent activities in Haditha, Haqliniyah, and Barwanah. Marines net nine car bombs, 28 other explosive devices, and capture 36 suspected insurgents.
October 1	Marines from Regimental Combat Team 2 conduct Operation Iron Fist to disrupt insurgents filtering into the country from Syria.
October 4–19	Marines conduct Operation River Gate in Haditha, Haqlaniyah, and Barwanah to disrupt insurgent activities and secure the triad region.
October 15	The referendum on the Iraqi Constitution, and the first phase of Operation Liberty Express.
October 18	The deputy governor of Anbar Province, Talib al-Dulaimi, is assassinated in Ramadi.
November 5–17	Regimental Combat Team 2 participates in Operation Steel Curtain against insurgents in al-Qa'im along the Iraq-Syria border.
November 19	Haditha Incident: Marines from the 3d Battalion, 1st Marines, are attacked by an insurgent land mine. In the aftermath, several civilians are killed or wounded in questionable circumstances.
November 19	Roughly 150 Iraqi Army soldiers and 300 U.S. Marines and soldiers launch Operation Dhibbah (Bruins) in Ramadi.
November 26	Approximately 400 U.S. Marines and 150 Iraqi Army troops launch a new offensive in the Ma-Laab district of eastern Ramadi, Operation Tigers (Nimur).
November 30	Operation Iron Hammer conducted by Marine and Iraqi armed forces to rid the Hai al-Becker region of insurgents traveling from Syria into Iraq.
December 2	Three hundred Marines from the 3d Battalion, 7th Marines, and 200 Iraqi Army soldiers from the 1st Brigade, 7th Division, conduct Operation Harba (Shank) in Ramadi to secure the Anbari capital for elections on 15 December.

December 15	The election for the Iraqi National Assembly. Operation Liberty Express provides security for polling.
December 17	Iraqi soldiers begin Operation Moonlight to disrupt insurgent activity along the Euphrates River near the border with Syria.

2006

January 15–27	Marines with Battalion Landing Team 1/2, and Iraqi Army soldiers conduct Operation Koa Canyon along the western Euphrates River Valley.
February 22	The bombing of the Golden Mosque in Samarra sparks an outbreak of sectarian violence.
February 28	I Marine Expeditionary Force (Forward) assumes control of the Multi National Force–West area of operations from II Marine Expeditionary Force (Forward).
March 9	U.S. Army LtGen Peter W. Chiarelli, commander of Multi National Corps–Iraq, directs further investigation into events surrounding the 19 November 2005 attack in Haditha.
April 7	The battalion commander of 3d Battalion, 1st Marines, as well as two company commanders, are relieved of command amid the investigation into the Haditha shootings.
April 17	Marines repel an attack by Sunni Arab insurgents in Ramadi, when the insurgents launch a coordinated assault against the city's main government building and two U.S. observation posts. No U.S. casualties result from the 90-minute attack.
May 26	Gen Michael W. Hagee, Commandant of the Marine Corps, announces Marines will face criminal charges for the November 2005 shootings in Haditha.
June 7	Al-Qaeda in Iraq leader Abu Masab al- Zarqawi killed in an air strike.
June 14–July 20	Operation Together Forward: U.S. and Iraqi Security Forces establish curfews, security checkpoints, and more patrols in cities across Iraq.
June 17	1st Brigade Combat Team of the 1st Armored Division launches operations to prevent Ramadi from become a center of al-Qaeda in Iraq.
August 8–October 24	Operation Together Forward II: 15,000 U.S. soldiers clear disputed areas and cede security responsibilities to Iraqi soldiers. Iraqi troops ultimately fail to secure the cleared cities.
Summer-Fall	U.S. Army LtCol Sean B. MacFarland of the 1st Brigade Combat Team begins forging anti-al-Qaeda alliances with Iraqi tribal awakening councils.
September	Sheikh Sattar al-Rishawi of the Dulaimi confederation's Albu Risha tribe launches a campaign against al-Qaeda in Iraq.
October	Marines from 1st Battalion, 6th Marines, commanded by LtCol William M. Jurney fight to secure Ramadi in support of Awakening operations.

November 6   Saddam Hussein found guilty by Iraqi tribunal for the 1982 murder of 148 Shi'ites in Dujail and sentenced to death.

November 7   U.S. midterm elections end Republican control of both houses of Congress.

November 8   Secretary of Defense Donald H. Rumsfeld resigns. His successor, Robert M. Gates, is confirmed by the Senate on 8 December 2006.

December 21   Eight Marines are charged for the killings of 24 Iraqi civilians in Haditha in November 2005. Four of the Marines, all enlisted, are charged with unpremeditated murder while four officers are accused of dereliction of duty for failures in investigating and reporting the deaths.

December 30   Saddam Hussein executed.

Appendix E

Reviewers

Gen James T. Conway

Gen Michael Hagee

Gen James N. Mattis

LtGen James F. Amos

LtGen Richard S. Kramlich

LtGen Richard F. Natonski

LtGen John F. Sattler

LtGen Keith J. Stalder

MajGen Joseph F. Dunford Jr.

MajGen Dennis J. Hejlik

MajGen Richard A. Huck

MajGen Stephen T. Johnson

MajGen John F. Kelly

MajGen Robert E. Milstead Jr.

MajGen Michael R. Regner

MajGen James L. Williams

BGen David H. Berger

BGen Charles M. Gurganus

BGen Ronald J. Johnson

BGen Kenneth F. McKenzie Jr.

BGen Thomas M. Murray

BGen Lawrence D. Nicholson

BGen Charles S. Patton

BGen David B. Reist

BGen John A. Toolan Jr.

BGen John E. Wissler

Col Scott M. Anderson

Col John R. Ballard

Col Elvis E. Blumenstock

Col Paul W. Brier

Col Larry K. Brown Jr.

Col Thomas L. Cariker

Col Robert H. Chase

Col Guy M. Close

Col Mark R. Cyr

Col Stephen W. Davis

Col Robert W. Destafney

Col Paul K. Durkin

Col Thomas C. Greenwood

Col Curtis E. Haberbosch

Col Anthony M. Haslam

Col John P. Holden

Col Michael E. Kampsen

Col John C. Kennedy

Col Stuart L. Knoll

Col John T. Larson

Col James K. La Vine

Col Kenneth J. Lee

Col Clarke R. Lethin

Col Ron R. McFarland

Col Steven E. McKinley

Col Jonathan G. Miclot

Col W. Lee Miller

Col David J. Mollahan

Col Glenn T. Starnes

Col Michael A. Shupp

Col Darrell L. Thacker

Col Craig A. Tucker

Col Michael Walker

LtCol Francis X. Carroll

LtCol Joseph A. L'etoile

Index

www.ingramcontent.com/pod-product-compliance
Lightning Source LLC
Chambersburg PA
CBHW050412110426
42812CB00006BA/1875